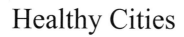

Healthy Cities

Healthy Cities

An Annotated Bibliography

Namir Khan
Willem H. Vanderburg

with the collaboration of Lynn Macfie,
Nina Nakajima, Pamela Robinson, and
Esther Vanderburg

The Scarecrow Press, Inc.
Lanham, Maryland, and London
2001

SCARECROW PRESS, INC.

Published in the United States of America
by Scarecrow Press, Inc.
4720 Boston Way, Lanham, Maryland 20706
www.scarecrowpress.com

4 Pleydell Gardens, Folkestone
Kent CT20 2DN, England

British Library Cataloguing-in-Publication Information Available

Library of Congress Cataloging-in-Publication Data

Khan, Namir, 1955–
    Healthy cities : an annotated bibliography / Namir Khan and Willem H. Vanderburg ; with the
    collaboration of Lynn Macfie, Nina Nakajima, Pamela Robinson, and Esther Vanderburg.
        p. cm.
    Includes bibliographical references and index.
    ISBN 0-8108-4034-0 (alk. paper)
        1. Cities and towns—Effect of technological innovations on—Bibliography. 2. Cities
    and towns—Environmental aspects—Bibliography. I. Vanderburg, Willem H. II. Title.
Z7164.U7 K44 2001
[HT119]
016.30776—dc21   2001020297

CONTENTS

PREFACE

There is mounting evidence that modern cities can be designed to constitute a more supportive environment for a great many activities, provide a more livable habitat, and reduce the burden imposed on the biosphere. They can be made healthier (in terms of the definition of the World Health Organization) and more sustainable by means of new and emerging preventive approaches. The growing evidence confirms what should have been obvious all along: it is both cheaper and better to prevent social and environmental problems than first to produce and then to mitigate them. The focus is on those preventive approaches that can make cities healthier and more sustainable.

Healthy, sustainable cities involve two interdependent sets of reciprocal relationships. The first is between their inhabitants involved in a variety of daily-life activities and the social and physical contexts in which these activities take place. The latter impose a number of demands on these activities including sensory overload, social overload, crowding, crime, noise, pollution, the separation of daily-life activities in space (and thus usually also in their social contexts), and alienation. Superimposed on these are the demands of the activities themselves, such as physical and intellectual difficulties, time pressures, and psychological stresses. People meet these demands by drawing on their own resources including past experience, education, health, and emotional preparedness. The health and sustainability for this set of reciprocal relationships are determined by the demands placed on people relative to their abilities to meet them. On one end of the spectrum, if the demands completely outstrip people's resources, their health and well-being will greatly suffer. The "human capital" of the city is being mined. On the other end of the spectrum, when people's resources are little challenged by the demands placed on them, the results are equally detrimental. Somewhere in between, there exists a range where people's resources are stretched to meet the demands in a way that permits learning and growth, thus providing the satisfaction of a challenging job well done.

The second set of reciprocal relationships are those between cities and the biosphere via local ecosystems. Since the activities carried out in cities can neither create nor destroy matter and energy, these are temporarily borrowed from the biosphere and returned in an altered form. Solar radiation is included here because it is "prepared" by the ozone layer. Activities involving the transformations of matter and energy therefore depend on other activities or the biosphere for their input and output flows of matter and energy. As a result of this constraint, expressed as the first law of thermodynamics, such activities constitute a network of flows of matter and energy for which the biosphere acts as the ultimate source and sink. A city is sustainable from a metabolic point of view only when the biosphere can indefinitely sustain this network. Hence, as cities transform the biosphere, the latter simultaneously affects cities in its role as ultimate source and sink, habitat and life-support. If the demands placed on local ecosystems and the biosphere undermine their capacity to perform these roles, "natural capital" is being mined.

These two sets of reciprocal interdependencies show that as people change cities and local ecosystems, these simultaneously change people. As human intentions and aspirations are *externalized* (including the evolution of the built habitat), these activities become *objectivized*, thereby helping to constitute the social and physical setting for human life which, when experienced, is *internalized*, thus influencing the human mind.

Although the effects of individual experiences may be small, it must be remembered that the mind as a symbolic mapping of experiences permits the living of a life. This becomes painfully obvious with the onset of diseases such as Alzheimer's or short-term memory disorders, which can break human lives apart into relatively isolated moments of existence that the mind can no longer connect into a life. A particular social and physical setting promotes human freedom when people have a greater effect on these contexts than these have on them. Alienation results when the reverse is the case.

The preventive approaches that can help make cities more sustainable with respect to the biosphere are further developed in two accompanying annotated bibliographies dealing with industrial ecology and energy. Preventive approaches dealing with work as a significant factor in making cities more sustainable with respect to individual and collective human life have also been developed in a separate annotated bibliography. It is essential to integrate all relevant preventive approaches into a comprehensive strategy to ensure that reducing the burdens cities impose in one area will not lead to additional burdens in others.

These bibliographies are the result of a twelve-year research project carried out at the Centre for Technology and Social Development at the University of Toronto. The overall results have been published under the title *The Labyrinth of Technology* (Toronto: University of Toronto Press, 2000). The point of departure was an examination of professional education related to the engineering, management, and regulation of technology in the context of making modern ways of life more sustainable by reducing the harm done to human life, society, and the biosphere. During undergraduate education, future practitioners gain little knowledge of how technology affects these contexts and even less of how such understanding can be used in a negative feedback mode to adjust design and decision-making to prevent or greatly reduce harm. As a result, a great deal of design and decision-making occurring from the vantage point of a particular discipline or professional specialty externalizes those consequences that fall beyond its boundaries. The result is that, in modern technology, problems tend to be first created and then remedied. This is needlessly costly and harmful.

Specialists tend to cope with this situation by implicitly and explicitly saying that they do the best they can in their area of competence, and that those consequences of their actions and decisions that fall beyond these areas are best dealt with by others who have a competence there. We cannot help but sound a little defensive because we all know that our effectiveness and responsibility require both a frontier knowledge of our areas of competence and a context knowledge of those areas in which the consequences of our decisions and actions will fall. Only then will we be able to use this context knowledge to assess the consequences of our actions and decisions in order to adjust them to prevent or greatly reduce harm and, in the best of all worlds, ensure that the result will be technological and economic development instead of mere growth. At present, the intellectual and professional division of labor allows the consequences of the decisions and actions of one specialty to be dealt with only in an end-of-pipe or after-the-fact manner by specialists in whose areas these fall. It precludes dealing with the root of any problem. There is growing evidence that this is costly and ineffective because it frequently merely displaces symptoms from one area to another. In the areas of technological and economic growth, educating the practitioners involved in these enterprises as both specialists and generalists could make a fundamental difference in ensuring that any advances are not undermined by the problems they simultaneously create. This would lead modern civilization to adopt preventive approaches in order to get us out of the labyrinth of the social and environmental implications of technology in which we are now lost because the "system" makes it almost impossible to get to the root of any situation or problem by means of specialized knowledge and practice.

The above situation is both cause and effect of the kinds of values that guide technological and economic growth. Performance values such as efficiency, productivity, cost-effectiveness, profitability, risk-benefit ratios, and GDP are ratios of desired outputs obtained from requisite inputs. For example, GDP measures the value of all goods and services produced by a society using its "social and natural capital." Hence performance values give us no indication to what extent any technological or economic gain in output has partly or wholly been achieved by degrading the human, societal, and biospheric contexts on which it depends. In other words, they give us no indication to what extent we are using our "social and natural capital" sustainably and to what extent we are "mining" them. For example, a new production system may lead to an increase in labor productivity and profitability and also produce more unhealthy workers, in turn affecting the fabric of their social relations and their communities. New materials may be particularly advantageous in terms of their technical and economic performance, but collectively such materials may undermine the health of ecosystems on which all life depends. In general, it may be said that technological and economic growth is characterized by gains occurring predominantly in the domain of performance values and problems in the domain of context values. The latter assess compatibility with the human, societal, and biospheric contexts.

As a consequence, the members of contemporary civilization individually and collectively "steer" technology, much like driving a car with the windows covered over by concentrating on the performance of the vehicle as indicated by the instruments on the dashboard. Each time a scream is heard or a bump is felt, we frantically attempt to rip holes in the covers over the windows to see what is happening, but this is an after-the-fact reaction. After two centuries of technological and economic growth, there are many small holes in the window covers but we still do not have a clear view of how technology is related to everything else on the road of human history.

Following this diagnosis of the present situation, the research program undertook an exhaustive comparison of the state-of-the-art methods and approaches for dealing with the social and environmental implications of technology and their conventional counterparts. The latter deal with any technological situation or problem in two stages. The first seeks to obtain the highest possible desired outputs from the requisite inputs. Success is measured in terms of performance values. A second stage deals with those undesired outputs that are prohibited or constrained by laws and regulations. The state-of-the-art methods collapse these two stages into one, at least with respect to one dimension of sustainable development. Pollution prevention is paradigmatic. It goes back to the root of the problem and asks why a particular product or process produces pollutants in the first place. How can material inputs and/or the process be modified to avoid producing these pollutants? The possibilities do not end with pollution prevention. There are other approaches, and it is only after all these fail that end-of-pipe abatement should be attempted. This led to the formulation of the concept of preventive approaches, which incorporate into design and decision-making a proactive consideration of the implications to "steer" technology to avoid collisions with its contexts. The research findings led to the development of a new conceptual framework and strategy aimed at converting technological and economic growth into development that would gradually become more

x PREFACE

sustainable. It was put into practice in a set of courses and a certificate program at the University of Toronto aimed at graduating engineers with a difference. The present bibliography brings together that portion of the literature that can make a significant contribution to preventive approaches in the areas of urban planning, architecture, civil engineering, and others.

It is hoped that this annotated bibliography will facilitate specialists becoming generalists in those domains where the consequences of their actions are most important, help policy-makers and politicians come to grips with the broader implications of "steering" technology, and help members of the public gain a better all-around understanding of the complexity of the many issues that surround technological and economic growth. A better understanding of the ecology of technology and the ecologies of individual technologies is essential to create a humane and sustainable future. The bibliography is therefore not intended to be encyclopedic. It is designed to support the development of preventive approaches, and the selections have been made with this general purpose in mind. In terms of the division of labor between co-authors, the overall direction of the project and the development of the conceptual framework have been my primary responsibility, while the gathering and abstracting of the particular contents of this bibliography have been under the direction of my co-author.

The research into professional education and the development of the conceptual framework for preventive approaches, including the database from which this annotated bibliography was drawn, have been generously supported by the Social Sciences and Humanities Research Council of Canada.

Willem H. Vanderburg
Toronto January 2001

HEALTHY CITIES BIBLIOGRAPHY

1. Association of Collegiate Schools of Architecture West Central Regional Conference. *Design for the Environment: The Interdisciplinary Challenge.* Urbana-Champaign: School of Architecture at University of Illinois, at Urbana-Champaign, 1995.

Keywords: current, built environment, design, green space, sustainability

Changes in technology and culture are requiring planners, architects, engineers, and landscape architects to make a concerted effort to resolve complex environmental problems. This book targets architects and calls upon them to include environmental policy-making as an essential component of practice. Areas covered include: architectural history/culture, building environmental systems, collaborative and team-based learning, socially responsible design, collaborative design, design theories and paradigms, collaboration on public policy, and cross-disciplinary design studios. This book has obvious value for architects but it will also be helpful to those professionals who work with architects or in design-related fields.

2. Adams, John. *Transport Planning: Vision and Practice.* London: Routledge & Kegan Paul, 1981.

Keywords: energy, transportation, urban planning

Adams takes issue with the theory that development is a process that allows "progress" to gradually diffuse equitably to all, a view held firmly by transport planners. Since this is believed to be a global phenomenon, Part 1 (chapters 1-7) investigates global transport planning. Adams questions the popular belief that all people share the goal of greater mobility and that it is the transport planner's duty to help them achieve this goal. He relates this belief to theories of economic development suggesting that history is a transition from poverty to affluence. This transition of course involves mobility, which increasingly connects distant parts of the world, creating global transport problems. The problems created by mobility and the urban transition are examined in some detail, followed by a description of the transport problems in London, problems common to most large cities in developed countries. Adams notes that the mobility transition involves an energy transition and emphasizes that current plans for mobility require quantities of energy that are either impossible to attain or result in unacceptable costs. He next argues that conventional traffic statistics misrepresent the importance of traffic accident casualties and examines why countries with high levels of car use are reluctant to implement policies that would reduce the death toll.

Part 2 (chapters 8-12) begins by examining how transport planners rationalize their methods and practices and outlines the steps involved in the design and construction of a new road, emphasizing the lack of a public consensus regarding the goals of any such project. Adams suggests that traffic forecasts are akin to covert operations since neither forecasters nor policy-makers appear to assume any responsibility for them. He notes that the economic assessment of transport planning does not include considerations of the desirability of traffic growth. Chapter 12 suggests that independent inquiries are not truly independent and this is why they have failed to convince the public of the wisdom of certain planning decisions.

Part 3 (chapters 13-16) begins by exploring the subconscious motivations involved in pro-growth planning. It is suggested that transport planning has the unidimensional goal of eliminating distance, and the costs of achieving such a goal are examined. The book concludes with a general criticism of modern economics, which is seen as the reason why transportation planning remains ineffective.

3. Adams, John, Mayer Hillman, and John Whitelegg. *One False Move: A Study of Children's Independent Mobility*. London: Policy Studies Institute, 1990.

Keywords: automobiles, children, risk assessment, transportation, Britain

Child road accident fatalities in Britain have almost halved while traffic volume has nearly doubled. The British government thus concluded that streets are now safer. This report from 1990 is based on a study of school children ages seven to fifteen in five communities in England and five similar areas in Germany. It claims that child fatalities related to traffic accidents are not a true measure of safety. It proposes that the only reason the fatalities have decreased is because children have been removed from the danger of the streets. In fact, streets are now more dangerous than ever before. Growing automobile use has caused increases in noise, pollution, danger, and unpleasantness that have all contributed to an insecure society. Car travel has also led to a loss of street life, increasing the number of people considered to be strangers. This increases the fear of molestation. Comparing the 1990 study to one made in 1971 reveals that parents have greatly reduced their children's freedom in response to the danger caused by traffic. Children are increasingly escorted by adults, usually by car, especially to and from school. This supervision has its costs: it increases resource costs, decreases adult opportunities, increases traffic congestion, limits a child's physical fitness, and limits the opportunity for a child to develop independence. As this cycle increases traffic volume, the safe space available for children's activities is bound to decrease. This study suggests new measures of safety and freedom, such as the annual number of hours spent escorting a child, that would discourage the use of the automobile rather than encourage it. Furthermore, simple street design proposals are made that have already been implemented with much success in Germany.

4. Alexander, Christopher. "The City as a Mechanism for Sustaining Human Contact." In *People and Buildings*, ed. R. Gutman, pp. 406-34. New York: Basic Books, 1972.

Keywords: support, alienation, architecture, design, health, housing, psychological health, urban planning

Alexander was one of the first design professionals to recognize the possibility of using behavioral research to deal with both the ends and means of design, and this is a classic article on behavior-environment interactions. The subject of this article is the problem of loneliness, anomie, and alienation in the contemporary urban environment. Alexander redefines this problem as the absence of human contact. He summons a substantial body of empirical research to show that lack of human contact is the cause of many individual and social pathologies, such as psychosis and juvenile delinquency. He also discusses the evidence for the view that anomie is largely the consequence of the highly fragmented social and physical organization of urban society.

The author proposes a design scheme for reducing the amount of loneliness in the city. He uses a model that assumes social pathology is the consequence of need frustration and explains this in terms of the absence of compatibility between buildings and urban forms and between basic psychological or group process requirements.

5. Alexander, Christopher, Murray Silverstein, Shlomo Angel, Sara Ishikawa, and Denny Abrams. *The Oregon Experiment*. New York: Oxford University Press, 1975.

Keywords: architecture, built environment, case studies

"This book is the master plan for the University of Oregon. It also defines a process which can, with minor modifications, be adopted as a master plan by any community, anywhere in the world. And it is also the third in a series of books which describes an entirely new attitude to architecture and planning—the first one of the series which explains in full practical detail how these ideas may be implemented." (From the Introduction.) The first two volumes of the series (*The Timeless Way of Building* and *A Pattern Language*—also by Christopher Alexander) are listed in this bibliography.

Each of the chapters applies one of the six principles needed to create an environment that meets human needs. These principles of implementation are the principle of organic order, the principle of participation, the principle of piecemeal growth, the principle of patterns, the principle of diagnosis, and the principle of coordination.

6. Alexander, Christopher. *A Pattern Language: Towns, Buildings, Construction*. 3rd ed. New York: Oxford University Press, 1979.

Keywords: sociocultural, architecture, buildings—social aspects, built environment, community, urban design, urban planning, classic

Alexander's *Pattern Language* has been hailed as a great achievement in resurrecting building traditions "on the verge of extinction" (James Howard Kunstler). Like any other language, a pattern language presents us with a vocabulary, in this case, a vocabulary of building. Elements of this vocabulary go back to building traditions thousands of years old; others are derived from common sense. The key factor is the ability to see all aspects of the built environment as a series of connecting relationships. In the absence of this ability, the built environment becomes fetishized and discontinuous, with all the accompanying ugliness and discomfort. Thus people who have acquired this language perceive a window not as a hole in the wall but as expressing a relationship between the outside and the inside, between light and dark, and cold and warmth. Similarly, a picket fence is not coeval with its material existence; it makes sense only in light of the fact that it delineates a relationship between the yard and the sidewalk.

The authors summarize the language as follows: "The elements of this language are entities called patterns. Each pattern describes a problem which occurs over and over again in our environment, and then describes the core of the solution to that problem in such a way that you can use this solution a million times over, without ever doing it the same way twice."

7. Alexander, Christopher. *The Timeless Way of Building*. New York: Oxford University Press, 1979.

Keywords: sociocultural, architecture, buildings—social aspects, built environment, community, urban design, urban planning, classic

"There is one timeless way of building. . . . The great traditional buildings of the past, the villages and tents and temples in which man feels at home, have always been made by people who were very close to the center of this way. It is not possible to make great buildings, or great towns, beautiful places, places where you feel yourself, places where you feel alive, except by following this way. . . . It is so powerful and fundamental that with its help you can make any building in the world as beautiful as any place that you have ever seen." This work lays out the principles of this timeless way. That is, it describes how a building or town can be brought to life. It is meant to be read with Alexander's other works in mind. These are listed in this bibliography.

In the section entitled "The Quality," Alexander describes the quality without a name which we must first discover in order to understand the timeless way. "There is a quality which is the root criterion of life and spirit in a man, a town, a building, or a wilderness. This quality is objective and precise, but it cannot be named." Alexander first helps the reader to recognize this quality within themselves, and then to recognize it in buildings and towns.

The next section is entitled "The Gate." "To reach the quality without a name we must then build a living pattern language as a gate." The living patterns refer to patterns of events that repeatedly occur in a place. The more living patterns there are in a building or town, the more it can come alive. Pattern language refers to the power to create an infinite variety of buildings, just as the language we speak provides us with the ability to create an infinite variety of sentences.

"Once we have built the gate, we can pass through it to the practice of the timeless way." In the final section ("The Way"), the timeless way is described as a process of unfolding parts from the whole. All of this is described in a lyrical style that is quite accessible to readers.

8. Alexander, Christopher, Hajo Neis, Artemis Anninou, and Ingrid King. *A New Theory of Urban Design*. New York: Oxford University Press, 1987.

Keywords: sociocultural, architecture, buildings—social aspects, built environment, community, urban design, urban planning, classic

The most beautiful towns and cities of the past impress us because they somehow feel to be "organic"; that is, it feels as though each of these towns grew as a whole, under its own laws of wholeness. This wholeness, the authors suggest, is not something vague and should not be taken as a biological analogy. It is very real and quite palpable. We can feel this wholeness, not only at the largest scale, but also in every detail: in the restaurants, shops, houses, markets, roads, parks, gardens, and sidewalks.

This book is an attempt to recreate this wholeness through urban design and outlines the process by which this can be achieved. The authors are all too aware that no specific plan can achieve this feeling of wholeness; they thus delineate the proper prerequisites that must inform the design process. These prerequisites are presented as a list of seven rules, which are then applied in an experimental fashion for the development of thirty acres on the San Francisco waterfront. The rest of the book describes the development of this hypothetical little town as it emerges on paper.

9. Alexander, Donald, and Ray Tomalty. *Urban Policy for Sustainable Development: Taking a Wide-Angle View.* Winnipeg: Institute of Urban Studies, University of Winnipeg, 1994.

Keywords: urban metabolism, sustainability, ecology, population, public policy

This brief and concise review of literature relevant to urban policy for sustainable development includes both "empirical writings" and "visionary work." The empirical literature focuses on the problem of environmental and economic efficiency while the visionary literature looks at culture and the built environment. Together, these articles establish the goals of urban sustainability as: ecological integrity; reaching a cultural state necessary for sustainability; making the built environment livable; reducing resource use and environmental impact; and maximizing the efficiency of the urban infrastructure.

10. American Planning Association, ed. *Planning and Community Equity: A Component of APA's Agenda for America's Communities Program.* 1st ed. Chicago: APA Planners Press, 1994.

Keywords: support, community, housing, neighborhood, transportation, urban planning

Each chapter in this book addresses a different urban issue. The topics are wide-ranging: from affordable housing and citizen participation, to transportation and the university's role in urban development. The chapters are a concise summary of the issues and make proposals for how urban life can be improved through planning and other initiatives.

11. Amit-Talai, Vered, and Henri Lustinger-Thaler, ed. *Urban Lives: Fragmentation and Resistance.* Toronto: McClelland & Stewart, 1994.

Keywords: support, community, public policy, urban planning, Canada

Scholars from five different disciplines explore the challenges and conundrums of late twentieth-century life in Canadian cities. Case studies and ethnographies illuminate the theory of global economic restructuring, grassroots municipal politics, housing, urban planning, community, communication, collective rights, peer relations, and fieldwork practices. Two central themes animate this portrait: actual practices and resistance. The problematic relationships between urban research and policy development are highlighted. The focus of this collection is on resistance, that is, on people struggling to construct everyday routines, relationships, and collectivities in the midst of complexity.

12. Anderson, Terry L., ed. *Breaking the Environmental Policy Gridlock.* Stanford, Calif.: Hoover Institution Press, 1997.

Keywords: environmental planning, public policy, U.S.

This book sets out to "demonstrate how the principles of fiscal responsibility and individual accountability have been applied to social and economic policies." By using American examples it reinforces the potential for success of market-based incentives to promote environmental protection. The performance-based (as opposed to technology-based) approach of the proposed reforms will help those interested in taking a preventive approach to their work. Although the policies discussed are federal government initiatives, there are good lessons to be learned from this book for those who work in policy development at all levels of private and public sector policy development.

13. Andrew, Caroline, and Beth Moore Milroy, ed. *Life Spaces: Gender, Household, Employment.* Vancouver: University of British Columbia Press, 1988.

Keywords: support, built environment, democracy, economics, housing, work, Canada

Existing theories on urban structure focus solely on the male experience. But inaccurate descriptions, explanations, and prescriptions for cities result from neglecting women as a category of urban actors. The articles presented in this book reinforce the importance of gender considerations in urban studies. By exploring the interrelationship between gender and urban structure, they present feminist analyses of how and why urban areas are structured as they are. This book presents a Canadian perspective on issues such as access, equality of treatment, dominance, and power. All of the contributors share the belief that gender relations can be best understood by studying the relationship between two things: the organization of the production of goods and services, and the way in which society maintains and reproduces the labor force (outside the labor process itself). Other common foci throughout the articles are about how theory, research, and policy are inextricably linked.

14. Andrey, Jean Clara, and James Gordon Nelson, ed. *Public Issues: A Geographical Perspective.* 1st ed. Geography and Public Issues Series. Vol. 2. Waterloo: University of Waterloo, 1993.

Keywords: support, public policy, transportation

This volume touches on a wide range of issues on the nexus between geography and public issues, but some of the topics relate directly to urban problems. One such example is the chapter entitled "Employment Opportunities of the Urban Poor: An Assessment of Spatial Constraints and the Mismatch Hypothesis." This chapter discusses the paradox of the presence of white-collar workers and blue-collar jobs in the suburbs and the presence of blue-collar workers and white-collar jobs in the inner cities.

15. Angotti, Thomas. *Metropolis 2000: Planning, Poverty and Politics.* New York: Routledge, 1993.

Keywords: support, case studies, community, developing countries, neighborhood, urban planning, poverty

Attempts to achieve the physical integration of the city without economic equality will always fail. This book looks at metropolitan development and planning under the various economic and environmental conditions that prevail in different parts of the world. The author proposes the principle of "integrated diversity," which emphasizes linking neighborhood planning with a broader vision of an integrated metropolis. Applying an approach derived from political economy, the author argues for new, pro-urban, ecologically sound thinking. Individual chapters focus on the dominant regions of the former Soviet Union and the developing nations of the South. The author argues that "only when the metropolis is understood as a necessary and beneficial accompaniment to social progress can a progressive, human approach to city planning be developed."

16. Appleyard, Donald. *Livable Streets*. Berkeley: University of California Press, 1981.

Keywords: social fabric, neighborhood, streets, traffic, transportation, urban planning, case studies, U.S., Britain

The street is defined as the social center of towns and cities—a place where children grow up and learn to confront strangers and their environment, a mediator between the home and the environment, a place with social and personal meaning for adults and elders. Yet surveys reveal that traffic is a more widespread problem than crime on many streets in the United States. It is suggested that this problem should be solved immediately via urban and transportation planning that involve an understanding of the problems in different residential areas, strategies to create livable streets, public planning participation programs, and reliable methods of assessing the costs and benefits of any changes. In compliance with these requirements, this book has two purposes: (1) to provide an understanding of what it is like to live on streets with varying volumes of traffic, and (2) to investigate ways in which streets can be made more livable.

Part 1 (chapters 1-8) is a social, psychological, and environmental analysis of street life in San Francisco. This involves a study of specific streets along with an outline of the existing relationships involved. A study is made of the impact of traffic on people of different social classes and their response. The traffic and street variables that aggravate or alleviate the problem are examined. Part 2 (chapters 9-12) involves a study of the obstacles involved in designing a livable street. Three British projects that followed the Buchanon Report, *Traffic in Towns* (Harmondworth: Penguin, 1963) are examined, as are efforts to protect residential neighborhoods in San Francisco. Part 3 (chapters 13-15) concludes with recommendations for achieving livable streets. This involves a review of goals to be attained, an outline of how to plan and carry out a program and the policies this involves, and a listing of systems and devices currently used to control street traffic.

17. Arendt, Randall, Elizabeth Braebec, Harry L. Dodson, Christine Reid, and Robert D. Yaro. *Rural by Design: Maintaining Small Town Character*. Chicago: APA Planners Press, 1994.

Keywords: current, built environment, community, environmental planning, green space, land use, quality of life, urban design, United States

"If you're a fan of strip malls, pedestrian-free gated subdivisions, twelve lane freeways and treeless horizons—avoid this book," the authors warn the prospective reader. This is a compendium of practical answers to the wide range of questions that arise from the application of environmental planning principles. Indeed, it can be seen as a manual for creating a "sense of place" or "community" and is full of examples from American communities. Although complex issues are tackled, the approach will be readily understood by all.

18. Arendt, Randall. *Conservation Design for Subdivisions: A Practical Guide to Creating Open Space Networks*. Washington, D.C.: Island Press, 1996.

Keywords: current, built environment, community, environmental planning, green space, land use, quality of life, urban design, United States

Arendt takes on the challenge of trying to balance conservation with development, of preserving our environment while simultaneously creates living landscapes. He details information describing the actual techniques that are available to landowners, developers, local officials, and construction organizations who are interested in conserving land through the development process so that their communities may enjoy the benefits of an interconnected network of open, green spaces for years to come. This is a practical handbook, profusely illustrated, showing how homes can be built in a less land-consumptive manner. Supplementing the innovative designs are model zoning and subdivision ordinances that can benefit citizen and local officials. This, along with its companion volume, *Growing Greener*, is an indispensable guide to sustainable subdivision development.

19. Arendt, Randall. *Growing Greener: Putting Conservation into Local Plans and Ordinances*. Washington, D.C.: Island Press, 1999.

Keywords: current, built environment, community, environmental planning, green space, land use, quality of life, urban design, United States

Like its sister volume, *Conservation Design for Subdivisions*, this is an illustrated, practical handbook demonstrating how subdivisions can be so designed that green space and ecologically sensitive areas are preserved. Arendt's strategy revolves around modifying or establishing a municipal comprehensive plan, a zoning ordinance, and a subdivision ordinance to entrench conservation. The value of the book is enhanced by eleven case studies of actual conservation developments and two exercises suitable for group participation.

20. Archibugi, Franco. *The Ecological City and the City Effect: Essays on the Urban Planning Requirements for the Sustainable City*. Aldershot, England: Ashgate Publishing, 1997.

Keywords: urban planning, current, economics, public policy

The first round of policies and legislation adopted by the European Union and the United States—once the environment became a cause for concern—largely ignored the city and concentrated instead on the natural unbuilt environment. This effectively robbed the policies of their teeth, because most of the damaging environmental consequences actually emanate from cities and their needs. Once this realization struck home, the authorities responded with a host of end-of-pipe mitigation measures that were only partially successful. This is because most of these measures were technology driven and created a positive feedback loop requiring an unending amount of energy and materials for more and more mitigation technologies. This, Archibugi correctly asserts, is a case where the greyhound never catches the mechanical hare as the mitigation technologies themselves cause problems leading to the need for more technologies and so on.

Planning attempts to get beyond this impasse have been unable to overcome a fundamental contradiction between two desirable aspects of cities which Archibugi identifies as the *city effect* and the *livability of cities*. The first of these refers to those aspects of cities that developed nations must bring to all their citizens: access to social, medical, and educational services, mobility, jobs, affordable housing, and so on—all of which can be most effectively delivered within the context of a city. The *livability of cities* refers to the fact that urban air and water quality are never the best, and overcrowding, noise, crime, homelessness, and traffic gridlock are perennial problems. Urban planners have always assumed that the *city effect* would be an automatic consequence of urbanization and have thus concentrated their efforts on the *livability of cities* only. They have forgotten, Archibugi claims, that it is precisely the engendering of the *city effect* that leads to the generation of conditions that adversely affect the *livability of cities* (e.g., mobility and jobs may both lead to smog and industrial pollution).

This extremely valuable book clearly demonstrates that, so long as planning remains focused on the *livability of cities,* the dreams of an ecological or sustainable city will never be achieved because all efforts will be end-of-pipe in nature. A truly preventive approach must also concentrate on exactly how the *city effect* itself is delivered. For this, a holistic and integrated approach is needed; an approach that calculates all the consequences of a *city effect* and uses this information in a negative feedback mode to adjust the way in which the *city effect* is delivered. The essays in this book suggest many ways in which this can be done.

21. Ashley, Robert, and John S. Reynolds. "Overall and Zonal Energy End Use in an Energy Conscious Office Building." *Solar Energy* 52, 1, 1994: 75-83.

Keywords: transformation, energy, energy efficiency, office buildings, work environment

This article describes the design of an unusual "energy conscious" building. It goes on to analyze the results of a three-year effort to monitor energy use through submeters in various locations. The use of daylighting and some passive solar heating, as well as night ventilation cooling, are analyzed for the different areas of the building, and some suggestions regarding the use of daylight-sensing controls of indirect electric lighting, "task heating," and night ventilation are presented.

22. Ashton, John, ed. *Healthy Cities*. Philadelphia: Open University Press, 1992.

Keywords: sociocultural, health, quality of life

This book is edited by one of the leading researchers in the field. Ashton's introduction gives a concise history of the notion of healthy cities, from the formation of the Health of Towns Association in Exeter, England in 1844, to initiatives taken in more contemporary towns. Part 1 distinguishes the art of the possible regarding healthy cities, as opposed to more utopian conjectures, and includes a chapter on various indices for measuring health in cities. Part 2 consists of more specific studies of the emergence of healthy city concepts in Canada, Australia, and the United States as well as in developing countries. Parts 3 to 5 consist of case studies from Europe (Liverpool, Sheffield, Horsens, Gothemburg, Eindhoven, Barcelona, the Basque country, Valencia, and Zagreb); North America (Toronto, California, and Indiana); and the Antipodes (Palmerston North, Canberra, and Noarlunga).

23. Asterita, Mary F. *The Physiology of Stress*. New York: Human Sciences Press, 1985.

Keywords: health

This volume offers a comprehensive view of the various physiological effects of stress. Subject areas discussed include the human nervous and endocrine systems and their response to stress.

The main purpose of the book is to present a scientific exposition of the physiology of stress based on general knowledge and current research findings. The major emphasis is on the changes resulting in the nervous and endocrine systems of the body due to stress, which produce specific end-organ activity. Since many factors that contribute to stress (such as crowding, noise, and high-rise living) are endemic to cities, researchers on healthy cities will find the book useful.

24. Atash, Farhad. "Redesigning Suburbia for Walking and Transit: Emerging Concepts." *Journal of Urban Planning and Development* 120, 1 (March 1994): 48-57.

Keywords: pedestrians, public policy, suburbs, transportation, urban planning, new urbanism

Traditional Neighborhood Development (TND) and Pedestrian Pockets (PP) are identified as two neo-traditional modes of town planning to counteract suburban sprawl, overreliance on the automobile, and lack of alternative modes of transport. The article suggests that the concepts of TND and PP offer a unique opportunity to integrate suburban development policies with transportation policies to prevent sprawl and create compact, mixed-use communities. Both these concepts later evolved into the New Urbanism.

25. Atkinson, Adrian, Julio D. Davila, Edesio Fernandes, and Michael Mattingly, eds. *The Challenge of Environmental Management in Urban Areas*. Aldershot, England: Ashgate Publishing, 1999.

Keywords: environmental planning, urban planning, public policy

Environmental management practice in the countries of the North and South is examined in the papers presented here. The emphasis is on the policies, politics, and management dilemmas of urban environmental problems. The book is particularly rich in case studies that illustrate both environmental and social sustainability initiatives around the world. A good guide for anyone interested in policies regarding solid wastes in cities as different as Copenhagen, Colombo, and Madras; air pollution policies in Accra, Sao Paulo, and Santiago; and community-based environmental management in Tanzania and Britain. Other topics covered include homelessness, municipal fiscal policies, local and central government partnerships, and the management of flood relief activities.

26. Ausubel, Jesse H., and Robert Herman, eds. *Cities and Their Vital Signs: Infrastructure Past, Present and Future*. Washington, D.C.: National Academy Press, 1988.

Keywords: input-output, transportation, water, urban metabolism

The book discusses infrastructure—the built environment in which we live, how we use it, and how it can evolve in the future. Infrastructure is broadly defined to include sewers, water delivery systems, telecommunications, roads, and airports. This book looks at the role that infrastructure has played in shaping our future and the public and private motives for infrastructure development. Our relationship with the infrastructure is then examined in some detail—for example, how we control it, how we regulate access to it, and so on. The impacts of urban form on infrastructure are also discussed. The relationship between infrastructure and natural vs. human made disasters is probed. The crumbling state of some infrastructure is discussed as well as planning for new types. Issues raised here include: the benefits of retrofitting or building new systems, and what the ideal life span of new systems should be. The strength of this book is derived from its illustration of how the problems of physical infrastructure and related human activity are an overwhelming yet inviting task for researchers.

27. Bacow, Adele Fleet. *Designing the City: A Guide for Advocates and Public Officials*. Washington, D.C.: Island Press, 1995.

Keywords: social fabric, community, democracy, public policy, urban design

This book is intended as a practical guide for improving the design, planning, and building of communities and will be of use to concerned citizens, policymakers, planners, designers, and environmentalists. Little information is given regarding which design is good or bad. Instead, the focus is on how to approach and influence design decisions, thus filling the gap that exists between those directly involved in design and development and the remaining community. The goals of this manual assist the reader to:
- establish productive partnerships
- develop resources with which to accomplish a project
- increase expertise and expand perspective
- establish a program as legitimate
- educate the community in the design and development process
Chapter 1 describes all those involved in the design process, while chapter 2 offers answers to popular criticisms such as "it can't be done." Chapters 3 to 8 document successful strategies and programs for a range of projects including bridge and highway design, grant programs, and education. The final chapter outlines the approach through which an idea is put into action, with the aim of improving a neighborhood or community.

28. Baechler, M. C., et al. *Sick Building Syndrome: Sources, Health Effects, Mitigation*. Park Ridge, N. J.: Noyes Data Corp., 1991.

Keywords: transformation, buildings—health aspects, indoor pollution, sick building syndrome

This book discusses the "Sick Building Syndrome." Sources and health effects of various indoor air pollutants, and methods for mitigation of the problem, plus suggested analytical methods for detecting and measuring environmental carcinogens found in indoor air, are covered here.

Part 1 of the book discusses the syndrome itself as well as specific pollutants—including mitigation techniques, ventilation, and the interaction between energy conservation activities and indoor air quality. Part 2 reflects information currently available on the health effects associated with each of the selected contaminants. Part 3 presents suggested sampling procedures and analytical approaches for known and suspected carcinogens found in indoor air. The table of contents is organized in such a way as to serve as a subject index and provides easy access to the information contained in this book.

29. Bakacs, T. *Urbanization and Human Health.* Budapest: Akademiai Kiado, 1972.

Keywords: environmental pollution, health, sewage, toxins, water, traffic

Expectations of a healthy urban milieu have not been fulfilled. It has become evident that the engineering aspects of city building have to be complemented with a biological approach and an anthropocentric attitude. The need for an even wider range of cooperating specialists has emerged, involving, among others, the municipal economist and sociologist, and it has been realized that the problems can only be solved by broad interdisciplinary activities and by the integrated efforts of many professions. In this co-operation, due regard should be given to the principles of ecology and the laws of biology if we want the city of the future to guarantee a better way of life and fulfil the expectations of its residents.

The author is inspired by these considerations and has attempted to follow the train of events in the changes of the urban process, to point to some cause-and-effect relations, and to make a few suggestions from the viewpoint of one of the cooperating disciplines: environmental health and hygiene.

Although an increasing number of books have been published discussing the urban problem from the technological, demographic, or sociological aspects, a monographic elaboration of the topic from the viewpoint of public health focussing on the hygienic problems of human settlements seems justified.

The author attempts to unfold the problems of urban life starting from the principles of human biology and to arrive at conclusions pointing to the tasks ahead. A general approach rather than a "jungle of details" is what emerges as a result.

30. Baldassare, Mark, ed. *Cities and Urban Living.* New York: Columbia University Press, 1983.

Keywords: support, urban sociology, modernization

New topics in urban sociology and older issues that have regained relevance are represented in this collection. It is a standard, but comprehensive, urban sociology text. Questions have been raised about the usefulness of traditional urban sociology and the need for a newly formed discipline. The critics claim that traditional urban sociology lacks relevance to modern problems, is politically conservative, is not attuned to the most significant socioeconomic factors, disregards cultural and historical considerations, and refuses to admit the importance of the resident's actions and beliefs. The defenders claim that their urban paradigm presents the most holistic and integrated study of urban conditions and that it can inform urban practitioners of policy options, thus they see no need for incorporating other perspectives. The reader is therefore warned that urban sociology has been shaped by disciplinary controversy as well as actual city events. Specific issues dealt with are: "Recent Ideas About Modern Urban Communities," "Neighborhood Revitalization in the Inner City," "Population Growth in Rural Localities," "Renewed Interest in Residential Crowding," "Vulnerable Populations in the City," and "New Perspectives in Urban Sociology."

31. Baldassare, Marc. *Trouble in Paradise: The Suburban Transformation in America.* New York: Columbia University Press, 1986.

Keywords: support, urban sociology, modernization, suburbs

A slightly older but still useful study of the problems facing suburbia in the United States Baldassare uses sociological theories about suburban communities, translates these concepts into testable hypotheses, and then tests them empirically. The core analysis of the book identifies six challenges that face suburbia.

A suburban housing crisis is looming as prices rise steeply. Secondly, there is a growth controversy fueled by the changing landscape of suburbia. Trust in local government is also a problem since many suburbs are fragmented into many jurisdictions and thus suffer the consequences of not having a central authority.

Tax revolts and fiscal strains present a fourth challenge. The suburbs themselves have created a shortage of funds with the federal and state governments. As suburban residents oppose taxes, service delivery and service expanses are threatened. This leads to the fifth challenge, which is the special need for services in the suburbs. The sprawling and politically diffuse nature of the suburbs creates problems for delivering services and meeting needs that emerge as suburbs "mature," such as a transportation network and a more diverse health, education, and welfare program.

A final challenge is posed by the increasing social diversity of the suburbs. Social heterogeneity increases the potential for conflict, and the provision of social services to those with special needs becomes difficult.

32. Banerjee, Tridib, and Michael Southworth, eds., *City Sense and City Design: Writings and Projects of Kevin Lynch.* Cambridge, Mass: MIT Press, 1990.

Keywords: sociocultural, case studies, urban design, urban planning

The editors note that "Kevin Lynch (1918-1984) was the leading environmental design theorist of our time. His productive career was devoted to research, writing and teaching. He has left behind a rich legacy of ideas and insights about human purposes and values in built form, and possibilities for designing human environments. . . . In this volume we have assembled almost all of Lynch's previously published journal and anthology articles, as well as a broad selection of his unpublished work, including drawings and sketches, essays, and excerpts for professional reports and travel journals." Each of the chapters presents a key article by Lynch preceded by pithy introductions by the editors that provide context and background to it.

33. Barlow, James. *Public Participation in Urban Development: The European Experience*. London: Policy Studies Institute, 1995.

Keywords: support, community, democracy, public policy, urban planning, Britain, France, Sweden

The history of urban planning in Britain is briefly reviewed, concluding that a government that viewed public participation in planning as a hindrance in the 1980s now encourages it as much as possible. This was an outcome of the realization that planning is a powerful tool for the promotion of a more sustainable society, based on the values of its citizens. Despite such initiatives, public planning participation has been underresearched. Virtually no comparative research has been undertaken. The purpose of this book is to fill in this gap. A comparative study is made of the three drastically different planning approaches of Britain, France, and Sweden.

In chapter 1, the influences on planning participation in the UK are discussed. Chapter 2 focuses on the differences between each country's political structures and urban planning strategies and how these influence urban development politics. Chapters 3 and 4 outline the difference in public participation and urban development politics between countries. In chapter 5, the differences discovered between countries are analyzed and used to arrive at implications for public participation in urban planning in Britain.

34. Barnett, Jonathan. *The Elusive City: Five Centuries of Design, Ambition and Miscalculation*. New York: Harper & Row, 1986.

Keywords: urban planning, urban design, economics

"All purpose" city design concepts have been with us from well before industrialization. Most of these have failed because economic and social changes were too rapid to be contained within any static pattern. This engagingly written and profusely illustrated book examines four such "all purpose" design concepts that have led to today's city. Barnett starts with a brief discussion of pre-industrial design strategies—mostly influenced by Vitruvius—before examining the "monumental city" most ably represented by Christopher Wren's work. The "garden city" of Ebenezer Howard is discussed next. The advent of modernism in architecture, best exemplified by Le Corbusier and the "modern city," is critically assessed. A final design strategy encapsulated in the "city as a building" rounds out the discussion.

The solution to the problems faced by contemporary cities lies not in searching for yet another "all purpose" design concept but in finding new ways of integrating city design with processes of economic and social change.

35. Barnett, Jonathan. *The Fractured Metropolis: Improving the New City, Restoring the Old City, Reshaping the Region*. New York: HarperCollins, 1996.

Keywords: suburbs, current, economics, transportation, United States

Most suburban sprawl may be considered as constituting a new city—one that robs resources from the older city from which it spun off. This has left the older cities fighting for their lives with diminished tax bases, deteriorated housing, high crime areas, and poor schools. The new city in the meanwhile has its own problems. For years, the most rapidly growing suburban towns and counties continued to assume they were satellites of established city centers. They were not prepared to become centers themselves. Their zoning and subdivision ordinances had been written when a major change meant adding a few dozen houses or building a new supermarket on Main Street. Planning boards struggled with development proposals for huge shopping centers, office parks, and residential subdivisions of hundreds or even thousands of acres. There were no precedents for the scale of these developments or the speed with which they were constructed. Since each component was proposed separately by competing developers, the shape of the new city did not emerge until it was an accomplished fact. Thus the new city is usually fragmented, ugly, and inefficient with traffic gridlocks, despoiled nature, shoddy construction, and bad planning. The new city thus also breeds social isolation and alienation.

Barnett looks at what can be done to restoring older cities and correcting the problems of new cities by extrapolation from actual strategies that have worked in both older and new cities. Through all of this the reader gets a good tour of major and some not so major U.S. cities along with a good introduction to the do's and don'ts of competing planning theories and redevelopment and redevelopment strategies.

36. Baron, R. *The Tyranny of Noise*. New York: St. Martin's Press, 1970.

Keywords: transformation, health, noise—physiological effects, noise—psychosocial effects

This book considers the physiological effects of noise as well as its social and economic implications. The difficulty of reducing and fighting noise in the city because of weak laws is also discussed. Part 4, entitled "Design for Quiet," explores the potential for noise control and what citizens can do to reduce and avoid the noise in their environment.

37. Bartone, Carl, Jais Bernstein, Josef Leitmann, and Jochen Eigen. *Toward Environmental Strategies for Cities: Policy Considerations for Urban Environmental Management in Developing Countries*. Washington, D.C.: World Bank, 1994.

Keywords: biosphere, developing countries, environmental planning, environmental overload, land use, case studies

In response to the rapid urbanization occurring in the developing world, this paper offers a strategic approach to urban environmental planning and management based upon the principles of participation, building commitment, and choosing effective policy interventions. Through a series of case studies, the strategic planning process outlined in this paper is used to show how institutional, political, and technical problems can be addressed. Problems discussed include: the "Brown" agenda, poverty, variability in urban environmental problems, and economic and political trade-offs.

38. Bartsch, Charles, and Elizabeth Collaton. *Brownfields: Cleaning and Reusing Contaminated Properties*. Westport, Conn: Praeger, 1997.

Keywords: transformation, case studies, environmental pollution, ground pollution, hazardous waste, toxins, waste

Large areas of American urban land currently lie unused because of contamination from previous industrial activity. While the existing infrastructures go unused, money is being spent to develop new urban sprawl developments. This pattern can be reversed to bring growth and investment back to cities, argue the authors, by paying careful attention to development priorities. This book is an invaluable resource for policies regarding the reclamation of old industrially and environmentally contaminated urban land (referred to as brownfields).The policies are specific to the United States but with insights that are applicable elsewhere in the developed world.

The first chapter presents a framework of environmental and economic development concerns in specific community situations. Barriers to brownfields development, the perceived fears of the lender, and relevant banking policies are discussed. The second chapter deals with environmental policies governing brownfield cleanup and reuse. It reviews several important federal and local programs that could assist in brownfield cleanup and reuse. Chapter 3 features a similar treatment of economic development policies. Finally, the challenges encountered and solutions sought by communities with brownfields are noted in the fourth chapter. The background, financial information, solutions, regulations involved, impacts, and lessons learned are given for brownfield projects in nine American cities.

39. Bartuska, Tom J., and Gerald L. Young, eds. *The Built Environment: Creative Inquiry into Design and Planning*. Menlo Park, Calif.: Crisp Publications, 1994.

Keywords: current, buildings—health aspects, built environment, green spaces, housing, indoor pollution, land use, office buildings, sick building syndrome

Context is all-important in developing an understanding of the things people build and how they affect human life. To this end, all design and planning fields are examined in terms of their connection with the rest of the world.

As a collaborative work, the text draws from the knowledge and experience of internationally renowned environmental designers, planners, and ecologists. This book is comprehensive, interdisciplinary, and well integrated, with each section building on the previous one to form an overall study of how humans create and respond to the built environment. Engineers, architects, planners, interior designers, and others who work with built form will find this book a valuable resource.

40. Baum, Andrew, and Stuart Valins. *Architecture and Social Behavior: Psychological Studies of Social Density*. New York: John Wiley & Sons, 1977.

Keywords: support, architecture, crowding, psychological health

The social and psychological effects of architectural design are studied by first reviewing the literature. The rest of the book is largely devoted to the presentation of the authors' own research findings. The behavior of dormitory residents in different social density situations was observed. Stress and social interaction of subjects were studied while they waited in a laboratory and in a dental office. The effects of cooperative orientation, competitive orientation, and being ignored were studied in the waiting period as well. Group interaction studies were also performed under various crowding conditions. The effects on group development, group consensus, cooperation, competition, and task performance were studied.

The authors conclude that crowding-related stress and divergent social behavior are present in high-density college dormitories. They also suggest "that the ways in which interior design variables arrange space and distribute social resources are important in considering quality of life in residential environments."

41. Baum, Andrew, and Yakov M. Epstein, eds. *Human Response to Crowding*. New York: Lawrence Erlbaum Associates, 1978.

Keywords: housing, crowding, psychological health

This comprehensive book is considered a classic text in the field. It describes theoretical developments, examines research methods, and considers evidence of human response to crowding. No aspect of crowding goes undiscussed here, whether it be an historical account of crowding itself or an historical account of crowding research. Personal and social consequences of crowding—at what density crowding causes helplessness; what its effects are on preschool children; the experience of dormitory living; human spatial behavior—all these topics receive detailed attention. All in all, the articles in this book are an excellent asset for urban planners and designers, as well as architects.

42. Baxter, Diana. *Health in the Urban Environment: Health Status Indicators and Their Use in Measuring Quality of Life*. Project Ecoville (in cooperation with UNESCO). Working Paper #10. University of Toronto (Institute for Environmental Studies), 1984.

Keywords: sociocultural, health, quality of life

The importance of this work lies in the fact that it directly relates the broader environmental concerns of urbanization to the quality of life. It demonstrates clearly that not all the key choices are those taken by public decision-makers. The importance of lifestyle is emphasized as it demonstrates that at least some of the outcomes of the urbanization process are within the control of the individual. Considerable space is allotted to measuring health and developing indices of health.

43. Bayley, Stephen. *Sex, Drink and Fast Cars*. New York: Pantheon Books, 1986.

Keywords: automobiles, consumerism, transportation

There is no better introduction than this to the mystery of why cars have become fetishized cultural icons full of symbolism rather than a mere means of transport. Cars as symbols of sex, money, speed, status, art, and design and cars as a means of escape, freedom, beauty, and power are discussed. The automobile has gone beyond a means of transport, the author says, and has gained magical, inspirational qualities that are tied to eroticism. This book relates the values and meanings assigned to cars to a lack of depth in culture, poor public transport, and an economic system that encourages consumption. The author, a graphic artist, has written a humorous and ironic book with some wonderful insights about why cars are so addictive.

44. Beatley, Timothy. *Ethical Land Use: Principles of Policy and Planning*. Baltimore: Johns Hopkins University Press, 1994.

Keywords: biosphere, case studies, land use, public policy, urban planning

All land-use decisions—whether to build an interstate highway or maintain a suburban lawn with chemical fertilizers—invariably involve ethical choices. The author observes that historically many such decisions were made on narrow legal, technical, or economic grounds rather than on a full consideration of their complex ethical and moral dimensions. Drawing on a combination of actual land-use conflicts and hypothetical scenarios, Beatley offers a full description and analysis of the difficult issues faced by policy makers as well as individual citizens. He concludes by proposing a practical set of principles for ethical land use to guide future policy and planning.

45. Beatley, Timothy, and Kristy Manning. *The Ecology of Place: Planning for Environment, Economy and Community*. Washington, D.C.: Island Press, 1997.

Keywords: community, economics, environmental planning, privacy

Conventional planning has often seen a disjuncture between the needs of the economy and the necessity of maintaining a healthy environment, between the need for community and the need for individual privacy. Thus a vibrant economy is seen as involving some trade-off by generating pollution and wastes. Growth, which enables cities to increase their tax base and thus offer more services, is often seen as involving a trade-off with overcrowding, gridlocked streets, etc. Beatley and Manning suggest that these trade-offs are a result of the faulty methods used by conventional planners in the first place. They go on to describe ways in which land can be used sparingly, cities and towns can become vibrant and green with thriving economies, and citizens and agencies can create places of enduring value. This work is heavily influenced by the New Urbanism—and this is acknowledged—but tries to go beyond it by making its environmental goals a little more explicit. A valuable contribution to the literature on sustainable cities.

46. Beavis, Mary Ann, ed. *Colloquium on Sustainable Housing and Urban Development*. Winnipeg: The Institute of Urban Studies, 1991.

Keywords: housing, sustainability, urban design, urban planning, Canada

This is a collection of papers based on presentations delivered at a colloquium hosted by the Institute of Urban Studies at the University of Winnipeg. "The Origins of Sustainable Development and Its Relationship to Housing and Community Planning," by David D'Amour, introduces the background of the concept and argues that sustainable housing has social, economic, and ecological implications and that a transition must be made from a technocentric to an ecocentric approach. "The Politics of Sustainable Urban Development Policy in Canada," by Philip H. Wichern, exposes conflicts between the different levels of government. "The Relativity of Sustainability," by William R. Code, challenges the idea that residential intensification of the downtown area is the key to urban sustainability. The multi-nodal city with multi-use suburbs is the proposed alternative. "The Regulatory Framework and the Development of Sustainable Housing and Communities: Can We Achieve Sustainable Objectives?," by Julie Tasker-Brown, identifies key characteristics of sustainable communities and proposes regulatory changes. "Reconsidering the Dream: A Report on Research Undertaken Regarding Contemporary Suburbia With a View Towards a New Morphology" shows how limited familiarity with the vast literature now available on urban sustainability is in discussions of suburbia. Ian MacBurnie, the author, refers to interesting literature on the history of suburbia. He is optimistic about the viability of the suburb and suggests gridded streets and mixed density as fixes for suburbia. However, he does not evaluate whether his proposed fixes are sustainable. "Linking Affordable Housing and Environmental Protection: A New Framework for Sustainable Urban Development Policy," by Mark Roseland, critiques the Brundtland Commission's version of sustainable development, and offers an example of integrating equity into urban development. He also describes the use of Community Land Trusts to promote sustainable use of land.

47. Beavis, Mary Ann, and Jeffrey Patterson. *A Select, Annotated Bibliography on Sustainable Cities*. Winnipeg: Institute of Urban Studies, 1992.

Keywords: current, sustainability

This is a useful and thoughtfully annotated work. It covers a range of issues in urban sustainability including design, air quality, energy, agriculture, environmental policies, water issues, developing countries, and financial constraints. However, the present bibliography is more comprehensive and up-to-date.

48. Benello, C. George, Robert Swan, and Shann Turibul. *Building Sustainable Communities*. New York: Bootstrap Press, 1989.

Keywords: community, economics, sustainability

Based on the Schumacher Society Seminars on Community Economic Transformation, this book is a valuable guide to building sustainable communities. It is divided into three major sections:
    1) community land trusts and other community ownership of national resources
    2) worker-managed enterprises and other self-management techniques
    3) community currency and banking.
    A lexicon of social capitalism and a bibliography of key works on self-reliant economic change are also included. Concepts are linked with concrete ideas and examples. A "bottom-up" rather than a "top-down" economic transformation is envisaged. Unemployment, the depletion of nonrenewable resources, and tools for community economic transformation that place the well-being of people and sustainability ahead of economic activity are at the center of concern. A good bibliography rounds off this work.

49. Bertuglia, Cristoforo Sergio, G. P. Clarke, and Alan Geoffrey Wilson, eds. *Modelling the City: Performance, Policy and Planning*. New York: Routledge, 1994.

Keywords: public policy, quality of life, urban planning

While there has been substantial progress with a wide range of theoretical problems in urban modeling, modelers have not paid enough attention to the usefulness of their model outputs in terms of indicators that offer new insights into the workings of the city or region. Too often in the past, modelers have focussed on the direct use of model predictions for planning without fully exploring the rich information base created from both data input into models and the outputs of model simulations. In addition, contemporary concern with performance measurement in many service organizations makes it appropriate to review the development of performance indicators in urban planning as a whole, and urban modeling in particular. *Modelling the City* examines the changing role of urban models with respect to both the need to re-address measures of urban well-being and the perceived need to bring model outputs more in tune with key planning problems.

The book offers a new geography of performance indicators for the public and private sector based on the principles of spatial interaction. This new geography includes definitions of both residence- and facility-based indicators. The spatial interrelationships between these two sets of indicators are likely to offer new insights into the age-old equity-efficiency problem.

50. Billinghurst, Lucy, and Elizabeth Crowther-Hunt. *Inner Cities, Inner Strengths*. London: Industrial Society, 1990.

Keywords: social fabric, community, inner cities, urban design, urban planning

The future of viable urban communities lies in its people. It is argued that the skills, aspirations, and courage of a city's citizens are essential tools for building a stable urban environment through regeneration. The involvement of local people in planning, management, and execution of inner-city initiatives is stressed as a solution to problems such as poverty, housing for the poor, and unemployment. Increasing public involvement also allows morale to evolve in a community as its citizens develop a sense of political efficacy.

51. Birnbaum, Charles A., and Cheryl Wagner, eds. *Making Educated Decisions: A Landscape Preservation Bibliography*. Washington, D.C.: Department of the Interior, National Park Service, Cultural Resources, Preservation Assistance Division, 1994.

Keywords: current, architecture, ecology, green space, public space

This useful bibliography contains over 500 citations with very brief annotations. The works cited cover the areas of landscape preservation philosophy, research, preservation planning, practice, treatment, management, and maintenance. Many of the citations are case studies from forty-eight states in the United States and from twenty-seven other countries. A geographic as well as a subject and author index is also included. Each citation is assessed in terms of its compatibility with the *Secretary of the Interior's Standards* whose mission it is to promote and achieve "a wise use of our land (and) preserving the environmental and cultural values of our national parks and historical places." The bibliography is designed for practitioners, stewards, educators, scholars, and students.

52. Blackman, Tim. *Urban Policy in Practice*. London: Routledge, 1995.

Keywords: community, economics, health, public policy, Britain

Local governments can provide democratic, strategic, and sustainable policies that allow for the management of services close to the consumer. This book is a detailed, practical, and critical guide to urban policy in Britain. It aims to study the policies regarding issues such as quality of public services, community development, the local economy, environmental issues, public health, and education and training. A critical assessment of recent policies and case studies is included.

The opening chapter discusses urban policy as framework for allocating resources to meet needs. How to define "need" and how to assess it are major themes of the book. Subsequent chapters explore how policy is put into practice using objective setting, performance indicators, and evaluations of its effects.

53. Blake, Peter. *Form Follows Fiasco: Why Modern Architecture Hasn't Worked*. Boston: Little Brown, 1977.

Keywords: architecture, modernism, classic

This book exposes the flaws of modernism in architecture, which the author once promoted. An article in the *Atlantic Monthly* (September 1974 issue) outlined nine fallacies and attempted to deal with each one. The author's new perceptions on the subject have been developed to form this book, after much experience as an architect who both designs and builds. Commonly accepted concepts of nature, planning, and urban design began to make little sense after the author began practicing architecture. He decided to question every assumption. Le Corbusier, Mies van der Rohe, and Frank Lloyd Wright— the founders of modern architecture—all come under the author's critical scrutiny. This is a book of questions that are not normally asked, but should be. Much of the technical data for this book was gathered over the twelve years that the author served as editor-in-chief of the *Architectural Forum* and then *Architecture Plus*.

54. Blowers, Andrew, ed. *Planning for a Sustainable Environment: A Report by the Town and Country Planning Association*. London: Earthscan, 1993.

Keywords: energy, environmental pollution, public policy, sustainability, urban planning, waste, Britain

Sustainable forms of development *are* possible but can be achieved only through an integrated, strategic, and long-term approach. The authors in this work show how responsible and responsive planning in the UK must take more account of the environmental contexts and social impacts. They offer both practical suggestions and broader perspectives on sustainable development, and examine all the main elements of planning policy, including energy, pollution and waste, construction, transport, the economy, and urban form. In the final two chapters, the authors indicate what a sustainable environment would be like and how it could be achieved.

55. Boardman, Brenda. *Fuel Poverty: From Cold Homes to Affordable Warmth*. London:

Belhaven Press, 1991.

Keywords: energy, energy efficiency, poverty, Britain

Boardman's contribution is an important one, for it highlights what policies should and shouldn't do. It contains information regarding energy efficiency in homes and how poverty affects the quality of home life, home heating, in particular. Chapter 1 sets out the framework for studying fuel poverty in Britain. Next, the author places fuel poverty in an historical context and provides a profile of the fuel poor. Chapter 4 looks into sources of heat loss in homes, what added insulation can do, government-funded insulation programs, and other initiatives. The subsequent two chapters report on the energy efficiency of homes and the required temperatures within them. It is shown, through a study of household trends, that the fuel poor do not meet the required temperatures. Cost-effective energy efficiency improvements, a proposed program for affordable warmth, and other solutions conclude the book.

56. Bocock, Robert. *Consumption.* New York: Routledge, 1993.

Keywords: social fabric, consumerism

Consumption is a specifically urban phenomenon, and the culture of consumerism defines the very nature of many of our most ubiquitous social institutions. This book is a good introduction to the field. The author, a senior lecturer in Sociology at the Open University, presents one of the best critical reviews of sociological approaches to consumption and consumerism in modern and postmodern societies. The contributions of writers such as Veblen, Simmel, Marx, Gramsci, Weber, Bourdie, Lacan, and Baudrillard are discussed concisely as are structuralist and "critical theory" contributions to the analysis of consumption. This is not a book about the economic dimensions of consumption but deals with the notion as a sociocultural category.

57. Boerner, Deborah A. "Trees and Your Health." *American Forests* 1989 (Sept./Oct. 1989): 37-41.

Keywords: green cities, green space, health, psychological health

This article discusses new research that suggests that trees and urban vegetation can have a powerful positive effect on city dwellers, by speeding up human healing, easing stress, and helping us choose a better lifestyle.

58. Boivin, Robert, and Jean-François Pronovost, eds. *The Bicycle: Global Perspectives.* Montreal: Vélo Québec, 1992.

Keywords: case studies, public policy

The bicycle is the most socially affordable and environmentally friendly mode of transportation. This volume contains 170 papers (some in French, some in English, some in both languages) that were presented at the Conférence Vélo Mondiale—Pro Bike— Vélo City held in Montreal September 13-17, 1992. The articles seek to explore constructive approaches to integrating the bicycle into transportation policies. The papers are divided into five sections. The first one, "Around the World," contains papers on bicycle policies in Nigeria, France, Ghana, Uganda, the former Soviet Union and Baltic States, Czechoslovakia, Poland, and various cities and provinces in Canada. The other four sections survey current work in the fields of planning and implementation, safety, political strategies, and recreation and tourism.

59. Bookchin, Murray. *Urbanization Without Cities: The Rise and Decline of Citizenship.* Montreal: Black Rose Books, 1992.

Keywords: biosphere, community, democracy, ecology, environmental overload, philosophy of the urban environment, social ecology

Massive contemporary urbanization is sweeping away so many natural features of our planet that we can ignore the ecological consequences of urbanization only at our peril. Bookchin suggests that considering the city as an ecocommunity helps us better conceive of urbanization in ecological terms, and not merely as a phenomenon with social and cultural dimensions alone. While many researchers have directed their attention to the impact of urbanization on natural systems, Bookchin says that few have analyzed the changes urbanization has produced in our sensibility toward society and the natural world.

The present book attempts to remedy this oversight by developing the groundwork for a "social ecology" through which ecological thinking can be made more relevant to the modern human condition. In Bookchin's own words, "What I wish to do is to redeem the city, to visualize it not as a threat to the environment but as a uniquely human, ethical, and ecological community that often lived in balance with nature and created institutional forms that sharpened human awareness of their sense of natural place as well as social place."

The notion of social ecology allows Bookchin to redefine the city and citizenship in terms that include references to the natural world. Interesting and instructive parallels thus emerge between, for example, civic participation as the social counterpart to biological mutualism, citizenship as the social counterpart of biotic involvement in shaping the form of a natural ecocommunity, and civic history as the social counterpart to natural history.

60. Bottles, Scott L. *Los Angeles and the Automobile: The Making of the Modern City.* Berkeley: University of California Press, 1987.

Keywords: automobiles, democracy, traffic, transportation, urban design, urban planning, United States

The focus here is on the city of Los Angeles and its history from the turn of the century to the present. Through this historical approach, the author is able to critically examine the impact of cars upon American society. He successfully drives home the point that "Perhaps no technological innovation has affected the character of American cities as much as the automobile." Topics discussed in this excellent source include: effects on air quality, effects on community design, suburbs, the sense of community, and the influence on quality of urban life. Also discussed is the role of automobile corporations in the weakening of urban public transportation systems.

61. Bowman, Brian, Robert L. Vecellio, and David W. Haynes. "Strategies for Increasing Bicycle and Pedestrian Safety and Use." *Journal of Urban Planning and Development* 120, 3 (September 1994): 105-13.

Keywords: pedestrians, transportation

Passage of the 1991 Intermodal Surface Transportation Efficiency Act (ISTEA and pronounced ice-tea in popular parlance) has resulted in increased emphasis on alternative modes of transportation. Two old modes of transportation, bicycling and walking, are beginning to receive renewed attention. This attention is centered on those actions that are effective in increasing the safety and usage of bicycling and walking. With these goals in mind, many agencies are developing programs that use the elements of engineering, education, and enforcement directed toward all segments of the community. This paper presents the results of a project sponsored by the Federal Highway Administration that compiled considerations and inducements that could be used by local agencies to increase bicycle and pedestrian activity. Strategies addressed include: providing bicycle facilities for employees; linking bicycling and walking with mass transit; eliminating roadway hazards for bicyclists; removing sidewalk obstacles for pedestrians; regulating bicycle couriers; and maintaining pedestrian facilities through construction zones.

Many of these strategies for safer cycling and walking are rather obvious (such as prohibiting headphones and cycling under the influence of drugs or alcohol). The discussion of each strategy is brief and often uninformative.

62. Boyden, Stephen, Sheelagh Millan, Ken Newcombe, and Beverly O'Neill. *The Ecology of a City and its People: The Case of Hong Kong.* Canberra: Australian National University Press, 1981.

Keywords: urban metabolism, ecology, energy, food, land use, quality of life, case study, classic

Excessive fragmentation and specialization in education, research, and government are identified as the primary causes of global problems. On the other hand, human experience and the natural world involve a continual interaction, or interplay, of all facets of reality. Thus, in order to solve social and environmental problems there must be an increase in holistic or comprehensive knowledge concerning the interwoven nature of reality. This book is an account of a holistic ecological study of the urban settlement of Hong Kong by the Human Ecology Group at The Australian National University. This study became known as the Hong Kong Human Ecology Programme. It was adopted by UNESCO in 1974 as a pilot project in its Man and the Biosphere Programme. It is an attempt to holistically describe a human settlement in terms of its societal, cultural, physical, and biotic components, while considering the complex relations between components and how they relate to the well-being of humans and the biosphere. The book has three goals: to encourage holistic thinking through the comprehensive study of Hong Kong, to draw attention to global ecological problems, and to study the interrelationships between cultural and natural processes.

The authors hope that ecological studies similar to this can be used to find answers to global concerns such as the implications of our current way of life on civilization and the biosphere and the fulfillment of human needs. The first part of the book (chapters 1-3) consists of an ecological and historical background of Hong Kong. The second part (chapters 4-14) focuses on the ecology of Hong Kong, including a study of energy and nutrient flows and a study of the well-being and health of its population. In the third part, the findings arising from the ecological study of Hong Kong are used to discuss general implications for the future of urban settlements. This is a classic work in the field of urban metabolism.

63. Boyer, M. Christine. *The City of Collective Memory: Its Historical Imagery and Architectural Entertainments*. Cambridge, Mass.: MIT Press, 1994.

Keywords: sociocultural, architecture, built environment, experience of place, modernism

This work investigates representational images and architectural entertainments of present-day cities. By doing so, it attempts to critique the practice of architecture, city planning, and historic preservation in a specific manner. It recognizes that these arts still carry within their visual imaginations the influence of nineteenth-century procedures and representational views of city building. The book argues that the shift of view from the present to the historical, from the modern to the traditional, from twentieth-century to nineteenth-century city forms, leaves many questions unanswered and some not even posed. The fundamental relationship between architecture, urban form, and history is questioned, for the city is the collective expression of architecture and it carries in the weaving and unraveling of its fabric the memory traces of earlier architectural forms, city plans, and public monuments.

64. Breen, Ann, and Dick Rigby. *Waterfronts: Cities Reclaim Their Edge*. New York: McGraw-Hill, 1994.

Keywords: case studies, urban design

This book is a product of an award program organized by the Waterfront Center. Documentation and examples are given to show that the waterfront has been the most fertile area of planning and development in our communities. The waterfront is considered from many perspectives: cultural, environmental, historic, mixed-use, recreational, residential, planning, and work. Chapters 2 to 9 are analyses of prototypical examples of the wide variety of urban waterfront transformations. The authors love cities and see the transformation of the urban waterfront as playing a major role in efforts to test the health of our city centers. The urban waterfront phenomenon, the authors argue, is a leading indicator validating the value of the city core, and this is predicted to become stronger in coming years. Seventy-five projects are discussed in this book.

65. Breheny, M. J., ed. *Sustainable Development and Urban Form*. London: Pion Limited, 1992.

Keywords: current, energy, energy efficiency, land use, sustainability, telecommunications, transportation, urban design

A discussion of sustainability must include a significant urban focus, for cities are the major consumers of energy and natural resources and the major producers of pollution and waste. The contributors to this book are concerned with the urban and regional dimensions of sustainability and contemplate what changes would result through alternative kinds of urban form. The first few articles are general in focus and examine wide political, definitional, and technological issues. The focus becomes progressively less general, with the next set of chapters exploring the sustainability of different urban forms. The potential role of land-use planning, the conflict between green spaces and increasing urban densities, the Dutch planning doctrine, and the compact city are examined. The next two chapters: "Energy Use, Transport and Settlement Patterns" and "Patterns of Land Use in English Towns: Implications for Energy Use and Carbon Dioxide Emissions" deal with the energy efficiency of different urban forms. Specific aspects of sustainability are the subjects of the remaining chapters. Barton analyzes the potential benefits of a light rail transit system in Bristol, England. How market-based decisions frustrate environmental policy and how to change this situation are the subjects of Rydin's contribution. The role of geographic information systems (GIS) and the prospects of combined heat and power systems in reducing energy consumption are discussed in the final two chapters.

66. Brewster, George Burton. "A Better Way to Build." *Urban Land* 1995 (June 1995): 30-35.

Keywords: architecture, energy, energy efficiency, waste

The article contains a summary of green design principles. It also argues for the need for environmentally responsible development. The largest section of the article is devoted to outlining what environmentally responsible development is. It is defined here as "the production of buildings and communities that conserve resources and reduce waste through more efficient use of materials, energy, and water; that are more durable and useful; and that are designed for adaptive use or the recycling of their materials."

67. British Columbia Round Table. *State of Sustainability: Urban Sustainability and Containment.* Victoria, B.C.: Crown Publication, 1994.

Keywords: ecology, sustainability, Canada

This volume contains methods, definitions, approaches and, most important, indicators that pertain to urban sustainability. The main goal is to develop a long-term strategy to preserve and protect the planet's ecosystem internationally without government barriers and narrow social or economic interests.

The British Columbia Round Table has developed a provincial strategy for sustainability, but it requires a commitment to change for this strategy to succeed. The section on indicators is extremely important because, without the ability to measure the health of environmental, economic, and social systems, the effectiveness of proposed solutions is just a guess. Though applied to British Columbia, the ideas can be generalized. A thematic model is given for measuring sustainability. The indicators are applied to key issues such as population growth, the urban environment, and social well-being. Recommendations based on the proposed indicators are given. It is concluded that compact cities can improve the quality of life, protect environmental values, and reduce wasted travel time as well as the cost of development.

68. Brooke, Steven. *Seaside*. Gretna, La.: Pelican Publishing, 1995.

Keywords: urban design, new urbanism, architecture

Seaside, Florida was meant to be—and to a large extent is—a model New Urbanist development. Most people will be familiar with it since it was satirized in, and was the setting for, the popular 1999 movie *The Truman Show*. This book consists of text and photographs by the famous architectural photographer Steven Brook. It is instructive on how New Urbanist design principles translate into actuality, and also demonstrates the range of architectural styles that can be accommodated by these principles. The photographs, on their own, are quite beautiful.

69. Brotchie, John, Peter Newton, et al., eds. *The Future of Urban Form: The Impact of New Technology*. New York: Nichols Publishing, 1985.

Keywords: social fabric, technology, telecommunications, transportation, urban design, urban planning

This collection of exploratory essays is an outcome of a workshop held in Waterloo, Canada, in July 1983 as part of an international conference on technological change and urban form, convened by the International Council for Building Research Studies. The chapters in this volume are future-oriented and are concerned with exploring, often speculatively, the transition of technologically advanced Western societies to an information-based post-industrial state and the impact that such a transition is likely to have on national settlement systems. This is a valuable resource for anybody who wishes to examine the possible social and environmental impacts of different kinds of information systems authorities.

70. Brotchie, John F., Peter Hall, and Peter W. Newton, eds. *The Spatial Impact of Technological Change*. Beckenham, Kent: Croom Helm, 1987.

Keywords: technology, urban planning

While the subject of the book (the impact of technology on society) is not specifically urban, many of the chapters' topics relate directly or indirectly to life in cities, for example, "Urban Issues in an Advanced Industrial Society," "Cities and Regions in the Electronic Age" and "Spatial Planning in the Information Age." These chapters ask many important questions about the changes the new technologies will bring to urban planning and living.

71. Brower, Sidney. *Good Neighborhoods: A Study of In-Town & Suburban Residential Environments*. Westport, Conn.: Praeger, 1996.

Keywords: social fabric, housing, neighborhood, suburbs

Creators of neighborhoods are guided by their visions of a good neighborhood. But what is a good neighborhood? It is the position of the author that there are many different types of good neighborhoods for different types of lifestyles. In this book, he develops a typology of good neighborhoods based on the literature and on interviews with residents. In the first chapter, it is stated that a neighborhood typology should be based on differences in residential lifestyle rather than differences in geographic location that are conventionally used. The relationship between the housing unit and the neighborhood is the focus of chapter 2. How do neighborhoods get to be the way they are? This question is addressed in chapter 3 by looking to the changing attitudes toward housing and neighborhoods. The next three chapters look at popular images of desirable neighborhoods with examples of real-life, ideal, and mythical neighborhoods. A list of the thirty qualities associated with good neighborhoods is provided in chapter 7. Chapter 8 explores neighborhood typologies based on place, activity, personality, and culture. Chapter 9 states and supports the author's four-part neighborhood typology system, while the next chapter discusses and elaborates on it. The typology can be used by public planners, who should take a type-specific approach to public policy. This is the message of the concluding chapter.

72. Bruce, J. P., Hoe-song Yi, and Erik F. Haites, eds. *Climate Change 1995: Economic and Social Dimensions of Climate Change*. Cambridge: Cambridge University Press, 1996.

Keywords: quality of life, sustainability, economics

While this report may seem like "too much" information for planners and engineers, it provides a useful range of information for anyone interested in expanding their understanding of the social and economic impacts of climate change (global warming). Its discussion of no-regrets policies may provide options for those facing opposition to initiatives to combat climate change.

73. Bunting, Trudi, ed. *Canadian Cities in Transition*. Toronto: Oxford University Press, 1991.

Keywords: social fabric, poverty, public policy, social ecology, urban planning, Canada

The purpose of this collection is to provide a detailed overview of trends affecting Canadian cities. Intended as a textbook for urban geography students, the perspective of the city presented here is mostly that of geography, but planning, engineering, and political science approaches are also included. Throughout the book, Canada's unique urban situation is contrasted with the American situation. Part 1, "National Perspectives" studies urban characteristics that concern Canadian cities. Part 2, "Regional Perspectives" considers cities' zones of influence and the distributions of population and economic activity across Canada. The form of cities and the social forces that shape them are probed in part 3, while urban functions are investigated in part 4. Urban policy-making, urban planning and its history, and the poverty and limitations faced by disadvantaged groups are the focus of the final section. The appendices provide useful statistics on demographics, socioeconomic features, and other fields in Canadian census metropolitan areas.

74. Button, Kenneth John, and Jean-Philippe Barde, eds. *Transport Policy and the Environment: Six Case Studies*. London: Earthscan, 1990.

Keywords: case studies, pedestrians, public policy, traffic, transportation

In most countries, transport policy is a major government concern, yet it is rare for decisions to be made outside a narrow set of sectoral considerations. This book looks at seven countries: the UK, the United States, West Germany, France, the Netherlands, Greece, and Italy. Each case demonstrates the problems in transport policies produced by the failure to take into account the true social costs. This failure is a consequence of departmental divisions; transport, the environment, the exchequer, etc. all having their own, quite separate ministries. Here, a group of economists have demonstrated the folly of such partial ways of thinking and have provided models for ways to go forward.

75. Button, Kenneth. *Transport, the Environment and Economic Policy*. Brookfield, Vt.: Edward Elgar, 1993.

Keywords: economics, environmental planning, transportation

This book attempts to explain the environmental impact of transportation by the application of economic theories. Various policy options with which to resolve the problems are then suggested. While the book is primarily concerned with economics, not ecology, it argues that the two are not easily separated. The goal of attaining guidelines for environmental protection is maintained throughout.

Chapters 1-3 examine existing international transport systems, current trends, and the policies governing them. The main focus is on industrialized countries, but the developing world and Eastern Europe are also studied. With this background established, the environmental impact of transport is discussed.

Chapter 4 reviews the techniques used to evaluate the environmental impacts of transport and reports certain values currently used for decision making. It is concluded that although much work still needs to be done in this area, there exists substantial knowledge with which to make policy trade-offs. Chapters 5 and 6 examine the roots of environmental problems via welfare economics. While chapter 5 focuses on environmental problems caused by market failures, chapter 6 examines problems created by misguided government transport policies.

The remainder of the book deals with policy-making responses to environmental damage caused by transportation. Chapter 7 examines a variety of economic tools that may be used by government. These include tax refunds, emission charges, parking fees, and road pricing. Where these are not appropriate or feasible, chapter 8 discusses other approaches which include standards, land-use planning, and moral judgement. The final chapter briefly examines the political economy of environmental policy in the transport sector. The creation of international environmental policy is discussed along with the difficulties associated with such efforts.

76. Byrne, John, and Daniel Rich, eds. *Energy and Cities: Energy Policy Studies*. Vol. 2. New Brunswick, N.J.: Transaction Books, 1985.

Keywords: energy, transformation

The types and quantities of energy used by cities have played a fundamental role in their development as well as predicting the path they would follow in the future. Within each of the five articles that make up this book are issues brought to life by the changing relationship between cities and energy. The greatest debate among them is whether cities will "reconcentrate" as a result of the energy crisis or "deconcentrate." Other issues discussed are: "the role of cities as energy resource allocation systems"; barriers to saving energy in the urban built environment; the international economic and political power that energy can have over communities and the need for cities to change their role from "consumers of goods to producers of wealth"; hard vs. soft energy paths; methods of energy production where the consumer can become a producer in their own energy supply; the impacts that changing forms and uses of energy will have on society; and the social costs involved in these transformations. A selective bibliography by Cecilia Martinez on energy and cities rounds out the book.

77. Byrum, Oliver. *Old Problems in New Times: Urban Strategies for the 1990s*. 2nd ed. Chicago: APA Planners Press, 1992.

Keywords: housing, inner cities, neighborhood, poverty, public policy

As the title suggests, this book deals with perennial and ubiquitous problems faced by cities. Poverty and low income neighborhoods, urban decay, housing, and unemployment are all discussed in the context of new strategies appropriate for the last decade of this century. Starting with a short review of current research in the field, the impact of economic or market forces on inner-city developments is examined and various public policy responses are assessed. Chapter 3 presents a synoptic discussion of a "six-point metropolitan and city strategy" that can be used to ameliorate urban conditions. The subsequent chapters elaborate these strategies in detail. The six points revolve around: (1) employment generation to reduce poverty; (2) various interventions in the housing market to reduce concentration of poverty in the inner city; (3) ways in which the human development quality of low-income neighborhoods can be maintained and improved; (4) prevention of the deterioration of the marketplace value of city neighborhoods in the metropolitan housing market; (5) strategies whereby the inner city can be synergistically linked to metropolitan opportunities; and (6) the mobilization of metropolitan leadership toward creative problem-solving and shared responsibility vis-à-vis inner-city problems.

This book was sponsored by the Center for Urban and Regional Affairs at the University of Minnesota and published under the aegis of the American Planning Association.

78. Cadman, David, and Geoffrey Payne, eds. *The Living City: Towards a Sustainable Future*. New York: Routledge, 1990.

Keywords: urban metabolism, sociocultural, community, developing countries, sustainability

This is a collection of papers presented at "The Seminar on Future Cities," held at the Oxford Polytechnic in 1987. Section 1 of the book is a compendium of mainstream ideas, recent trends, and conditions in cities of the developed and developing world. Emphasis is given to present trajectories in these cities and emerging and existing policy responses. The overall suggestion is that many of these policy responses and mainstream ideas are too narrow or economistic in their approach.

Section 2 attempts to overcome the narrowness of conventional approaches and their supposed economic "neutrality" by widening the ways in which problems facing cities may be addressed, and questions the assumptions that underlie the "neutrality" of the economist's approach. A critique of conventional approaches is expanded into a presentation of other approaches—many acknowledging their value-laden assumptions—which, in the long term, may be of much greater significance. Some of these alternative approaches include notions of participation, ecological balance, local self-reliance, economic sustainability, and technological choice. This second section also includes Herbert Girardet's oft-cited essay "The Metabolism of Cities," as well as case studies on the Orangi project in Karachi, Pakistan, and the development of new towns in Tanzania and Malaysia.

79. Calabrese, Edward J., and Elaina Kenyon. *Air Toxics and Risk Assessment*. Chelsea, Mich.: Lewis Publishers, 1991.

Keywords: biosphere, air pollution, public policy, risk assessment

This volume presents a well-researched model for assessing potential risks to public health from exposure to air toxics. In addition to providing a decision tree framework that could be applied to any compound, the book applies the methodology to over 100 specific toxic agents. The information in the book is of both theoretical and practical value, especially for those in the standard-setting professions.

80. Caldwell, Lynton Keith and Kristin S. Shrader-Frechette. *Policy for Land: Law and Ethics*. Lanham, Md.: Rowman & Littlefield Publishers, 1993.

Keywords: environmental overload, ground pollution, land use, public policy, sustainability

This study of land use policy examines its aesthetic, ecological, economic, and ethical dimensions. It discusses several approaches to land use ethics as well as Lockean concepts of land ownership. It seeks to arrive at a consensus on what ethical land use is and to urge readers to critique current land management practices and laws pertaining to land and land use politics. The need for a sustainable land use policy is emphasized.

81. Calthorpe, Peter. "The Post-Suburban Metropolis." *Whole Earth Review*, December 21, 1991, 44-51.

Keywords: social fabric, architecture, automobiles, built environment, community, green space, identity, neighborhood, pedestrians, technology, transportation, new urbanism

The technology of the built environment is easy to criticize and difficult to change, particularly as it relates to our ever-increasing dependence on automobiles. Architect and planner Peter Calthorpe is designing alternatives that are actually getting built.

The author discusses how the scale and character of neighborhood streets must change to facilitate pedestrian-friendly connections and social places, rather than car-dominated driveways and high-speed collectors.

Calthorpe also discusses how town centers should combine civic functions, small businesses, and stores with parks, plazas, transit shops, and daycare—rather than "strip" retail centers lining heavily traveled arterioles. This is a very good introduction to what has lately emerged as the New Urbanism.

82. Calthorpe, Peter. *The Next American Metropolis: Ecology, Community, and the American Dream*. New York: Princeton Architectural Press, 1993.

Keywords: social fabric, case studies, community, urban ecology, urban planning, new urbanism, classic

This is not a study of the ecology of natural systems nor about urban ecology per se, whether construed in the sense of the urban sociology of the Chicago School or as "urban metabolism." Calthorpe is concerned here about the ecology of communities in terms of the interaction between diversity, interdependence, scale, and decentralization—principles drawn from ecology that can help us conceptualize the city, suburb, and region. With such a viewpoint, Calthorpe suggests we can more readily see the viability of communities that are simultaneously more "diverse and integrated" in use and population, built to human scale and pedestrian-friendly, communities organized along the formal acceptance of the fact of decentralization at work. Links are drawn between human nature and human patterns of settlement. How this has an impact on our environment and economy is discussed, and many suggestions are given as to how some of the more adverse effects may be changed.

83. Canada Mortgage and Housing Corporation. *The Ecological City: Canada's Overview*. Ottawa: Canada Mortgage and Housing Corporation, 1995.

Keywords: current, energy, environmental pollution, green cities, green space, hazardous waste, health, housing, public policy, sewage, sustainability, transportation, urban design, urban ecology, water, Canada

The Project Group on Ecological Cities was established by the Organization for Economic Cooperation and Devlopment's Group on Urban Affairs in order to identify innovative strategies aimed at creating more sustainable cities. This report, which provides a valuable overview of Canada's ecological cities programs, represents Canada's contribution to the OECD Group.

The first section discusses the definition of the ecological city or region and the theory behind the ecological approach to urban policy. The second section provides background information regarding Canada's social, political, demographic, geographic, and economic climate. The status of Canada's progress toward ecological cities is reported in the next section. Here, the planned and already implemented initiatives of various Canadian cities are summarized under the headings of land-use, transportation, energy consumption and conservation, water resources, wastewater treatment, air quality and atmospheric change, storm water, solid waste management, hazardous waste management, green space, housing, crime, social spending and child poverty, gender issues, and health. While the initiatives appear to be numerous, the conclusion is that there is still a very long way to go. The challenges to and opportunities for urban sustainability are analyzed in section 4 in terms of values and beliefs, information, education, institutions, public participation/consultation, and economics. Section 5 features Vancouver and Hamilton-Wentworth's sustainability strategies along with seven innovative policy tools which may be used to overcome the previously mentioned challenges. Since the Project Group on the Ecological Cities emphasizes *integrated* approaches to sustainability, the various institutional structures and integrative institutions and their roles are described in the final two sections.

84. Canadian Urban Institute. *Dialogue on Urban Issues: A Series of Discussions with Prominent Speakers on Current Urban Issues.* Toronto: Canadian Urban Institute, 1991.

Keywords: urban planning

This report is based on the Urban Focus Series of breakfast seminars initiated by the Canadian Urban Institute, the aim of which was to hear views on urban issues from prominent speakers. Issues pressing to the Greater Toronto Area are emphasized but some universal topics are discussed as well. Summaries of the various presentations are provided along with the minutes of the discussions that followed. Issues of equity, employment, and the economy, as well as environmental protection, are discussed by Environment Minister Ruth Grier in the second section. A key suggestion here is the creation of a social planning mechanism that is integrated with those for environmental and economic planning.

"Cities and Environment," by Jeb Brugmann, is directed towards the International Council for Local Environmental Initiatives, which tried to establish a model for a well-managed community. It considers their suggestions in terms of human settlements overall.

Local planning problems are also discussed. The concept of the Urban Ecosystem is fleshed out and a full systems approach is encouraged for recognizing the interdependence between issues. Other topics are "Social and Community Services: Who's in Charge? Who Should Be?" by Don Richmond, "The Future of the Greater Toronto Area: A View From Mississauga" by its mayor, Hazel McCallion, "Quebec's New Approach to Provincial-Municipal Relations" by Robert Courboyer, and "Montreal Faces its Challenges" by Serge Carreau.

85. Canter, David, Martin Krampen, and David Stea, eds. *Environmental Policy, Assessment and Communication.* Vol. 2. Ethnoscapes. Aldershot, England: Avebury, 1988.

Keywords: support, built environment, community, housing, policy

This collection deals with the human-environment relation in such areas as crime, housing, and the natural environment. Most of the chapters report the results of case studies or surveys. The volume does not have a specific urban focus, but many topics such as crime and community, mass housing, and others give insights to a discussion of healthy cities.

86. Canter, David, Martin Krampen, and David Stea, eds. *Environmental Perspectives.* Vol. 1. Ethnoscapes. Aldershot, England: Avebury, 1988.

Keywords: support, built environment, experience of place

This collection of papers exemplifies the increasing importance of environmental psychology for the design of the built environment. They include an explanation of how environmental variables may be used for the prediction of human behavior; cultural specificity and its relationship to the uniqueness of various built forms in Africa; the study of built forms autonomous from the cultural practices that shape it; and an overview of the work of William Morris, for whom architecture was an art "made by the people for the people as a joy for the maker and user."

87. Carew-Reid, J., R. Prescott-Allen, S. Bass, and D. B. Dalal-Clayton. *Strategies for National Sustainable Development: A Handbook for their Planning and Implementation.* London: Earthscan, 1994.

Keywords: current, public policy, sustainability

Any National Sustainable Development Strategy (NSDS) has a great impact on the sustainability of cities. This handbook is included in the Healthy Cities bibliography to assist practitioners in developing and implementing NSDSs. The book summarizes the lessons learned from over sixty national and provincial conservation strategies, environmental action plans, development plans, and other multi-sectoral strategies in Africa, Asia, Latin America, and some OECD countries. It emphasizes strategies that focus not only on the environment, but rather integrate environmental considerations with social and economic aspects. Part 1, "An Approach to National Strategies" includes "Ten Lessons and Features for Success," contributions made by NSDSs, and the issue of participation. Part 2, "The Strategy Cycle" gives useful advice on "Getting Started," "Planning the Strategy," "Implementing the Strategy," and "Keeping Strategies on Track." Financing strategies and external agencies' roles are discussed in part 3.

88. Carr, F. Housley. "Client Backing Crucial to Ecological Building." *ENR* 233, 20 (Nov. 14, 1994).

Keywords: energy efficiency, sustainability

This article is about a Pet Shelter designed with sustainability in mind. It outlines the features that make the building sustainable, such as high-performance heat-mirror glazing; high-efficiency heating; ventilating and air-conditioning systems; floor tiles made from byproducts of glass manufacturing; adhesive-backed carpeting installed without toxic glues and rigid insulation free of ozone-damaging chlorofluorocarbons, both made from at least 50 percent recycled materials; floor mats composed of recycled tire rubber; and benches and bathroom partitions composed of 65 percent recycled plastic. The author emphasizes that the Pet Shelter was not difficult to build compared to conventional buildings and will save money in energy and maintenance costs that will amply repay the slightly higher costs of initial construction.

89. Carr, Stephen, et al. *Public Space.* New York: Cambridge University Press, 1992.

Keywords: public policy, public space, urban design

This is a collaborative work between an architect/environmental designer, a landscape architect, an environmental psychologist, and an open-space administrator. Together, the authors pool their expertise in the subject common to all: public space. The emphasis is on the actual use and value attributed to public space by the people most involved in it. This in turn informs the way such spaces should be designed and built. The authors thus establish a direct link between social use of public space and design. This would seem trivial were it not for their extensive examination of the history of public life and public space, evidence from current research on this area, and their own experience in professional planning, design, management, and analysis of this relationship.

The authors develop three guiding principles from this research—namely, that the design and management of public spaces should evolve from three principles: (1) the essential needs of the users; (2) their spatial rights; and (3) the meanings the users seek in such spaces. Several original case studies along with illustrations serve to amplify the above considerations and reveal how each of the three principles can be adapted to the unique social and environmental context of different public spaces. The book is aimed at a large and varied audience, including planners, developers, concerned citizens, and designers.

90. Carstensen, Edwin L. *Biological Effects of Transmission Line Fields*. New York: Elsevier, 1987.

Keywords: electromagnetic fields and health, health, risk assessment

This work has been prepared for those professionals or lay readers who have an interest in the potential for biological effects of the electric and magnetic fields associated with power transmission lines—in particular, the extra high voltage transmission lines that pervade our modern world, and the ultra high voltage transmission lines that are technically feasible and offer prospects of greater efficiency in the transport of power in the future.

Chapter 3 discusses the electrical properties of biological materials and their relationship to the structure and composition of the tissues. Chapter 4 contains world literature describing observations of plants and animals that have been exposed to electric and magnetic fields. Chapters 5 to 9 compose a series of well-documented effects on a subject-by-subject basis. The topic of chapter 10 is magnetic fields and cancer.

91. Cartwright, Fraser. *Urban Dynamics*. Toronto: Oxford University Press, 1991.

Keywords: current, social ecology, urban planning, Canada, case study

This senior high school urban geography textbook provides some preventive perspectives with considerable Canadian content. It is filled with maps, diagrams, photos, and exercises to assist students in discovering the complex and intriguing nature of cities. Unit 1, "Urbanization" explains the various ways in which urbanization has shaped the modern world. Unit 2, "Urban Activities" deals with the functions of cities, with a specific focus on the economy, and how this enlarges the city's sphere of influence. Various urban patterns such as those of inner cities, central business districts, inter-urban networks, intra-urban networks, and information networks are examined in unit 3. Unit 4, "Urban Life" summarizes some of the sociocultural aspects of cities such as social structures, poverty, neighborhoods, housing, and gentrification. The final unit is a new town planning project for Seaton, Ontario, in which students can integrate the material learned in the course to plan their own communities. The text contains case studies of cities in Latin America, Texas, Hong Kong, Cape Town, Melbourne, and Calderdale (England). The glossary at the end of the book is a valuable summary of many of the basic terms associated with urban studies. Land-use maps provided in the appendix serve as useful resources as well.

92. Castells, Manuel. *The Urban Question: A Marxist Approach*. London: Edward Arnold, 1977.

Keywords: social fabric

Castells develops the Marxism of French philosopher Louis Althusser to criticize traditional urban sociology as represented by the Chicago School. He suggests that his redeployment of Marxist sociology gives us greater insight into the formation of metropolitan regions, the urban malaise in the United States, urban political and economic structures as well as urban social movements, than the tools provided by the Chicago School. Castells suggests that the competitiveness, impersonality, and loneliness that the Chicago School theorists attribute to the city can be better understood as caused by a particular moment (in Althusserian terms a "conjuncture") in capitalist evolution.

93. Castells, Manuel. *The City and the Grassroots: A Cross-Cultural Theory of Urban Social Movements*. London: Edward Arnold, 1983.

Keywords: social fabric, community, democracy, neighborhood

Castells sketches the outlines of a new theory of urban change that can help to develop a new kind of city based on principles of social justice. He situates the study of social movements at the heart of a broader theory of urban social change. The relationship between urban forms and functions and urban movements is elaborated with the help of case studies from different sociocultural contexts. The case studies also reinforce explanations regarding the development of social movements, the different social and spatial effects of these movements, and what elements account for the internal structure and historical evolution of movements.

The detailed case studies include the Grands Ensembles of Paris, San Francisco, squatters in Latin America, and the Citizen Movement in Madrid. Castells' analysis reveals that social movements arise because the citizens want to reassert the value of their neighborhoods and to have a sense of autonomous local culture and more power in the local government.

94. Castells, Manuel, and Peter Hall. *Technopoles of the World: The Making of 21st Century Industrial Complexes*. New York: Routledge, 1994.

Keywords: technology, case study

Technopoles, defined as planned centers for the promotion of high-technology industry, are the subjects of this study. The authors argue that these new technopoles are having a major impact on the conditions and processes of local and regional development.

This point is made through various case studies including Silicon Valley; Boston's Highway 128; Akademgorodok in Siberia; Taedok in South Korea; Science Castle in Japan; Kansai Science City, also in Japan; Sophia-Antipolis in France; Cambridge, England; and Hsinchu in Taiwan. A chapter is also devoted to Japan's Technopolis program. The chapter entitled, "The Metropolis as Innovative Milieu" discusses London, Paris, and Tokyo, the "metropolitan survivors." Their lessons on the dynamics of innovative growth are studied in hopes of capturing their best elements in future technopoles. Then, the "new metropoles" of Munich and Southern California are studied in order to determine the reasons for their sudden success in the mid-twentieth century. After all the case study work, the lessons learned from them are summarized. A discussion of how these lessons can be applied to the design of future technopoles ends the book.

95. Caulfield, Jon. *City Form and Everyday Life: Toronto's Gentrification and Critical Social Practice*. Toronto: University of Toronto Press, 1994.

Keywords: support, economics, housing, inner cities, neighborhood, urban sociology, Canada

This book is a case study of urban change in Toronto. It focuses on the recent widespread pattern of middle-class residential settlement of older inner-city neighborhoods formerly occupied mainly by working-class and underclass communities. Part 1 ("Context") sets the stage for exploring the middle-class settlement of Toronto's older downtown neighborhoods by examining the main forces that shaped urban form in the decades immediately preceding the emergence of gentrification. Part 2 ("Theory") explores theoretical issues germane to gentrification that helped shape the fieldwork and suggests a framework for understanding gentrification distinct from neoclassical and structuralist approaches. Part 3 ("Fieldwork") reports on fieldwork carried out among a specific subgroup of middle-class inner-city resettlers in Toronto, at a specific moment in time, with an eye toward issues of critical social practice.

96. Caulfield, Jon, and Linda Peake, eds. *City Lives and City Forms: Critical Research and Canadian Urbanism*. Toronto: University of Toronto Press, 1996.

Keywords: current, built environment, case studies, economics, neighborhood, sociology, urban design, urban sociology, Canada

There are many issues confronting Canadian cities and city-dwellers today, and several of these are addressed in this book. The primary focus is on the interaction between social relations and urban landscapes; on the status of Canadian cities in the new world economy; on the sociocultural complexity of Canada's urban populations; and on urban social movements oriented to altering existing patterns of power and privilege. Part 1 looks at aspects of the social and physical fabric of everyday life in Canadian cities. Within its six chapters are two case studies on the issues of race in urban life and the manner in which myths are fabricated and play themselves out in the social relations of cities, as well as chapters on the nature of urban space and its links with social relations. The theme for part 2 is the economic and political analysis of the complex, deeply embedded relationships between the marketplace, the state, and people's everyday lives. The significant shift in the economic character of Canadian urbanism that has affected the social and physical landscapes of cities is addressed here. Part 3 probes urban social movements in terms of social conflict, economic production, gender, race, values, urban planning, and class structure.

97. Cervero, Robert. *Suburban Gridlock*. New Brunswick, N. J.: Center of Urban Policy, 1986.

Keywords: automobiles, traffic, transportation

This book examines traffic problems along America's urban fringes and emphasizes how behavioral, institutional, and logistical problems provide difficulties in finding a solution to the problem. The most difficult barriers to overcome, says the author, are behavioral and institutional. He describes how the traffic problem will increasingly have a negative effect on people's lives, on how they build, and what public initiatives they take if it is left unresolved. The goal of this book is to stimulate constructive discussion and to create initiatives toward solving the suburban traffic problem. The author suggests subtle changes in land use patterns and employment densities which can be used to control traffic.

98. Chermayeff, Serge, and Christopher Alexander. *Community and Privacy: Toward a New Architecture of Humanism*. Garden City, N. Y.: Doubleday, 1963.

Keywords: social fabric, architecture, privacy, urban design, suburbs, classic

Nascent in this important early work are many of the ideas that Alexander would develop in *A Pattern Language* and other later works (included in this bibliography). The concepts and critiques presented undoubtedly inspired many of the themes of the New Urbanists. This is an ambitious work that tries to balance the needs of community with those of privacy, the demands of the built habitat with the importance of respecting ecosystem integrity. In its approach to architecture it tries to achieve a synthesis between art and science. It is prescient in its critique of the automobile and automotive culture—and even more so of the destructive effects of suburbia, which is presented as a nowhere land which is neither nature or city. Beautifully designed and illustrated.

99. Cherulnik, Paul D. *Applications of Environment-Behavior Research: Case Studies and Analysis*. Cambridge Series in Environment and Behavior. Cambridge: Cambridge University Press, 1993.

Keywords: social fabric, built environment, community, housing, neighborhood, public space, case study

Paul Cherulnik brings a large array of social scientific research, ranging from basic behavioral theory and classic works in psychology to urban sociology, into a common conceptual framework to analyze various urban contexts. Cherulnik uses this framework to look at a variety of settings such as public housing, city centers, offices, parks, and neighborhoods.

Part 3 of the book consists of four case studies of community design including: (1) a minipark that was modified to increase its attractiveness to midtown Manhattan's office workers, shoppers, and tourists; (2) a neighborhood that underwent traffic-diversion; (3) a housing project where modifications were made in an effort to reduce crime; and (4) a neighborhood's community-development plan.

In all four cases, the behavior and attitudes of residents/users were compared before and after the modifications.

100. Cisneros, Henry G., ed. *Interwoven Destinies: Cities and the Nation.* New York: Norton, 1993.

Keywords: support, economics, poverty, public policy

The first part of the book takes a look at city and population data and dynamics in order to ask questions or theorize about the occurrence of problems that basically revolve around racism and poverty. In the second part of the book, the economic and political structure of cities is examined in terms of their exacerbation or alleviation of the problems of racism and poverty. In Part 3, the authors examine policies and initiatives to deal with problems raised in parts 1 and 2.

101. Clark, David. *Urban Geography: An Introductory Guide.* London: Croom Helm, 1982.

Keywords: social fabric, public policy, urban planning

Urban geography is that branch of geography that concentrates upon the location and spatial arrangement of towns and cities. This is a standard introductory text in urban geography with some indirect implications for the study of healthy cities. It seeks to add a spatial dimension to our understanding of urban places and urban problems. Urban geographers are concerned with identifying and accounting for the distribution of towns and cities and the spatial similarities and contrasts that exist within and between them. Emphasis in urban geography is directed towards the understanding of those social, economic, and environmental processes that determine the location, spatial arrangement, and evolution of urban places. In this way, geographical analysis both supplements and complements the insights provided by allied disciplines in the social and environmental sciences that recognize the city as a distinctive focus of study.

102. Clark, Terry Nichols, ed. *Urban Innovation Creative Strategies for Turbulent Times.* Thousand Oaks, Calif.: Sage Publications, 1994.

Keywords: public policy

The "turbulent times" in the title of this book refer to the extreme conditions that have constrained the operation of city governments in North America in the past few decades. These constraints are wide-ranging and include a curtailment of transfer payments and grants from regional and federal governments, citizen apathy as revealed in low voter turnouts, taxpayer revolts, and a disgruntled and cynical urban citizenry, and the growing problems of race and class. All of these are examined in some detail. Later articles move on to discuss the various ways in which cities can respond to these challenges.

Using data from the Fiscal Austerity and Innovation Project survey, other readings reassess traditional notions of political leadership and decision-making and examine the evolution of various innovations tried by city governments.

103. *Climate Variability, Atmospheric Change and Human Health Conference.* Downsview, Ontario: Environment Canada, 1996.

Keywords: urban planning, policy, urban metabolism, Canada

These proceedings from a conference devoted to the education of government policy makers, corporate decision-makers and the public on the impacts of climate change are a useful resource. They provide background information on stakeholder involvement, current policy responses and issues at all levels of Canadian government, and alternative policy proposals. There is also an interesting investigation of the impact of atmospheric change in the Toronto-Niagara Region.

104. Clunies-Ross, Tracey. "Urban Renewal in Denmark: Fighting for Control." *The Ecologist,* 24, 3 (May/June, 1994): 110-12.

Keywords: sociocultural, community, democracy, energy, green city, neighborhood, public policy, Denmark

This article outlines the attempts by the residents of Vesterbro, an inner-city district of Copenhagen, to revitalize their neighborhood. The residents proposed dividing Vesterbro into urban villages with schemes for the treatment of their own sewage, a reduction in water and energy demands, and an improvement of existing facilities and recreational areas. All these schemes, however, were undermined because they were at variance with official plans for neighborhood renewal.

105. Cohen, Anthony P., and Katsuyoshi Fukui, eds. *Humanizing the City? Social Contexts of Urban Life at the Turn of the Millennium.* Edinburgh: Edinburgh University Press, 1993.

Keywords: developing countries

Authors from many different disciplinary backgrounds express their views regarding the future of the city. Foci range from the role of culture, family, and kinship in the twenty-first century city to discussions of the "post-industrial city" and the role of the "world city." Some chapters deal with specific areas of the world such as Britain, Japan, Africa, and other parts of the developing world. The essays were originally presented at the symposium "The Age of the City: Human Life in the Twenty-First Century," held at the International House, Osaka, Japan, March 27-30, 1990.

106. Cohen, Michael A., Blair A. Ruble, Joseph S. Tulchin, and Allison M. Garlands, eds. *Preparing for the Urban Future: Global Pressures and Local Forces.* Washington, D.C.: Woodrow Wilson Center Press, 1996.

Keywords: support, housing, poverty, community

The purpose of this book is to debate the context in which a new paradigm for a city can be developed. The contributors look at the present urban situation and suggest paths for the future. They find both problems (such as intolerance, violence, ethnic hatred, and destruction) and bright spots (such as the fact that cities are still the core of civilization and culture). Twenty-two social scientists and public officials debate various urban issues in preparation for the 1996 United Nations Conference on Human Settlements (Habitat II). The implications of the global economy for cities, culture, and public policy are also studied. The other major theme running through this book is the power of local community groups to provide solutions to local problems.

The final chapter by Richard Stren provides an excellent overview of major works of urban research in this century.

107. Collins, Tony. *Living for the City: Urban Australia: Crisis or Change?* Sydney: ABC Books, 1993.

Keywords: community, land use, suburbs, transportation, Australia

The Australian dream is to own a spacious plot of land and one's own detached home. The author argues that this dream will lead to extreme urban sprawl and the destruction of Australian cities. The purpose of this book (based on a radio documentary) is to convince the general public of this point. Chapter 1, "The Sprawl," highlights the environmental degradation, costs, and isolation brought on by suburban development. Chapter 2, "Consolidation," discusses urban planning policies and an equitable provision of urban infrastructure that will encourage urban density. Chapter 3, "Transport," presents the long list of problems arising from Australian dependence on the car. It includes an interview with former Toronto mayor Art Eggleton, who speaks about Toronto's decision in the late 1960s to not build any more urban expressways and instead focus on the development of public transit. It also cites other examples of public policies to deal with the car problem. Chapter 4, "Water," outlines the poor state of Australian bodies of water. The sources of pollution are examined, as well as new ways of dealing with the pollution and over-use problems. Major changes to the planning system are urged in chapter 5, "Planning." The improvements should give town planners more authority, for Collins states that they believe in, and have always advocated, energy-efficient and pedestrian-friendly cities. The importance of community is stressed in chapter 6, "Culture." The problematic suburban, low-density, car culture is recalled and examples of urban revitalization projects are given.

108. Colquhoun, Ian. *Urban Regeneration: An International Perspective.* London: B.T. Batsford, 1995.

Keywords: support, transportation, case studies, community, green city, housing, health, inner cities, land use, transportation, urban design, United States, Britain

It is axiomatic that the design of a city has a direct impact on its residents. If this impact is detrimental, the function of the city as an economic, social, and cultural center in society is threatened. Urban environments must often be regenerated to avoid this outcome. The first chapter is an in-depth focus on crises faced by the modern city such as poverty, unemployment, and health problems. Different approaches to the organization and management of urban regeneration are discussed, including new housing, conservation, the re-use of old buildings and the revival of waterfront areas. The second, third, and fourth chapters illustrate these approaches with specific examples of cities from the United States, Britain, and Europe.

109. Commission of the European Communities. *Solar Architecture in Europe: Design, Performance and Evaluation.* Bridport, England: Prism Press, 1991.

Keywords: transformation, architecture, energy, energy efficiency

This book is one result of a project to study houses, schools, factories, and offices with features using passive solar energy. Thirty schemes appear in this book, and each is explained and evaluated. Full details are provided about the aims of the schemes, the design features, their actual performance, and cost-effectiveness.

110. Common, Michael. *Sustainability and Policy: Limits to Economics.* Cambridge: Cambridge University Press, 1995.

Keywords: economics, environmental planning, sustainability

There are environmental constraints on economic growth, a thesis set out in *The Limits to Growth* (Meadows et al. 1972) and *Our Common Future* (The Brundtland Report, World Commission on Environment and Development, 1987). The concern in this work is with sustainability and the policies used to address threats to it, with an emphasis on the role of economics. Five related themes are presented. The first, "interconnectedness," involves the complex nature of the sustainability problem because of the interrelationships existing between the natural environment, economics, and human actions and aspirations. The second, "poverty," is concerned with the issue of inequality, methods of resolving the problem involving economic growth and redistribution, and the potential for social conflict if some fundamental changes are not made. The theme of affluence emphasizes the pursuit of higher material living standards via economic growth in developed countries and their refusal to redistribute wealth. A better understanding of what human welfare entails is called for. The theme of economics presents the limitation of economics in analyzing the issue of sustainability. It is emphasized that economics ignores history, the laws of nature, and consideration of the nature of human beings, all of which are topics that must be considered when addressing sustainability. The final theme, "solutions," is a recognition that a blueprint for sustainability does not exist, but rather that sustainability largely depends on context. Thus, it is argued that efforts to achieve sustainability should directly address factors that threaten it.

111. Consultative Programming Committee for Spatial Research (PRO), Working Party on Sustainable Human Settlements Planning. Henri van der Vegt, Henk ter Heide, Sybrand Tjallingii, and Dick van Alphen, eds. *Sustainable Urban Development: Research and Experiments.* Dordecht, Netherlands: Delft University Press, 1993.

Keywords: biosphere, case studies, energy, public policy, sustainability, transportation, urban ecology

This publication aims at providing inspiration for further research and planning, contributing to the development of guidelines for sustainable human settlements, planning, and identifying possibilities for research cooperation. Three major issues are discussed in these proceedings.

Sustainable flow management is about the concept of the city as a system of ingoing and outgoing flows. The city should be seen as a link in a chain. The challenge for urban planners is to develop urban systems that assume responsibility for what happens on both sides.

Sustainable planning for areas is concerned with the planning dilemma of reconciling spatial claims, on the one hand, for housing and business areas and, on the other hand, for green areas and open spaces. The challenge is to widen the scope of possible solutions by generating innovative types of land use and by trying to reach political consensus on regional spatial structures.

Participation means that not only governmental agencies, but also citizens and companies should accept responsibility for the quality of the urban environment. All actors have to participate in ecologically sound urban development. The book is divided into four parts: Introduction, Case Studies, Strategies and Models, and Conclusions and Recommendations.

112. Conway, Donald, ed. *Human Response to Tall Buildings*. Stroudsburg, Penn.: Dowden, Hutchinson, and Ross, 1977.

Keywords: urban metabolism, buildings—health aspects, buildings—social aspects, built environment, health, megastructures, office buildings, psychological health, quality of life

This volume is a significant contribution to the literature on tall buildings. It is concerned with active user and client involvement in problem identification and problem solving and the systematic searching out of patterns, relationships, and behavioral settings as a prelude to design. The author has a high regard for the physical interdependence of communities and ecological ethics.

The rest of the book is concerned with the design, building, and management of tall buildings. A wide range of subject areas is discussed, including the physiological stresses from the sway and movement of tall buildings; the psychological reaction to tall buildings; the impact of high-rise structures on users, neighbors, and the community; the visual impact of high-rises; children in high-rise buildings; residential responses to tall buildings; design guidelines for high-rise buildings; and emergencies in tall buildings.

113. Cooper, James. *European Logistics*. Oxford: Blackwell Publishers, 1991.

Keywords: production, green companies, industrial pollution, transportation

In considering the logistics of European companies, it is often the location of the country and not the companies' country of origin that matters. The scope of this book is therefore fairly broad, having relevance for companies as diverse as Kodak and Sony. Logistics refers to the management of supply chains in industry, the movement and storage of goods and information flows from the beginning to the end of the chain. This entails (1) the movement of raw materials, (2) production processes, and (3) final distribution. It is the conclusion of this book that many companies have benefited by taking an integrative approach, considering all three aspects as a whole. The structure of the marketplace for logistics is also considered at length. This has importance for users concerned with what services are available and what will happen to the prices of logistics service providers, who want to know what future opportunities can be exploited. Also, managers from either side of logistics can make business more effective only by developing and understanding the market.

Logistics planning can allow decreased inventory levels, reducing lead times as well as providing other benefits for companies. The thirteenth chapter on green logistics is of special importance for research on healthy cities. A better use of inventory and reduced inventory levels are possible through environmental audits, the author argues. With increasing regulation, neither governments nor companies can ignore the environment. It is also beneficial for a company to provide a green image to the public. Transport and storage of goods are at the center of logistics, including the transport of hazardous materials. The environmental impact of such activities can no longer be dissociated from economic considerations. Freight transport, such as the use of lorries, also has environmental impacts. One of the goals of this book is to allow logistics managers in Europe to incorporate environmental considerations into their planning.

114. Coupland, Andy, ed. *Reclaiming the City: Mixed Use Development.* London: E & FN Spon, 1997.

Keywords: current, land use, urban design

By mixing different types of development, it is hoped that cities will become more sustainable through decreased car use and that safer neighborhoods will ensue. Information and ideas covered in this book include the history of mixed uses in British cities; the debate surrounding mixed use development as an agent of sustainable development; the impact on cities of tourism, arts, and culture; a discussion of the attitudes of property developers and funding agencies to mixed use development; an examination of the link between crime and built form; a discussion of the impacts changing government policy on mixed use development through a series of case studies; an investigation into developers' motivation to build mixed use developments; and a look at the segregation of mixed use development in large-scale land use proposals.

115. Cozic, Charles P., ed. *America's Cities: Opposing Viewpoints.* Opposing Viewpoints Series. San Diego, Calif.: Greenhaven Press, 1993.

Keywords: support, housing, public policy, safety, United States

This is an anthology of articles debating key issues related to America's cities. Each chapter poses a single question (Chapter 1: Why are America's cities in decline? Chapter 2: How can urban homelessness be reduced? Chapter 3: How can urban crime be reduced? Chapter 4: What measures would improve urban housing? Chapter 5: How can urban conditions be improved?). The questions are followed by four to eight "answers" in the form of articles, book excerpts, and speeches from various writers. These articles present a wide range of often contradictory "answers." Critical thinking activities such as evaluating sources of information and recognizing stereotypes are included at the end of each chapter.

116. Crowe, Norman. *Nature and the Idea of a Man-made World: An Investigation into the Evolutionary Roots of Form and Order in the Built Environment.* Cambridge, Mass.: MIT Press, 1995.

Keywords: architecture, built environment, new urbanism, modernism, classic, philosophy of the urban environment

This is an ambitious and exhilarating work that aims at nothing less than a general theory of the human environment "in which the built world is seen as a kind of nature unto itself." To accomplish this daunting task, Crowe successfully surveys a broad range of disciplines in sight, drawing insights from each, and reweaving these threads into a rich theoretical tapestry. Philosophy and political theory, anthropology and sociology, history, architectural theory, psychology, and theology are all asked to yield their wisdom about building and dwelling and what it means to live in a city and be a citizen. Plato and Aristotle mingle with Vitruvius; Hannah Arendt, Leo Strauss, and Heidegger consort with Leon Battista Alberti; Gaston Bachelard, R. G. Collingwood, William McNeil, Mircea Eliade, J. T. Frazer, Thomas Kuhn, and Claude Levi -Strauss all become fellow passengers on a quest for the meaning of the built habitat in itself and for humanity.

Along the way, Crowe sprinkles his arguments with acute observations about the environmental crisis (and its relationship to our habit of narrowing our understanding of our built world in relation to nature to an almost exclusively technological one) and the shallowness of contemporary experience (and its relationship to the dispirited mythos of contemporary life). He also denounces the modernist hubris, which attempted to reinvent the architectural world "free of the inhibiting constraints of the past." Ultimately, Crowe argues that overlooking the long-evolved ways of doing things puts us in peril. In many ways this book may be seen as providing a theoretical foundation for many contemporary movements that are salutary for sustainability, such as the New Urbanism. This is an indispensable work for those interested in sustainable cities.

117. Cullingworth, J. Barry, ed. *Energy, Land, and Public Policy.* New Brunswick, N.J.: Transaction Publishers, 1990.

Keywords: current, energy, energy efficiency, fossil fuels, land use, public policy

One of the main ideas uniting this collection of papers is that different energy supply systems significantly influence land use patterns, and hence the structure and livability of cities. The range of topics is quite vast, from a historical analysis of the relationship between energy supply technologies of the nineteenth century and the structure of cities to an analysis of the spatial structure of modern cities. The first essay of this volume analyzes how energy supplies and technologies of the nineteenth century served to initiate, and characterize, the development of present-day large modern cities. The second essay deals with the relationship between the spatial organization of society and issues of energy demand and conservation. The third paper examines the links between land use and the environmental impact of energy development. The next article analyzes issues related to nuclear waste sites, and examines case studies from the United States in order to draw lessons from their experiences. The following paper discusses the regional implications of energy price fluctuations. The next essay analyzes trends in energy consumption per unit of output in the manufacturing sectors of the United States and Canada. In the final paper, the author makes a personal statement regarding actions that need to be implemented in order to achieve sustainability.

118. Cullingworth, J. Barry. *Planning in the USA: Policies, Issues and Processes*. London: Routledge, 1997.

Keywords: current, land use, urban planning, United States

This book touches on all of the current issues in planning including: land use regulations (zoning, institutional and legal frameworks, development charges); quality of the cultural environment in terms of aesthetics and historic preservation; growth management; development issues (housing, transportation, community, and economic development); environmental policies like the National Environmental Protection Act, the Clean Air Act, clean water and waste initiatives, and carrying capacity.

119. Dalal-Clayton, Barry. *Getting to Grips With Green Plans: National-Level Experience in Industrial Countries*. London: Earthscan, 1996.

Keywords: case studies, public policy, sustainability

Agenda 21 emerged from the 1992 UN Conference on Environment and Development, urging nations to develop and implement national sustainable development plans. Dalal-Clayton has studied numerous developed countries' green plans and summarizes and analyzes them in this useful book. Part 1, "Overview and Synthesis," begins by providing a background to the study and goes on to compare approaches taken by different countries in developing green plans. A further analysis includes a consideration of duration, time frames, mandates, management approaches, degree of participation, coordination with regional plans, and political influences. The different approaches to green plans taken by developing versus developed countries are compared; the author recommends more communication between the two groups to facilitate better green planning. Conclusions are drawn regarding the ability of the various green plans to meet the goal of sustainable development. Part 2 consists of case studies of Australia, Canada, Denmark, France, Latvia, The Netherlands, New Zealand, Norway, Sweden, the United Kingdom, the United States, and the European Union. The sustainable development plans of these nations are analyzed using considerations similar to those in part 1. Less detailed studies of Austria, Germany, Ireland, Japan, Portugal, and Russia are also included.

120. Dandaneau, Steven P. *A Town Abandoned: Flint, Michigan, Confronts Deindustrialization*. Albany: State University of New York Press, 1996.

Keywords: broader sociological issues, case studies, economics, sociology

Flint, Michigan, is the hometown of General Motors (the largest American industrial firm) and United Auto Workers (the largest American industrial union), yet since the massive plant closings began in the 1980s, it has become a deserted, poverty-stricken wasteland. Dandaneau presents a critical sociology of Flint, a victim of dependent deindustrialization. He posits that "most of America's chief social problems and evident cultural pathologies can be traced, not to our nation's crackhouses, unwed mothers, and homeless, but rather to our collective unwillingness to fully appreciate the destructive and corrosive nature of our *capitalist* society." While examining Flint's response to its own decline, Dandaneau analyzes class and culture in a late capitalist society. The lessons learned, namely that Flint is essentially powerless because it is trying to confront large-scale problems such as the internationalization of American business, can be applied not only to Flint, but to all Western cities.

121. Davidson, Joan. *How Green is Your City?* London: Bedford Square Press, 1988.

Keywords: community, environmental planning, green cities, Britain

This book focuses on the local environmental actions of Britain's "voluntary sector," an independent, self-managing, community-based group concerned with the unemployment and declining quality of the environment that has struck their communities. This sector is increasingly involved with social services such as health care, housing, the care of disabled and old people, and the welfare of children. As the environmental movement gains momentum, this voluntary sector is also increasingly eager to apply principles of resource conservation and sustainable development to the city. It is emphasized that urban regeneration depends on self-reliance and socially and ecologically sustainable economic development. This book examines local environmental action of the voluntary sector in a number of British cities as a promoter of self-reliance and sustainable development. Other objectives of this work include further documenting the environment's role in communities and emphasizing the potential for the creation of paid, unpaid, temporary, and permanent work associated with environmental activity. The community-based projects studied focus on three issues: city greening, energy conservation, and waste recycling.

122. Davies, John K., and Michael P. Kelly, eds. *Healthy Cities: Research and Practice.* London: Routledge, 1993.

Keywords: transformation, case studies, health, public policy

"What is a healthy city?" and "How can the theory of a healthy city be put into practice?" are the main questions addressed in this work. Healthy cities projects around the world are evaluated. The connections between healthy cities projects and housing, health policies, community development, and health education are also discussed.

123. Davies, Wayne K. D., and David T. Herbert. *Communities within Cities: an Urban Social Geography.* London: Belhaven Press, 1993.

Keywords: social fabric, community, experience of place, neighborhood, urban design, urban sociology

This textbook draws together various approaches to the study of communities and neighborhoods within cities and assesses their function and role in modern urban systems. It reviews the historical roots of the idea of community and its modern relevance, together with its philosophical base and its practical limitations.

124. Day, Christopher. *Places of the Soul: Architecture and Environmental Design as a Healing Art.* London: Aquarian Press, 1990.

Keywords: support, health, architecture, experience of place, buildings—health aspects

How architecture affects people and places, how design and construction can be approached to bring health rather than illness, is the subject of this book. In many ways, the book is reminiscent of the works of Christopher Alexander. The chapter headings give a good indication of the topics covered: Architecture with Health-Giving Intent; Architecture as Art; Building for Physical Health; Space for Living In; Design as a Listening Process; Creating Places with Users and Builders; Ensouling Buildings; Building as a Health-Giving Process; Healing Silence—the Architecture of Peace; The Urban Environment—Cities as Places; Cities for People; Cities for Life; and Building for Tomorrow. Throughout the work, Day uses insights from many disciplines, and his use of tutorial examples of what contributes "health" generating architecture and design are always illuminating.

125. De Soto, Hernando. *The Other Path: The Invisible Revolution in the Third World.* New York: Harper & Row, 1986.

Keywords: support, developing countries, economics, housing, poverty, work

This work about Peru's informal economy in Lima presents a novel theory regarding the success of black-marketeers. The first four chapters present an in-depth study of the workings of Peru's black market for housing, trade, and transport. De Soto has collected all of the detailed material for this study not from books, economists, or government records, but from the poor people of Lima themselves. He presents his argument very convincingly, with statistics that show that the black-marketeers have built 83 percent of the city's markets, 50 percent of its houses, and own 95 percent of public transportation.

De Soto has scathing criticisms for those who believe that black-marketeers are sneaky tax-evaders and cheats. He shows that it is the government that prevents most poor people from owning land or operating businesses because of prohibitive costs in time and money. The informal sector actually has high levels of organization and rules, showing that people will develop their own democratic systems when the state fails to provide for them.

De Soto calls for a truly liberal economy. Chapters 5 to 8 contain his political analysis regarding the prerequisites for economic development, effective democratic institutions, and appropriate foreign policy. His suggestions for economic development by using the creativity and hard work of the urban poor apply to all developing countries, not only Peru. He outlines his plan for dismantling what he has termed the mercantilist apparatus. He proposes more accessible property rights, the simplification of legal institutions, decentralization, and deregulation.

126. Dear, Michael J., H. Eric Schockman, and Greg Hise, eds. *Rethinking Los Angeles.* Thousand Oaks, Calif.: Sage Publications, 1996.

Keywords: support, case studies, community, identity, urban ecology

Los Angeles may be the prototype of the urban future, but it is understudied and is probably the least understood American city. So argue the editors of this collection of essays which attempt to rethink Los Angeles in order to better understand not only the city but the future of all North American urban centers. The essays re-examine all aspects of the city's livelihood, people, environment, economy, politics, society, culture, history, geography, art, health, education, policing, immigration, and race and ethnicity. The book brings together viewpoints of community leaders, artists, poets, and others who search for the "lost soul" and are committed to "rewriting the social contract that brings people together in Southern California." It is loosely organized around the following seven themes, with one, two, or three essays on each:

1) The problems involved in understanding what we observe in the landscapes of Southern California

2) The past and future Southern Californian economy

3) The politics of reform in the governments of the city and county of Los Angeles

4) Dealing with pivotal questions of race and ethnicity

5) The environment

6) The issues of public (and private) services including education, health, and transportation

7) Envisioning the urban future

127. Degobert, Paul. *Automobiles and Pollution*. Paris: Technip, 1995.

Keywords: air pollution, automobiles

This book begins by presenting general information on atmospheric pollution and regulation. The share of pollution that can be attributed to automobiles is discussed, followed by an in-depth analysis of how pollutants can be eliminated from car exhaust. The consequences for the general environment are examined by considering potential effects on plant and animal species. The limits imposed by regulation and standard procedures for taking the corresponding measurements are covered. A later chapter deals with analytical methods for measuring various car exhaust pollutants which have been ignored until now. The mechanisms of the engine that creates pollution are examined, as well as the influence of fuel choice and lubricants to find the best compromise between performance, pollution, and fuel consumption. The book ends with a chapter on the economics of car pollution control. Many useful bibliographical references are included.

128. Dicken, Peter, and Peter E. Lloyd. *Modern Western Society: A Geographical Perspective on Work, Home and Well-Being*. London: Paul Chapman Publishing, 1981.

Keywords: social fabric, work

Despite the subtitle, this is more than a geographical perspective on the two "key nodes" of most people's lives in the urban-industrial milieu of western society: work and home. The authors range freely and smoothly over topics usually under the province of other social scientists, yet manage to draw these topics within a single framework.

The central theme uniting the work is an examination of the strategies of living adopted by people in the face of the complex and ever-changing reality of modern urban life. The authors consider the roles of rapidly evolving technologies, the influence of giant business organizations and governmental bureaucracies, and the constantly changing urban landscape in the dual process of people seeking employment in a volatile labor market and subsequently entering the complex, institutionalized housing market. Work and home within this shifting reality are studied as the two anchors which influence a household's capacity to access the "goods" of life as well as determining their proximity to the "bads" of life.

129. Dittmar, Hank. "A Broader Context for Transportation Planning." *American Planning Association Journal* (Winter 1995): 7-13.

Keywords: automobiles, sustainability, transportation

The Intermodal Surface Transportation Efficiency Act (ISTEA), passed in 1991, is seen as the turning point in American transportation planning. ISTEA is described as "an approach that sees transportation as society's servant rather than its master. At the heart of this new approach lies the concept that transportation should contribute to building a more sustainable society—a premise counter to the old notions about transportation's function in society." The history of transportation planning, current transportation planning principles, and the move toward healthy and sustainable transportation systems are the subject of this article. The ISTEA's policy directions, such as its emphasis on a systems approach and on alternative modes, are listed. Following these, further transportation goals that support a sustainable society and are not addressed by ISTEA are considered. The article concludes that while ISTEA is a positive start, other initiatives are necessary for health and sustainability.

130. Doering, Ronald L., et al. *Planning for Sustainability: Towards Integrating Environmental Protection Into Land Use Planning.* Ottawa: Minister of Supply and Services Canada, 1989-1991.

Keywords: environmental planning, land use, sustainability, urban planning, Canada

Building on the final report of the Brundtland Commission's "Our Common Future" and the Royal Commission's "Watershed," this work (prepared for the Royal Commission on the Future of the Toronto Waterfront) addresses the lack of integration between environmental and land-use planning in the Greater Toronto Bioregion. This negligence results in devastating consequences for the environment, especially under population growth pressures. Divisions in the legal and administrative arrangements are blamed for this lack of integration. The current process is described as an "unrelated collection of procedures carried out under different pieces of legislation for which different provincial ministers are responsible." Segregating a bioregion that functions as a whole into manageable pieces of land for planning purposes is also identified as a problem. Achieving environmentally sustainable economic development in the Toronto region requires that these issues be addressed for the purpose of integrating environmental and land-use planning.

131. Downey, John, and Jim McGuigan, eds. *Technocities.* Thousand Oaks, Calif.: Sage

Publications, 1999.

Keywords: urban planning, current, technology

The articles collected here provide a wide-ranging discussion of urban planning issues in relation to computer-mediated communications and cyberspace. Optimistic and pessimistic views of how cyberspace is changing the face of the city, communities, gender perceptions, political participation, and so on are given equal time in this book. This is a timely collection of differently informed approaches that allows us to make some sense of a field of dynamic and contradictory forces.

132. Downs, Anthony. *Stuck in Traffic: Coping With Peak-Hour Traffic Congestion.* Washington, D.C.: Brookings Institution, 1992.

Keywords: automobiles, transportation, public policy, economics

Peak-hour traffic congestion in the United States has become a serious environmental and economic problem. It is one of the primary causes of air pollution and it misallocates various scarce resources. In economic terms, the time lost through delays amounted to a sum in excess of $34 billion in 1988 alone. In ensuing years the problem has become worse as more suburban developments have been added.

This policy-oriented book provides a good overview of recent research on the subject by transportation experts and land-use planners before examining the advantages and disadvantages of the principal strategies proposed to reduce traffic congestion. Downs focuses his discussion around three questions: Why has traffic congestion become worse? What remedies might reduce it? Which remedies would be most effective?

The proposed remedies for reducing peak-hour congestion range from supply-side strategies that expand the carrying capacity of an area's transportation system, to demand-side strategies that reduce the number of trips made during peak hours. Some of the strategies in both categories are further seen as being *market-based*, while others are seen as being *regulatory*. Downs, as an economist, suggests that market-based approaches are the most effective and should be used whenever possible.

133. Downs, Anthony. *New Visions for Metropolitan America.* Washington, D.C.: Brookings Institution, 1994.

Keywords: public policy, economics

Growth-related dilemmas are threatening the long-term viability of American society. Growth is seen as the primary factor responsible for traffic congestion, air pollution, higher taxes, and lack of affordable housing. This has led hundreds of local governments to adopt various growth management policies, with various degrees of success. Downs compares existing policies, especially in terms of their economic viability, and suggests a number of alternative policy strategies that he suggests are much more economically sound. This book should prove to be of interest to economists, policy-makers, and local and municipal politicians and administrators.

134. Driedger, Leo. *The Urban Factor: Sociology of Canadian Cities.* Toronto: Oxford

University Press, 1991.

Keywords: broader sociological issues, urban ecology, urban sociology, Canada

After briefly studying the Agricultural Revolution and the origin of cities, the author turns his attention to the influence of industrialization. The population explosion in less industrialized regions is considered, along with the need for capital, jobs, housing, welfare, protection, pollution control, transportation, and urban demography. The first part is a useful reference for Canadian data on urban growth, history of urban development, metropolitan areas, urban mobility, and other demographic information. Part 2, "Urban Ecology," consists of descriptions of various approaches to urban ecology including human ecology, the Chicago School, theories regarding patterns of urban growth and "recent ecological methodological advances." The section examines how social class shapes spaces such as suburbia, the central business district, and slums. Various sociological theories on segregation of space are also included. After presenting national segregation trends, the author provides studies of segregation of Blacks in Halifax, Jews in Montreal, and the Portuguese and Chinese in Toronto. Work, the industrial economy, politics, the government, and family networks are the subject of Part 3: "Social Organization." In Part 4, "Urban Planning," problems with poverty, housing, transportation, pollution, sprawl, crime, and discrimination are studied in the context of sociological theories and demographic factors such as socioeconomic class and changing household patterns. Another chapter in this section serves to provide a summary of prominent urban planning strategies of the past such as The Garden City, Broadacre, The Radiant City and The City Beautiful. The remainder of this chapter provides different authors' approaches to answering the important questions of "How do we decide which criteria should be used in designing greater quality of urban life?" and "What strategies can be employed actually to bring such desirable features into being?" This last section on what makes a healthy city is the most important contribution made by the book, although the large amount of Canadian data that Driedger has collected is also a notable addition to the healthy cities literature.

135. Duany, Andres, Elizabeth Plater-Zyberk, and Jeff Speck. *Suburban Nation: The Rise of Sprawl and the Decline of the American Dream.* New York: North Point Press, 2000.

Keywords: new urbanism, suburbs, urban design, architecture, sustainability

A definitive critique of all that is wrong with the modern American city from the perspective of the New Urbanism. The authors, who are among the founders of New Urbanism, are forthright in their condemnation of sprawl and conventional suburbs. One need go no further than this book to find out how these soulless and forgettable places negatively effect both social and environmental sustainability. The carefully reasoned and clearly yet passionately articulated critique is followed by a delineation of the alternatives that are themselves informed by the authors' considerable experience in designing new neighborhoods and community revitalization projects. The procedures through which the much more sensible mixed-use and pedestrian-friendly community can come about are clearly outlined.

This book ranks extremely highly in the literature on sustainable cities.

136. Duchin, Faye, et al. *The Future of the Environment: Ecological Economics and Technological Change*. New York: Oxford University Press, 1994.

Keywords: economics, environmental pollution, input/output analysis, technology

Our technological and economic choices will determine the sustainability of our way of life. The primary aim of this book is to develop various forecast scenarios to illustrate this. The authors begin by exploring the relationship between increasing affluence, pollution, and technological choices. The analysis then shifts to a consideration of the situations facing the world economy over the next few decades.

Part 1 gives an overview of the assumptions and methods used in scenario construction and gives some tentative conclusions. Part 2 presents a detailed examination of the case studies on which the scenarios are based. Together, the various scenarios are compared to a "reference scenario" which assumes no technological change after 1990. The comparison reveals the tremendous impact technological choice and economic policy can have on the future from the perspective of sustainability.

137. Duhl, Leonard J. *Health Planning and Social Change*. New York: Human Sciences Press, 1986.

Keywords: support, case studies, interdisciplinary studies, health, health care, urban planning

This superb collection of essays addresses issues of personal development and health, health planning, and health care systems, as well as various ways of conceptualizing health issues in the urban context. The chapter titles listed below indicate the range of topics:
  1. Our Selves and Social Change
  2. Health Planning Critique and Alternatives
  3. The Dimensions of Health: Traditional Healing and Modern Medicine
  4. The Health Planner Dreaming for Health and Wellness
  5. Rational and Nonrational Planning
  6. The Delivery of Health Care Services
  7. Health, Whole, Holy, Healing
  8. Mental Health: A Look into the Future
  9. The Promotion and Maintenance of Health: Myth and Reality
  10. The Social Context of Health
  11. Human Social Futures
  12. Newark—Community or Chaos: A Case study
Also included are explicit discussions of interdisciplinary teaching in health, participatory democracy, and healthy cities.

138. Duhl, Leonard J. "Conditions for Healthy Cities: Diversity, Game Boards and Social Entrepreneurs." *Environment and Urbanization* 5, 2 (October 1993): 112-24.

Keywords: support, community, public policy, urban planning

This paper suggests that the reason why city authorities are often ineffective in dealing with urban problems is because there is a lack of "systems of governance" which can respond to the shifting complexities of modern cities. The role of serial entrepreneurs in the move toward healthy cities is also examined.

139. Dunphy, Robert T. "Transportation-Oriented Development: Making a Difference?" *Urban Land* (July 1995): 32-36, 48.

Keywords: case studies, land use, transportation, urban planning

San Diego and Portland have "broken new ground in planning for land use and transportation linkage." The details of both projects are laid out while trying to answer the question "Is it making a difference?"

San Diego is working on transit-oriented development (TOD) which includes mixed use development near trolley stations. But sources of conflict between the city and the developer are numerous and are cited in the article. Beaverton Creek in Portland is another proposed TOD. The plan calls for relatively high density multi-family and single-family units. This project too is having problems. These are briefly described in the four-page article.

140. Eagle, Selwyn, and Judith Deschamps, eds. *Information Sources in Environmental Protection*. London: Bowker-Saur, 1997.

Keywords: biosphere, ecology, environmental pollution, health, noise, toxins, waste

Good information sources for healthy cities are identified in this useful guide to the literature on environmental protection. The subject areas covered are: the effects of hazardous chemicals on human health; effects of pollutants on wildlife; environmental effects on oceans, rivers, inland water, and the atmosphere; waste management; noise as pollution; energy and mineral sources; land use; economics and environmental management; technology and the environment; environmental law; statutory provision of environmental information in the UK; education, training, and research; and environmental information and decision-making. Although these topics do not represent a solely urban perspective, many areas are relevant to healthy cities and many of the identified problems are urban in nature. Each section consists of a brief introduction to the topic followed by a discussion of the most important and most recommended published works in the field. Each publication cited is evaluated in terms of its contents and how it may be of use to a researcher. The appendix provides a list of organizations and associations.

141. Eden, Michael J., and John T. Parry, eds. *Land Degradation in the Tropics: Environmental and Policy Issues*. New York: Pinter, 1996.

Keywords: biosphere, case studies, developing countries, ecology, ground pollution

All countries must deal with the legacies of exploitation and environmental mismanagement that have resulted in land degradation. Although in northern countries this need is now taken seriously, this is not the case in the tropics where the drive for rapid development and industrialization takes precedence. This collection attempts to assess and provide solutions for the problems of land degradation in the South. Part 1 provides an introduction to environmental, social, and policy issues of land degradation. Part 2 addresses tropical forests, and parts 3 and 4 look at deserts and wetlands, respectively. This book is a welcome addition to the *Healthy Cities* literature because in part 5, the important but not often discussed topic of urban and industrial degradation in the tropics is studied in detail. Chapter 17 provides an overview of the seriousness of problems in rapidly growing cities in the developing world. Chapter 18 reports on urban agriculture and environmental protection in Harare, Zimbabwe. Causes, problems, and policies regarding urban degradation of Georgetown, Guyana, is the focus of chapter 19. A summary of the environmental implications of urban development in the Caribbean is given in chapter 20. The final chapter in part 5 is an inquiry into a proposed mining project in Fiji and its potential for conflict.

142. Eder, Norman. *Poisoned Prosperity: Development, Modernization, and the Environment in South Korea.* Armonk, N. Y.: M. E. Sharpe, 1996.

Keywords: biosphere, case studies, democracy, ecology, economics, environmental pollution

Korea is in the midst of a giant experiment that may reveal whether or not environmental destruction is an inevitable and irreversible result of rapid industrialization. Eder studies the impact of rapid industrialization on South Korea and concludes that while South Korea shows the usual signs of environmental degradation, it also shows serious environmental concern not evidenced in most recently developed nations. He attributes the newly awakened concern for the biosphere to expanded democratization, affluence, and greater international involvement.

143. Eichler, Margrit, ed. *Change of Plans: Towards a Non-sexist Sustainable City.* Toronto: Garamond Press, 1995.

Keywords: current, built environment, community, food, green cities, health, housing, sustainability, transportation, urban ecology, women

What exactly is a non-sexist city? What is the relationship between non-sexist design and ecologically sustainable design? This relationship is clarified through eight articles which discuss how to go about building non-sexist sustainable cities. The focus is considerably Torontonian. Margrit Eichler concludes in her article that, while feminist and environmentalist concerns "are in no way marching in lock step unison," there is enormous overlap and both groups would benefit from a strategic alliance. Sherilyn MacGregor espouses the premise that rather than being a neutral backdrop to city life, the urban built environment is a man-made force which significantly shapes residents' lives. Housing, health, prevention of violence, urban agriculture, and transportation are explored from a feminist perspective and are related to sustainable urban design. The final chapter summarizes future areas of research and emphasizes the importance of community-led planning.

144. Elkin, Tim, Duncan McLaren, and Mayer Hillman. *Reviving the City: Towards Sustainable Urban Development.* London: Friends of the Earth, 1991.

Keywords: current, built environment, energy, environmental pollution, food, green space, land use, quality of life, sustainability, transportation, waste

The goal of sustainable urban development can be achieved by the use of a suitable mix of regulations and incentives. This book contains discussions of various practical ways to achieve this goal in the cities of the North. The first six chapters deal with specific topics in sustainable urban development: the built environment, transport, energy, the natural environment, food and agriculture, and waste and pollution. To summarize, the authors advocate more open space and "naturalistic" greenspace, farm land, urban forests, more re-use and recycling of materials, energy conservation and provision of secure, clean and rapid mass transit systems. The broader issues related to socioeconomic considerations are reflected upon in chapter 7. Chapter 8 takes a look at how equity and quality of life can be promoted through sustainable urban development. A useful summary of broad recommendations for government action concludes this report.

145. Ellin, Nan. *Postmodern Urbanism.* Cambridge, Mass.: Blackwell Publishers, 1996.

Keywords: current, community, experience of place, modernism

We no longer have clear divisions between city, suburb, and countryside. Due to this blurred set of divisions, we now seek urbanity and sense of community through the preservation of cities' centers, building new form to mimic the old, grassroots social movements, and a reassertion of traditional social values and institutions. This book investigates the reactions of planners and architects toward the recent trends of deterritorialization and placelessness. This book provides an excellent theoretical discussion.

146. Elliott, Glen R. *Stress and Human Health: Analysis and Implications of Research.* New York: Springer Publishing, 1982.

Keywords: support, urban metabolism, health, psychological health, sensory and social overload, work and stress

This volume offers the results of a comprehensive study carried out by the Institute of Medicine/National Academy of Sciences in the United States It is a broad, integrative inquiry which intends to promote interdisciplinary research into complex health problems, including those arising from environmental stress.
Research areas include:
   - Stress and Life Events
   - Stress in Organizational Settings
   - Work Stress Related to Social Structures
   - Psychosocial Assets and Modifiers of Stress
   - Biological Substrates of Stress
   - Stress and Illness

147. Elsom, Derek. *Smog Alert: Managing Urban Air Quality.* London: Earthscan, 1996.

Keywords: air pollution, case studies

This is a thorough discussion of the root causes and impacts of urban air pollution. A case is made for developing standards to protect air quality by identifying who is at risk from the pollution problem. This book considers a range of approaches, from end-of-pipe to preventive, and includes a number of "smog city case studies." *Smog Alert* is an excellent resource for those interested in urban air quality issues.

148. Engwicht, David. *Reclaiming Our Cities and Towns*. Philadelphia: New Society Publishers, 1993.

Keywords: automobiles, green cities, health, neighborhood, pedestrians, traffic, transportation, urban planning, Australia

The overuse of the automobile is identified as the main cause of the deterioration of the quality of urban life. In addition to pollution and the greenhouse effect, cars produce deafening noise, make the air unbreathable, and in general make urban life miserable. Technological innovations do deliver cleaner, more efficient automobiles, and traffic studies allow sophisticated street planning. However, these efforts only encourage further use of the automobile. In *Reclaiming Our Cities and Towns*, Engwicht presents the only logical solution to the traffic dilemma: incorporating the sensible everyday needs of people into the math and number crunching of urban planning to create an eco-city in which life is quieter, cleaner, safer, and more human.

149. *Environment and Urbanization*. Vol. 11, No. 1, April 1999. Healthy Cities, Neighborhoods, and Homes.

Keywords: developing countries, sustainability, case studies

This special issue of *Environment and Urbanization* looks at Healthy City projects around the world. Good case studies of Nicaragua, Bangladesh, and Mexico City are provided. Separate sections look at healthy neighborhoods from the perspectives of water, sanitation and drainage, and healthy homes. Marina Kenzer provides a brief guide to the literature on healthy cities.

150. *Environment and Urbanization*. Vol. 11, No. 2, April 2000. Poverty Reduction and Urban Governance.

Keywords: developing countries, poverty, social fabric

A wide-ranging view of how poverty undermines sustainability. Good case studies are provided from around the world. The challenge that poverty poses for urban governance is explored in some detail. This journal always has material relevant to the study of healthy/sustainable cities.

151. Etzioni, Amitai. *The Spirit of Community: Rights, Responsibilities, and the Communitarian Agenda*. New York: Crown, 1993.

Keywords: community, sociology

This is a trenchant account of communitarian political theory and the communitarian agenda, as well as a contemporary critique of Liberalism. The communitarian platform is described in the following chapters:

1) The Moral Voice (Civil society requires we be each other's keepers)

2) The Communitarian Family (The limits of institutionalizing young children in child care centers)

3) The Communitarian School (Education for values we all share and for character formation is more "basic" than academic skills. The way to teach is by formatting experiences.)

4) Back to We (Four ways to rebuild old and start new communities)

5) Rebuilding Community Institutions

The Communitarian Agenda is laid out in chapters dealing with how to respond to special interest groups, hate speech and fighting authoritarianism, crime, and AIDS.

152. European Foundation for the Improvement of Living and Working Conditions, *European Workshop on the Improvement of the Built Environment and Social Integration in Cities*. Jacqueline Miller and Voula Mega, eds. Berlin, European Foundation for the Improvement of Living and Working Conditions, 1991.

Keywords: support, built environment, land use, safety, sustainability

There is a link between environmental deterioration and social exclusion. The participants in this workshop discuss the plight of various vulnerable groups, and examine strategies that address both environmental rehabilitation and social integration. The integrative potential of various transport-oriented housing policies, preventive measures in the area of delinquency and crime, and ways in which more economic opportunities may be generated are examined. Consideration is also given to mixed-use land development as a means to enhance social integration and sustainability in the cities of the twenty-first century.

153. European Foundation for the Improvement of Living and Working Conditions. *Land Use Management and Environmental Improvement in Cities*. Lisbon: European Foundation for the Improvement of Living and Working Conditions, 1991.

Keywords: urban metabolism, case studies, land use, public policy, sustainability

Most current urban planning is inadequate in the face of emerging sustainability challenges. What planning changes are needed and the future evolution of planning were addressed by participants in this workshop. Specific issues examined by the work groups were: environmental deterioration and policy conflicts based on land-use patterns; the need for citizen input to determine policies and priorities for urban land use; current land-use policies and environmental regulations pertaining to urban areas in Europe; and land-use strategies for the future to enhance sustainability.

154. Evans, Gary W., ed. *Environmental Stress*. Cambridge: Cambridge University Press, 1982.

Keywords: support, air pollution, built environment, crowding, noise—physiological effects, noise—psychosocial effects, public policy

This book has four specific objectives. The first is to provide some conceptual integration across several environmental problem areas by utilizing the concept of stress as a unifying theme. Noise, heat, air pollution, and crowding can all be viewed as nonoptimal environmental conditions that may elicit behaviors designed to modify that suboptimal human-environment relationship.

The second objective is to demonstrate how the stress concept can be used to understand human behavior in designed environments. Most research on human responses to the built environment has been atheoretical, focusing on post-occupancy assessments of user satisfaction. Following a general introduction to the ways in which the stress concept can describe dysfunction between human needs and the designed environment, sources of stress are discussed in four specific settings: hospitals, schools, offices, and neighborhoods.

The third objective is to review existing knowledge about the effects on human behavior of four environmental stressors: noise, heat, air pollution, and crowding. Empirical findings about each stressor are organized around three main areas of impact: health and physiology, performance, and effect on social behavior. Research on designed settings is also reviewed, with an emphasis on physical features that influence user satisfaction.

The author's final objective is to stimulate thinking about the ways in which research on behavioral aspects of environmental problems can be integrated into decision-making processes.

155. Ewen, Stuart. *Captains of Consciousness: Advertising and the Social Roots of the Consumer Culture.* New York: McGraw-Hill, 1976.

Keywords: social fabric, consumerism

This is a classic account of modern consumerist society and how advertising has helped to shape it. The role of advertising in our definition of social progress and development, our view of the machine as a symbol of power, progress, and sensuality, and the general shaping of all our values are also discussed in an insightful manner. The notion that we can achieve the good life through purchasing the right products or consuming the right service comes under critical scrutiny. How advertising has altered our habits and memories and supplied us with stereotypical images of youth, femininity, success, and failure is traced historically and is well illustrated with actual advertisements.

This is an important book for healthy cities research because it points to our resource use and thus our capacity to achieve sustainability. It also suggests weaknesses in capitalist enterprise and that our basic needs are often ignored and our energies channeled into consumerism.

156. Falk, Nicholas. "Towards Sustainability—Lessons from Denmark." *Towne & Country Planning* (March 1995): 91-92.

Keywords: case studies, pedestrians, transportation, Denmark

This brief article outlines Danish strategies that have reduced car use. Copenhagen now has a pedestrian zone that contains the main shopping area and covers seven or eight streets stretching over a mile and a half. Various schemes to promote walking and cycling are discussed. The author analyzes why, compared to the UK, the Danes have achieved so much. He attributes Denmark's success to good design as well as cultural and geographical factors.

157. Fay, Thomas H., ed. *Noise and Health.* New York: New York Academy of Medicine, 1991.

Keywords: urban metabolism, health, noise—physiological effects, noise—psychological effects

This reference book for the study of the effects of noise on human health discusses its effects on cardiovascular, neuroendocrine, immunologic, and gastrointestinal systems, as well as on sleep, fetal development, hearing, learning, cognitive development, and social behavior. The book also deals with community responses and attitudes toward noise, noise abatement, public education, and awareness of the effects of noise.

158. Filho, Walter Leal, Frances MacDermott, and Jenny Padgham, eds. *Implementing Sustainable Development at University Level: A Manual of Good Practice.* Bradford, England: European Research and Training Center on Environmental Education, 1996.

Keywords: case studies, public policy, sustainability

The Association of European Universities (CRE)-Copernicus University Charter for Sustainable Development has been signed by 212 university rectors and is being implemented in universities throughout Europe. This book is based on the workshop "Implementing Sustainable Development at University Level," organized by CRE-Copernicus and the European Research and Training Center on Environmental Education (ERTCEE). It includes case studies of specific university programs as well as discussion papers such as "Environmental Ethics," "Problems in Operationalising the Ideal of a Multidisciplinary Curriculum in Environmental Studies," "Developing University Distance Education on Sustainability," "Networking," and "Environmental Education and Continuing Education." The purpose of the CRE-Copernicus Charter is to promote interdisciplinary education in the environment through the preparation of teaching materials on environmental law, environmental and resource economics, and environmental health. The success of these efforts at Utrecht University, Universitat Autonoma de Barcelona, University of Hertfordshire, University of Bucharest, Nottingham Trent University, Uppsala University, and The Swedish University of Agricultural Sciences is documented.

159. Fisher, Robert. *Let the People Decide: Neighborhood Organizing in America.* New York: Twayne Publishers, 1994.

Keywords: social fabric, neighborhood, quality of life, urban sociology

In this updated version of "Let the People Decide," the author shows how citizen action groups abounded in the 1980s, and emphasizes a practical, get-things-done approach that has become the norm with the now-popular community development corporation. What is observed in this book is the political and economic background on which neighborhood interests are played out. For the accomplishment of the much-needed revitalization of America's inner-city neighborhoods, the author suggests a compromise between the idealism of the 1960s and the realism of the 1980s. The book investigates three types of neighborhood organizing: social welfare, radical, and conservative. It addresses the neighborhood community organizing "revolution" of the 1960s; the new populism of the 1970s; community organizing in the conservative 1980s; and the nature, potential, and prospects of neighborhood organizing.

160. Fishman, Robert. *Bourgeois Utopias: The Rise and Fall of Suburbia*. New York: Basic Books, Inc., Publishers, 1987.

Keywords: support, case studies, community, housing, suburbs, utopia, United States

Many architects and planners routinely attack the suburban ideal, but their own utopian visions are often only theoretical, and disappointing if and when they are actually built. On the other hand, the suburban ideal exists and is being chosen by so many people that they are changing the structure of cities everywhere in the developed world. This realization led the author to embark upon a study of the history of suburbia asking: "What are the true sources of new urban forms that prove to be effective? What are the real forces that shape urban growth? What are the mechanisms whereby new ideas are transmitted to those who have the power to transform the built environment? In particular, who invented suburbia and why? What explains its extraordinary hold over the middle-class mind?" After exploring these questions, Fishman concludes that suburbia must be understood as a utopia. It represents a vision of the family that is wealthy, independent, freed from the city, and living in harmony with nature—a utopia for the Anglo-American middle-class. The history of suburbia is traced from its origins in late eighteenth-century England to the present. London, Manchester, Philadelphia, and Los Angeles are studied in detail.

161. Flanagan, William G. *Contemporary Urban Sociology*. Cambridge: Cambridge University Press, 1993.

Keywords: economics, urban sociology

William Flanagan states that "classical urbanism" and "urban community" theory dominated the field of urban sociology during the first half of this century. He characterizes these approaches as being preoccupied with the alienating effect of cities, and explains the reasons why they have continued to exert an influence on urban sociology today. His prime motive, however, is to trace other parallel and later developments that have shaped contemporary urban sociology. Chapter 2 examines the development of theories of "urban ecology" during the same period that classical urbanism and urban community theory held sway and how this expanded upon these by investigating the development of the underlying spatial form of cities.

In chapter 3, Flanagan provides a concise analysis of the contribution of the political economy approach that gained ascendancy during the 1970s. The imperatives of global capitalism and their impact on cities were the primary motivation that engendered this approach, he argues. He next analyzes the evolution of "world-system" theory to account for the burgeoning growth of cities in the developing world. The final chapter examines the impact of post-modernism on urban sociology—particularly from the perspective of human agency and its potential for urban transformation.

162. Flint, R. Warren, and John Vena. *Human Health Risks from Chemical Exposure: The Great Lakes Ecosystem*. New York: Lewis Publishers, 1991.

Keywords: environmental pollution, epidemiology, health, public policy, toxins, water pollution

This is a comprehensive source book which summarizes a significant body of knowledge related to the issue of chemicals in the Great Lakes environment and the potential risks to human health posed by exposure to these chemicals. In addition to synthesizing the body of knowledge available on this subject, the book also has recommendations for action in the areas of policy, communication, education, and research related to the issue of risks to human health from exposure to toxic chemicals in the Great Lakes.

Chapter 1 presents the background on toxic chemicals in the Great Lakes, and chapter 2 describes the process of assessing the impacts of these chemicals. Other chapters concentrate on the environmental chemistry of exposure to toxic chemicals and the impact on environment and wildlife, as well as the epidemiology of exposure.

163. Fodor, Eben. *Better Not Bigger: How to Take Control of Urban Growth and Improve Your Community*. Gabriola Island, B.C.: New Society Publishers, 1999.

Keywords: community, suburbs, quality of life, economics

According to some estimates, the United States loses about fifty acres an hour to suburban and ex-urban development. Obviously this trend cannot continue without having an adverse affect on sustainability. Why then is growth an unchecked phenomenon in North America? Fodor examines all the myths that have arisen to support growth—from growth providing needed tax revenues for municipalities and jobs for people, to beliefs that limiting growth will make the price of homes skyrocket or that vacant or undeveloped land is just "waste." Fodor does a convincing job of demolishing these myths and revealing the hidden "external" costs of growth for which all of us pay, not only in monetary terms, but also in a diminished quality of life and a tattered environment. The second part of this insightful book is a list of strategies that can put the brakes on growth and replace it with development that is much friendlier to the environment and our quality of life. In many respects, this is an action guide for taking apart the machinery of (often hidden) policies and political growth that support unfettered growth.

164. Ford, Larry R. *Cities and Buildings: Skyscrapers, Skid Rows, and Suburbs*. Baltimore: Johns Hopkins University Press, 1994.

Keywords: current, architecture, buildings—social aspects, built environment, experience of place, megastructures

Disappointed with the lack of scholarly discourse on how cities really *feel* and what it is like to *experience* them, the author has written a book about just such matters. The relationship between urban architecture and the culture of a city is explored. He is especially interested in vernacular architecture and the "nooks and crannies" of the urban built environment. Thus the emphasis is on houses, stores, and offices in the older parts of North American cities. The evolution and spatial organization of downtowns are the focus of the first three chapters. They focus on skyscrapers, the transition zone surrounding downtowns, shops, arcades, bazaars, and festival centers and how they shape and are shaped by the economics and social climate of downtowns. The next two chapters deal with similar issues, but this time regarding residential buildings such as single family homes, apartments, and tenements. The much-maligned commercial strip is examined in terms of its architecture and why it is successful. In the final chapter, the newer mega-development projects are considered.

165. Forester, John. *Bicycle Transportation: A Handbook for Cycling Transportation Engineers*. 2nd ed. Cambridge, Mass.: MIT Press, 1994.

Keywords: traffic, transportation

John Forester, an avid cyclist and professional engineer, takes the unpopular stance that bicycles belong on the road proper, and should be treated as equal to motorized vehicles. He calls this the vehicular-cycling hypothesis. Both traffic engineers and healthy city advocates normally prefer bicycles on separate lanes or paths. Forester states that there is no scientific evidence to demonstrate that this is safer or more efficient. This common belief is based upon myth and emotion, according to Forester.

The author has written a book that will give those involved in cycling transportation engineering not only the instructions on how to design and build, but will also provide the social and political context of bicycle transportation.

In order to provide this broad context, the author looks at historical and present information regarding the psychology of beliefs about cycling, demographics, governmental action, cycling accidents, traffic law, the effect of cyclists on traffic, the effect of bikeways on traffic, cycle traffic flow, prediction of bicycle traffic volume, cyclist proficiency and training, bikeways, cycling organizations, and cycling and environmentalism. The second part of the book shows readers how to implement the vehicular-cycling policy that Forester advocates through discussions of the practice of cycling transportation engineering, recommended programs, changing governmental policy and traffic law, city planning, law enforcement, road design, traffic calming, improving bicycle facilities, integration with mass transit and long-distance carriers, educational programs, and private-sector support.

166. Fothergill, Stephen, Sarah Monk, and Martin Perry. *Property and Industrial Development*. Built Environment Series. London: Century Hutchinson, 1987.

Keywords: land use, public policy

This book combines the findings of new research and previous empirical studies to evaluate property and industrial development. It is intended for students in planning and surveying courses and for those specializing in geography, economics, and management. The book examines the way in which trends in the national economy, including the downturn in manufacturing performance, affect the demand for and supply of industrial land and buildings. After a closer look at the development process through which factories are built, the text deals with the use of factory buildings, focusing on the mismatch between original design and present use. Later chapters discuss the role of the public sector and the special needs of small firms. The book concludes by looking at the requirements of the industrial property market for re-industrialization and suggests that bold changes in public policy are necessary.

167. Fowler, E. P. "Land Use in the Ecologically Sensible City." *Alternatives* 18 (1991): 26-35.

Keywords: transformation, energy, land use, transportation, urban design, waste

This article starts with an explanation of the reciprocal interaction between our behavior and the built environment. The author emphasizes the fact that our environment affects our behavior and choices as well as our interaction with other people, which is often overlooked in the decisions made by local governments. This ignorance is extended to the connection between land use regulation and local ecosystems as well, with consequences that are ecologically and socially disastrous. Urban development of this kind is analyzed in terms of its political, social, and psychological consequences.

The author next turns to ecological consequences of poorly planned land use patterns, and here the automobile, sewage, and other wastes as well as energy use are discussed. Large scale developments are criticized as being particularly wasteful; the separate planning of land use and transportation is particularly castigated since they are obviously connected. Many solutions are offered: these range from John Todd's greenhouse methods of sewage treatment to transport-oriented land use planning, and from urban agriculture to mixed use and more modest urban development. The article ends with observations on how all of these may help to mitigate the feelings of separation and powerlessness that modern city dwellers experience vis-à-vis the environment.

168. Fowler, Edmund P. *Building Cities That Work*. Kingston: McGill-Queens University Press, 1992.

Keywords: urban metabolism, built environment, community, democracy, emotional needs, urban design, urban planning

This is a social and economic critique of the North American built environment from a planning and design perspective. Particular emphasis is given to the importance of human values and community involvement in the design of the urban landscape. Attention is also paid to the revitalization of urban community life through democratic processes of public participation. A study of communities in Ontario enhances the value of this book.

169. Freestone, Robert, ed. *Spirited Cities: Urban Planning, Traffic and Environmental Management in the Nineties*. 2nd ed. Sydney: Federation Press, 1993.

Keywords: transportation, built environment, case studies, streets, traffic, urban planning

The principles and challenges of current urban planning are examined in this collection of articles. The book's chapter headings give a good indication of the topics addressed:

1. Planning, Professionalism and Practice

2. Cross-Cultural Perspectives (examples of different urban planning approaches in different countries)

3. Roads and Environments (roads, housing frontages, post-modern streets)

4. Society, Suburb and Home

5. Metropolitan Planning (case studies and future plans of Hobart, Adelaide, Sydney, and Canberra)

6. Improving the Planning System

170. Freund, Peter E. S. *The Ecology of the Automobile.* Montreal: Black Rose Books, 1993.

Keywords: automobiles, land use, transportation

The introduction to this work establishes the auto-centered nature of our society, summarizes its implications, and states the ensuing need to study the ecology of the automobile. The entire *system* of auto-centered transport is considered in this holistic approach, including its relationship to public policy, land use, culture, social relations, community, natural resources, and environmental quality.

Part 1 discusses the objective problems of auto-centered transportation, including its energy and resource intensiveness, environmental and health effects, social inequities, and impact on developing countries.

Part 2 examines the ideological assumptions shared by car owners and transportation planners. Also examined are the subjective dimensions of automobile use, as well as the relationship between automobility and socioecological issues.

Part 3 first analyzes the politics of transport policy and then presents ideas to reduce auto use.

171. Frieden, Bernard J., and Lynne B. Sagalyn. *Downtown, Inc.: How America Rebuilds Cities.* Cambridge, Mass.: MIT Press, 1989.

Keywords: social fabric, urban planning, United States, case studies

Contrary to mainstream attitudes, the 1970s and 1980s actually witnessed the success of downtown urban renewal projects. The authors of this book point out that downtown retail centers were at the heart of making these projects work. The book contains case studies of Faneuil Hall Marketplace in Boston, Pike Place Market in Seattle, Town Square/Saint Paul Center in St. Paul, and Plaza Pasadena and Horton Plaza in San Diego. The University Town Center just outside San Diego is also studied as a suburban benchmark. The purpose of this book is to provide students who intend to work in city development with information on how cities and developers went about planning and building downtown shopping centers and other renewal projects.

172. Friedman, Avi. "Narrow-Front Row Housing for Affordability and Flexibility." *Plan Canada* (September 1994): 9-16.

Keywords: social fabric, community, housing, identity, public space, traffic, transportation

This article attempts to solve the problem of suburban sprawl by examining the various ways in which architects and planners have looked at smaller housing prototypes and densification strategies to make sustainable communities possible. Friedman suggests that the above approaches are appropriate to the contemporary socio-demographic climate, economic constraints, and environmental concerns. Narrow-front row houses are a suitable design for both cost and resource reduction. The article explores issues of parking and traffic, private and public open spaces, and unit and community identity in the context of neighborhoods composed of this form of housing. Principles underlying the development of such communities as well as their design criteria are also explored, with reference to their practical application in new communities and how this has altered planning approaches.

173. Friedmann, Arnold, Craig Zimring, and Ervin Zube. *Environmental Design Evaluation*. 1st ed. New York: Plenum Press, 1978.

Keywords: sociocultural, architecture, buildings—social aspects, case studies

The focus of this volume is on environment, behavior, and design evaluation. The authors' backgrounds are in design, psychology, and landscape architecture, but the book may be of particular relevance to engineers and design professionals as well.

Chapter 1 introduces the subject of design evaluation and discusses major conceptual issues, drawing upon the case studies that follow as a means of illustrating them. The next three chapters consist of case studies dealing with interior spaces, buildings, and outdoor spaces, respectively. Each of these chapters has a brief introduction which directs the reader to important distinctions among the case studies. The final chapter summarizes the authors' thoughts on environmental design evaluation and discusses methods and techniques for evaluative studies.

174. Frisken, Frances, ed. *The Changing Canadian Metropolis: A Public Policy Perspective*. Vol. 1. Berkeley, Calif.: Institute of Govermental Studies Press, University of California, 1993.

Keywords: democracy, public policy, suburbs, technology, Canada

This compilation of articles and those in its companion volume (vol. 2, 1994) were funded by The Institute of Governmental Studies and The Canadian Urban Institute in an attempt to determine the influence of public policy on Canadian metropolises in general. The book begins with an historical overview of the Canadian metropolitan system. Changes in the Canadian metropolis due to the impacts of information technology, the environmental movement, gender and employment, ethnic segregation, gentrification, social polarization, and suburbanization are analyzed.

175. Garnett, Tara. "Farming the City: The Potential of Urban Agriculture." *The Ecologist*, 26, 6 (1996): 299-307.

Keywords: input, food, green cities

By the turn of the century, the majority of the world's people will live in cities and urban areas. In the South, growing one's food in cities is already a thriving response by the poor to the problems of obtaining food in an era of structural adjustment. In the North, the imperative to grow one's own food seems less immediate. But the arguments in favor of urban agriculture on the grounds of community and health generation are compelling, particularly for those living on low incomes.

176. Garreau, Joel. *Edge City: Life on the New Frontier*. New York: Doubleday, 1991.

Keywords: support, case studies, community, economics, suburbs, utopia, work, current

How does America work, really? This question is the driving force behind Joel Garreau's now-famous inquiry into American Edge Cities. He claims that Edge Cities represent the most radical change in how Americans build their world since the Industrial Revolution. An Edge City is defined by the following five characteristics:

1) It has at least 5,000,000 square feet of leasable office space (more than downtown Memphis).

2) It has at least 600,000 square feet of leasable retail space (equivalent to a fair-sized mall).

3) It has more jobs than bedrooms.

4) It is perceived by the population as one place that "has it all" (jobs, shopping and entertainment).

5) It was nothing like a city as recently as 30 years ago (it was probably cow pasture or a suburban residential area).

Basically, the Edge City represents a shift in location of jobs to formerly residential and shopping areas.

The book is based on Garreau's travels and interviews. He believes that by studying Edge Cities, we can gain insight into American values regarding working, playing, and living. In the first few chapters, Garreau discusses how Edge Cities operate and notes how successful they are at delivering "just about anything quantifiable—like jobs and wealth." New Jersey, Boston, Detroit, Atlanta, Phoenix, Texas, Southern California, the San Francisco Bay Area, and Washington are studied in detail. The later chapters reveal just how complex the issues surrounding Edge Cities are. Questions of community, civilization, and soul are addressed. While the creation of Edge Cities is an attempt at utopia, Garreau contends the only way we can truly achieve it is if we change our relationship to the land and come to see it as sacred.

177. Garreau, Joel. "Edge Cities." *Plan Canada* (January 1995): 16-17.

Keywords: community, suburbs

This article contains edited extracts from a speech by Joel Garreau, the author of *Edge City: Life on the New Frontier*. He defines and describes his edge city model and goes on to comment on its significance. He is quick to point out that "I am not recommending this structure. I am reporting on it. I am not saying this is the way I wish the world would work; I am saying this is the way the world *does* work." However, he does recommend that "It is time to start developing 'clever' solutions in which technology and nature walk hand-in-hand. Solutions such as these are good for the planet, profitable, and promote a preferred way of life. This isn't just about property values, tax ratable, or where people will and will not choose to live. It is about you, your children's children for generations to come. Because this is the place we're all going to call home."

Following this article is a response by Paul Maas. He challenged Garreau during the question-and-answer period following his speech for inappropriately applying American experiences to other situations from around the world. This article expands on the points he made in that session.

178. Garvin, Alexander. *The American City: What Works, What Doesn't*. New York: McGraw-Hill, 1996.

Keywords: current, built environment, case studies, green space, housing, public policy, public space, streets, urban design

While many books discuss features and principles of sustainable cities, it is rare to find a book such as this one that so explicitly states the ingredients of success. Garvin confidently espouses the premise that careful consideration of market, location, design, financing, entrepreneurship, and time is a prerequisite, but not a guarantee, of success. After describing what he means by these six ingredients, he applies this framework to analyze over 250 projects and programs in 100 cities. He uses the six ingredients, or the lack thereof, to explain why a project succeeded or failed. The comprehensiveness of Garvin's undertaking is impressive, as is apparent from the chapter titles "Parks and Playgrounds," "Palaces for the People," "Shopping Centers," "City of Tomorrow," "Planning for Pedestrians," "Increasing the Housing Supply," "Reducing Housing Cost," "Housing Rehabilitation," "Clearing the Slums," "Revitalizing Neighborhoods," "Residential Suburbs," "New-Towns-in-Town," "New-Towns-in-the-Country," "Land Use Regulation," "Preserving the Past" and "The Comprehensive Plan."

179. Gaster, Sanford. "Urban Children's Access to their Neighborhood: Changes over Three Generations." *Environment and Behavior* 23, 1 (January 1991): 70-85.

Keywords: growing up, children, neighborhood

There has been a remarkable decline in New York City since the 1940s in neighborhoods that are supportive of children at play, as well as of children's unsupervised access to their neighborhood. Apart from interviewing a number of adults about their experiences as children in one New York City neighborhood between 1915 and 1976, the author consulted other archival sources, such as U.S. census reports, for demographic changes. The interviews themselves were content analyzed for various changes in children's activities. Many changes were detected in: (a) "the age at which children were first allowed outdoors without supervision"; (b) "the number and quality of settings visited"; (c) "the number and nature of environmental obstacles"; (d) "the number and nature of parent-imposed restrictions" and (e) "the number of professionally supervised activities taken."

180. Geddes, Robert, ed. *Cities in Our Future: Growth and Form, Environmental Health and Social Equity*. Washington, D.C.: Island Press, 1997.

Keywords: current, democracy, ecology, inner cities, quality of life, urban design

This collection of critical analyses of cities was prepared for The Conference on Cities in North America, held in New York in 1996 in anticipation of Habitat II. The two topics of social equity and environmental health are approached from a conceptual perspective in the first two chapters. The remainder of the book is devoted to case studies of cities in terms of social equity and environmental health issues. The case studies of Los Angeles, Toronto, New York, Cascadia (Portland, Seattle, and Vancouver), and Mexico City bring home the point that although the goal of urban regions is to achieve a balance between economy, environment, and equity, only one factor—the economy—has received consideration to date. Although there is agreement on this goal, the various authors debate about how it can be achieved. They do, however, agree that centers and edges are the most socially equitable and environmentally healthy forms of city-regions.

181. Gehl, Jan. *Life Between Buildings: Using Public Space*. New York: Van Nostrand Reinhold, 1987.

Keywords: urban design, architecture, streets, public space, experience of place

An outstanding analysis of the factors that make the outdoor environment in urban areas desirable. Gehl's approach is primarily empirical, and the book is replete with examples and illustrations. Gehl suggests that people's outdoor activities can be divided into necessary activities, optional activities, and social activities. The quality of the outdoors determines which of these activities predominates in people's lives. A poor quality environment limits activities to the necessary only, thus curtailing community building and political engagement. Good design, through which Gehl patiently guides the reader, can contribute immensely toward outdoor activities that are optional and social.

182. Gerecke, Kent. *The Canadian City*. Montreal: Black Rose Books, 1991.

Keywords: sociocultural, democracy, green cities, housing, Canada

The modern Canadian city is marked by an increasing polarization of wealth and poverty, a loss of political efficacy by citizens, and an increase in central control. The wide range of the analysis in this book is evident from the various section headings: "The Changing City," "Urban Theory," "Urban Planning," "Urban Design," "Housing," and "Green Cities."

183. Gibert, Alan. *The Latin American City*. London: Latin America Bureau (Research and Action), 1994.

Keywords: quality of life, developing countries, housing, poverty, work

The transformation of Latin America into an urban society from a rural one within the course of a single generation has placed burdens on people and governments that are unique and unprecedented for the area. With Mexico City providing the lead with a staggering population of 20 million people, the area contains some of the world's largest cities. The author notes that, with the exception of five Latin American cities, more people live in urban areas than in the countryside and, even in the exceptions, the balance is expected to shift within a few decades.

184. Gilbert, Richard, et al. *Making Cities Work: The Role of Local Authorities in the Urban Environment*. London: Earthscan, 1996.

Keywords: public policy, green cities, sustainability, case studies

This guide to implementing sustainable development at the municipal level is important for those who work in planning, engineering, and local government. The book outlines the role of local authorities in environmental management and issues for local action and the role of local authorities in global sustainable development initiatives. It also provides useful recommendations to guide future action and a series of useful case studies that highlight local government initiatives from both the developed and developing worlds. The bibliography and addresses of local associations make this book an excellent resource.

185. Girardet, Herbert. *The Gaia Atlas of Cities: New Directions for Sustainable Urban Living*. New York: Anchor Books, 1992.

Keywords: urban metabolism, automobiles, efficiency, environmental pollution, housing, industrial pollution, megacities, quality of life, sustainability, transportation, urban ecology, waste, classic

The Gaia Atlas of Cities provides an excellent introduction to the topic of healthy cities. As an extension of the Gaia hypothesis, the city is seen as an organism. The book discusses the problems of cities such as overconsumption, congestion, pollution, lack of adequate housing, poverty (especially of women and children), stress, sick buildings, and the generation of enormous quantities of waste. Each problem is given one or two paragraphs' worth of attention. Thus it serves as a good introduction and overview rather than an in-depth analysis. The city is described as a parasite with little concern for Gaia, the host organism from which a steady flow of supplies such as timber, water, and fossil fuels are derived.

The Gaia Atlas also deals with strategies for "Healing the City." Here, as in the rest of the book, the focus is on the metabolism of cities. Metabolic cycles must be made circular instead of linear. Other ideas for healthier cities such as energy efficiency, recycling, urban parks, urban farming, planning for proximity instead of for cars, traffic calming, pollution prevention, and citizen-run projects are presented. Many pictures, diagrams, and over eighty case studies help to make this book a readable and informative one.

186. Gittell, Ross J. *Renewing Cities*. Princeton, N. J.: Princeton University Press, 1993

Keywords: urban planning, public policy, case studies, inner cities

This is an important empirical analysis of what works and what doesn't—and the reasons why—in urban renewal projects. The heart of the book is four case studies of Lowell and New Bedford in Massachusetts, Jamestown in New York, and Mckeesport in Pennsylvania, all in the Northeast United States These cities had to take aggressive actions to avert disaster following massive de-industrialization during the '70s and '80s. The actions met with varying degrees of success. Gittell indulges in some inductive theory-building based on the case studies. The result is a valuable contribution to the literature on urban renewal, especially for those interested in U.S. cities.

187. Glass, D. C., and J. E. Singer. *Urban Stress: Experiments on Noise and Social Stressors*. New York: Academic Press, 1972.

Keywords: noise—physiological effects, noise—psychosocial effects, psychological health

This volume is a collaborative effort between two experimental social psychologists. Most of the studies center around noise, but this is not a "noise" book per se. Rather, the use of noise stimuli in this research was simply a convenient device for studying antecedents and consequences of analogues of urban stressors.

There are three central concepts in this work: direct effects of stress, adaptation to stress, and adverse after-effects of stress. The researchers attempt to show that while people do adapt to stress, adverse after-effects remain which are detectable in behavior.

More specifically, topics covered include:
-environmental stress and the adaptive response
-effects of noise on physiology and task performance
-behavioral after-effects of unpredictable noise
-perceived control and behavioral after-effects of noise
-other cognitive factors and behavioral after-effects of noise
-behavioral after-effects of unpredictable and uncontrollable shock
-behavioral after-effects of social stressors
-psychic costs of stress: exposure or adaptation

188. Gold, John R. *An Introduction to Behavioral Geography*. Oxford: Oxford University Press, 1980.

Keywords: social fabric, built environment, psychological health

Part 1 of the book examines how psychologists and geographers have previously viewed human behavior; it also outlines relevant concepts and frameworks. Part 2 considers how people come to terms with their spatial environment and also examines the role of learning processes. Part 3 supplies an overview of current knowledge about the nature and characteristics of spatial cognition. Part 4 investigates the links between cognition and behavior.

189. Goldberg, Michael A., and John Mercer. *The Myth of the North American City: Continentalism Challenged*. Vancouver: University of British Columbia Press, 1986.

Keywords: current, economics, inner cities, sociology, urban planning, United States, Canada

How many times has the term "North American cities" been used? How many times have American urban studies' findings been directly applied to Canadian cities? Goldberg and Mercer criticize the continentalization of Canadian cities and explain exactly why Canadian and American cities cannot be treated interchangeably. First they compare the two countries' values and cultures. Then, social and demographic structures are contrasted using rather outdated data from the early 1980s. Economic and political structures are similarly scrutinized. Urban forms, institutions, social characteristics, and governments are then compared and contrasted in light of the differing contexts previously established. What emerges is a clear picture of two countries with significant and often fundamental differences. The authors conclude that the transfer of American urban policies would lead to less livable and less sustainable Canadian cities.

190. Goldsteen, Joel B., and Cecil D. Elliot. *Designing America: Creating Urban Identity*. New York: Van Nostrand Reinhold, 1994.

Keywords: social fabric, built environment, public space, urban design

This comprehensive volume considers the design and implications of urban forms, focussing on spaces between buildings such as parks and squares. It includes case studies from the past and present. The chapter entitled "Reacting to Spaces—The Psychology of Perception and Behavior" provides an interesting study of the effects on people of factors such as setting, time of day, purpose of trips, proxemics, and familiarity. Finally, the methodology and financing of human-centered design of spaces are outlined.

191. Goodman, Percival, and Paul Goodman. *Communitas: Means of Livelihood and Ways of Life*. Morningside Edition. New York: Columbia University Press, 1990.

Keywords: social fabric, community, democracy, utopia

This is a new printing of the original 1947 version but the ideas presented in it are as relevant today, if not more so, than in the '60s when the book achieved popularity. The central argument of the book addresses the retreat from public life into the private realm by modern "citizens"—i.e., inhabitants of cities who do not participate in the civic realm in any meaningful way. The notion of "communitas" stands in opposition to this retreat and its concomitant abdication from social responsibility. The authors argue passionately for the virtues of the public realm: public places, debates, ideas, and responsibilities in contrast to the narrow and private concerns of individuals. The essence of what makes a city a worthwhile place to live in, a place that can enhance the development of people, is also encapsulated in the notion of communitas with its emphasis on collectivity, shared place, and a conception of this space as "common ground." To implement this vision of the public realm the authors explore the notion of green belts, integrated planning, efficient patterns of consumption, the relationship between production and consumption, the role and location of industry, and planned security that obviates the necessity of excessive regulation.

192. Gordon, David, ed. *Green Cities: Ecologically Sound Approaches to Urban Space*. Montreal: Black Rose Books, 1990.

Keywords: community, ecology, green cities, neighborhood, green space

The works in this anthology (a project of the Pollution Probe Foundation) discuss the green city from three perspectives that pertain to definitions, illustrations, and a delineation of "greening" techniques. Other articles on culture, globalism, international economics, and local initiatives provide a thoughtful perspective on emerging models of green cities.

193. Gottmann, Jean. "Megalopolis and Antipolis: The Telephone and the Structure of the City." In *The Social Impact of the Telephone*, ed. I. Pool. pp. 303-17. Cambridge, Mass.: MIT Press, 1977.

Keywords: social fabric, technology, telecommunications

Has the telephone contributed to the formation of cities, or has it encouraged people to move away from them? That is, is the telephone a force for the megalopolis or the antipolis? Jean Gottmann explores this question by looking at the relationship between the invention and use of the telephone and settlement patterns. "Some opinions hold that the improvement of personal communications brought about by generalized telephone use fosters the growth of selected transactional centers and the sprawl of vast urban systems." At the same time, others insist that "the telephone encourages geographical scatteration of the places where telephone users live and work and that this trend will develop until it brings about a complete dispersal of settlement and the dissolution of compact cities." The author concludes that both views are valid and that the task of assessing the impact of the telephone is a difficult one. This is because considerations of other factors and other technologies influencing society and settlement patterns obviously exist and must be taken into account. Nonetheless, the author acknowledges that in many ways the telephone is a megalopolitan force that encourages the geographical concentration of people. But Gottmann also states that the telephone can have an antipolitan influence by weakening communities.

194. Goudie, Andrew. *The Human Impact on the Natural Environment*. 4th ed. Oxford: Blackwell Publishers, 1993.

Keywords: air pollution, environmental overload, environmental pollution, greenhouse effect, ground pollution, ozone, water pollution

This large, comprehensive volume on the impact of human activity on the biosphere describes and explains everything from the use of fire to the effects of soil erosion. Although it does not deal specifically with cities, it contains sections of particular relevance to healthy city studies, especially from the perspective of urban metabolism. The following topics, which are extensively covered, are particularly important in this regard:
 -deforestation
 -soil erosion associated with construction and urbanization
 -urbanization and its effects on river flows
 -thermal pollution
 -world climate
 -the CO_2 problem
 -other gases
 -aerosols

-urban climates
-smoke, haze, and photochemical smog
-air pollution
-water pollution
-projected sea-level rise
-landforms produced by construction and dumping
-accelerated sedimentation
-deliberate modification of channels
-modern industrial and urban civilizations

195. Government of Canada, Ministry of Supply and Services. "Urbanization: Building Human Habitats." In *The State of Canada's Environment*, pp. 13-1 to 13-31. Ottawa: Government of Canada (Minister of Supply and Services), 1991.

Keywords: crowding, energy, environmental pollution, green cities, transportation, urban design, Canada

This is a very good source book with a comprehensive listing of major urban problems and challenges currently facing Canadians. It contains five main sections: Perspectives; The Environment and Human Activities; Regional Case Studies of the Arctic, Lower Fraser River Basin, Prairie Grasslands, Great Lakes Basin, St. Lawrence River and Upper Bay of Fundy Dikelands; Current Issues; and Sustainable Development.

Most applicable to healthy cities is the thirteenth chapter, "Building Human Habitats." Here, it is emphasized that urbanization itself is not the main problem; it is our use of energy and materials that create waste and pollution. Topics related to greening the city are addressed. Air and water pollution are discussed in some detail, as well as energy use and the problems associated with its generation, transmission, and use. The urban form in its relation to the environment is then considered. The tools for achieving a greener city are within our reach, suggests the author. City planners must henceforth design cities with strict attention to the features of the local ecosystem. The advantages of giving the city a firm boundary, developing compact housing, providing convenient public transport, building tree-overgrown roads, allowing as few cars as possible, and other ideas lead to the conclusion of this section.

196. Government of Canada, Ministry of National Health and Welfare. *A Vital Link: Health and the Environment in Canada*. Ottawa: Government of Canada (Minister of Supply and Services), 1992.

Keywords: biosphere, air pollution, built environment, environmental pollution, health, risk assessment, Canada

Most of the information in this publication is based on studies conducted by federal government departments, particularly Health and Welfare Canada, and is intended to provide information about health and environmental risks to the ordinary citizen so that informed decisions may be made on issues affecting personal health. Basic information on the various ways in which our health is jeopardized by contaminants in our environment is provided in lay language. Other parts of the book move on to the effects of specific contaminants and toxics, ranging from heavy metals, micro-organisms, radiation, various organic compounds, and pesticides. Emerging problems associated with noise pollution and the limitations of waste management techniques are also discussed along with Canadian policies regarding climate change and chemicals. A description of monitoring efforts by various government agencies to ensure safety from contaminants rounds off this extremely useful resource.

197. Graham, Colin. "Planning for the Sense of Community." *City Magazine* 15, 2/3 (Spring/Summer 1994): 44-46.

Keywords: community, green cities, sociology

The author begins by stating that recent studies in evolutionary psychology "could provide significant insights for urban planning." This leads to an examination of ideal city size and problems of large cities in the context of human history and evolution. The author suggests that small, town-like communities within cities are ideal from the perspective of sustainability.

198. Gratz, Roberta Brandes. *The Living City*. New York: Simon & Schuster, 1989.

Keywords: support, community, housing, neighborhood

This is a book about urban revitalization, historic preservation, and neighborhood renewal. It is an account of the rebuilding of cities based on personal observations made in New York City.

Gratz claims that one can learn more from the residents and users of a community than from any number of planners and theoreticians. The author also suggests that, from the illustrations and firsthand observations provided, it is possible to draw lessons that are applicable to development patterns in almost every community in the United States.

199. Gratz, Roberta Brandes, and Norman Mintz. *Cities Back from the Edge: New Life for Downtown*. New York: John Wiley & Sons, 1998.

Keywords: urban planning, public policy, urban design, inner cities

Entertainment complexes, once restricted to the suburbs, are now sprouting up with increasing regularity in the urban environment, much to the detriment of the latter. These "square boxes" featuring dozens of movie theatres, formula chain stores, and formula restaurants are a drain on municipal resources that could have been better spent on other urban redevelopments. Gratz claims that most "big box" retailers "don't know how to be urban, even when they locate in a city. They don't understand that the urban pedestrian shopper does not require the same things as a suburban car driver. They don't even realize that they may have more customers within a ten minute walk than within a ten mile drive."

Gratz then goes on to give a wealth of examples where urban developments have been successful on the basis of breaking away from traditional urban and transportation planning policies. A useful and thought-provoking book on how citizens can have an impact on the urban development process.

200. Greed, Clara H. *Women and Planning: Creating Gendered Realities*. London: Routledge, 1994.

Keywords: support, feminism, patriarchy, democracy, urban planning

Women in Planning is the first comprehensive history and analysis of women and the planning movement, covering the philosophical, practical, and policy dimensions of "planning for women." Beyond the marginalization of women, modern, scientific planning hides a story of past links with eugenics, colonialism, artistic, utopian and religious movements, and the occult. Central to the discussion is the questioning of how male planners have rewritten planning in their own image, projecting patriarchal assumptions in their creation of "urban realities." Issues of class, sexuality, ethnicity, and disability are raised by the fundamental question of "Who is being planned for?"

201. Greed, Clara. *Introducing Town Planning*. 2nd ed. Harlow, England: Addison Wesley Longman, 1996.

Keywords: current, land use

The first chapter discusses the scope and nature of town planning by clearly showing the reader why town planning is relevant to variety of work. Chapter 2 examines the organizational framework of planning. Chapter 3 discusses the profession of land use planning. Chapter 4 traces the need for town planning back to industrialization, urbanization, and social change in the nineteenth century. Chapter 5 examines the reactions to the changes outlined in chapter 4. Chapter 6 examines the history of planning in the first half of the twentieth century. Chapter 7 looks at recent changes to planning in the last ten years by highlighting themes and issues. Chapter 8 looks at the historical development of the townscape prior to the nineteenth century. Chapter 9 discusses conservation of urban and rural areas at one of the pressing issues in twentieth-century planning. In chapter 10, the ins and outs of development control planning are discussed. Chapter 11 traces the development of social theories as a result of changing attitudes and unrest in community groups. Finally, chapter 12 reinforces the notion that town planning is all about "where you want to live."

This book is billed as "a comprehensive introduction to the scope and nature of town planning in the UK." Despite its UK focus, it is still helpful for those interested in learning more about planning in a North American context keeping in mind that since planning practice is based in legal precedent, development control and other planning practices differ country to country.

202. Greed, Clara. *Implementing Town Planning: The Role of Town Planning in the Development Process*. Harlow, England: Longman Group, 1996.

Keywords: current, land use

In this sequel to *Introducing Town Planning*, the various contributors discuss the theoretical and procedural aspects of town planning and show how planning implementation fits into the legal and governmental structure of the UK. This book provides coverage of development process for planners and developers; raises economic and social issues for further consideration; provides a wealth of case studies, legal frameworks, policy proposals, maps, and site plans; provides tools for self-assessment; and discusses issues like conflict resolution, legislation, professionalism, the process in practice, and power issues. This book, like its prequel, provides a useful primer for those wanting to learn more about planning.

203. Greenberg, Mike. *The Poetics of Cities: Designing Neighborhoods That Work*. Urban Life and Urban Landscape Series. Columbus: Ohio State University Press, 1995.

Keywords: automobiles, built environment, community, economics, neighborhood, urban planning

Misguided revisionist planning and suburban sprawl resulting more from the "needs" of the automobile rather than people have resulted in a geography that thwarts the very things that justify the existence of cities in the first place. These are identified as the fostering of social, intellectual, and economic exchange. A historical survey of American cities identifies the various aspects of the geography of a city that can foster such exchanges (which made the city possible in the first place) or inhibit them. Greenberg carefully looks at features of earlier American cities that allowed them to function in a way that enhanced exchanges. These range from such diverse features as neighborhood scales and structures, the rhythms of their streetscapes, the design of their sidewalks that served so well to foster such exchanges, and how their being "tossed aside" in contemporary planning has had deleterious effects on the urban economy, the public sphere, and the stagnation of city cores. Drawing on lessons of the past, Greenberg offers several practical solutions in terms of planning strategies and regulations that retain the best of the past without compromising the needs of modernity.

204. Greer, Ann Lennarson, and Scott Greer, eds. *Cities and Sickness: Health Care in Urban America*. Vol. 25. Urban Affairs Annual Reviews. Beverly Hills, Calif.: Sage Publications, 1983.

Keywords: support, health, health care, United States

This is a text outlining the history and composition of the American health care system in cities. Part 1 (The Status of Health Care in American Cities) deals with issues such as urbanization and health status, the reconfiguration of urban hospital care, mortality, morbidity, the Inverse Care Law, the mentally ill, and the elderly and disabled. Part 2 (The Making and Unmaking of Health Policy) discusses the politics behind urban health care. A study of New York's public and voluntary hospitals and a world perspective on urbanization and health services are also included.

205. Gugler, Josef, ed. *The Urban Transformation of the Developing World*. Oxford: Oxford University Press, 1996.

Keywords: developing countries

As the cities of the world continue to grow at an alarming rate, especially in developing countries, the percentage of people living in these densely populated regions will soon surpass those who call rural areas home. This compilation of papers by various experts examines many issues surrounding socioeconomic and demographic transformations. The first paper, "Regional Trajectories in the Urban Transformation," analyses the evolution of urban spheres, while the second jumps right into a specific study of the history of cities in Monsoon Asia. Reassessing an evolving model of urbanization in China is the subject of the third article. The fourth paper takes the reader a little farther south to examine patterns and emerging policy issues of urbanization in India. "Urbanization in Indonesia: City and Countryside Linked" is the title of the fifth article, while the sixth concentrates on "Urbanization in the Arab World and the International System." The last two papers look at urbanization in Africa south of the Sahara as well as urban development and social inequality in Latin America. Although these papers are fairly brief, the contents are informative.

206. Gunn, Angus M. *Habitat: Human Settlements in an Urban Age.* Toronto: Pergamon Press, 1978.

Keywords: support, developing countries, housing, nutrition, population

This book deals mainly with the urban problems of the developing world such as absolute poverty, starvation and malnutrition, and the population explosion. Five chapters are devoted to such urban issues. Chapter 1 discusses the increasingly blurred distinction between rural and urban life. Chapter 2 addresses the issue of slums and squatter settlements on the urban fringe. Chapter 8 provides an overview of the environmental problems of cities. The need for provision or improvement of urban shelter and the high cost of urban land is the topic of chapter 10. Finally, in chapter 11, new planning strategies for urban and surrounding rural areas are described. Many graphs, maps, and statistics are provided in this readable textbook-type collection of information gathered for the 1976 Vancouver United Nations Conference entitled "Habitat."

207. Gutman, Robert, ed. *People and Buildings.* New York: Basic Books, 1972.

Keywords: urban metabolism, architecture, buildings—health aspects, built environment, crowding, health, home environment, housing, privacy

The authors have tried to work in the middle ground between environmental design and sociology. Included are five important areas of converging interest between sociology and design. These are:

1. Current research and theory on human anatomy and physiology, on our sensory apparatus and our be havior in space, and on the requirements that these characteristics generate for the design of buildings.

2. The impact of spatial organization on social interaction and group relationships revealed through studies of friendship patterns, communication, and privacy.

3. Environmental influences on physical and mental health, with particular attention to the role of housing conditions, noise, aesthetic surroundings, urban relocation, and overcrowding.

4. The work that anthropologists, functional sociologists, and psychologists have done in demonstrating the significance of architecture as the expression of social values and the reinforcement of cultural patterns.

5. This section includes a series of readings that illustrate the ways in which architects and behavioral scientists are applying a variety of these ideas and approaches to the practical problems of the design process.

This collection is not intended as a manual or handbook to guide design decisions on specific projects. Included is Christopher Alexander's classic article, "The City as a Mechanism for Sustaining Human Contact" (pp. 406-34).

208. Guttenberg, Albert Z. *The Language of Planning: Essays on the Origins and Ends of American Planning Thought*. Urbana: University of Illinois Press, 1993.

Keywords: land use, urban planning

Albert Guttenberg sees the terminology of planning as affording a chance to shed light on the nature of the American planning movement and, simultaneously, to help bring greater order into planning discourse. This conviction is apparent whether he is considering "Linguistic Sources and Factors in Planning," "Planning as a Social Invention," "Regionalization as a Symbolic Process," or "How to Crowd but Still Be Kind." Like much work in land use planning, Guttenberg's scholarship reflects the influence of economics, sociology, history, the law, and other social sciences.

209. Hall, Carl W., and David Pimentel, eds. *Food and Energy Resources*. Orlando: Academic Press, 1984.

Keywords: energy, food, fossil fuels

Food and energy resources are basic to survival. The alternative of biomass fuels would further stress the already depleted resources required for food, fiber, and shelter. The authors of the ten sections are from different disciplines so that the influence that energy, land, and water resources have on food production are examined from different perspectives.

The first section, by David Pimental, outlines people's place in the biosphere which is the source of all necessities of life. The history of society from hunting and gathering, to agriculture, and then towards more mechanized food production is described. Carl Hall then reviews both internal and external energy sources. The concept of entropy is explained, followed by a discussion of carbon and carbon dioxide cycles. Finally, the role of energy in food production is discussed in processing, packaging, transport, and preparation. The goal is to provide engineers, economists, agriculturists, geographers, ecologists, nutritionists, and natural resource specialists a perspective that allows for a joint effort towards food production while protecting resources.

210. Hall, Peter. *Cities of Tomorrow: An Intellectual History of Urban Planning and Design in the Twentieth Century*. Oxford: Blackwell, 1988.

Keywords: classic, urban design, urban sociology, suburbs

This book has been described as "nothing less than a history of the ideology and practice of urban planning through this century under a series of headings which attempt to encapsulate all the changing fashions and theories." The author provides an interesting approach to the history of cities by examining the various urban planning theories that held sway at the time significant expansions were made to a particular city. Hall transcends basic chronology and engages the reader's attention through an analysis of the changing sociological patterns of cities as well.

211. Halpern, David. *Mental Health and the Built Environment: More than Bricks and Mortar?* London: Taylor & Francis, 1995.

Keywords: support, built environment, crowding, noise—psychosocial effects, psychological health

David Halpern examines the relationship between the built environment and mental ill-health. After providing an overview of current thinking on the causes of mental ill-health, the environment is identified as a source of stress that could contribute to it. In chapter 2, classical environmental stressors such as weather, air pollution, and noise are discussed. Chapter 3 explores the social environment stressors such as crowding, crime, and fear. The relation between social support and the planned environment is analyzed in chapter 4. The symbolic characteristics of the environment, the planning process, and various case studies make up the remainder of this overview of environmental psychology.

212. Halpern, Robert. *Rebuilding the Inner City: A History of Neighborhood Initiatives to Address Poverty in the United States.* New York: Columbia University Press, 1995.

Keywords: social fabric, community, inner cities, neighborhood, poverty, public policy

From settlement houses in the nineteenth century to President Clinton's enterprise zones in the 1990s, the author demonstrates a pattern by which the neighborhood is most often chosen as the locus for social problem solving, particularly in the struggle against poverty and urban decay. This book shows how neighborhood-level initiatives, although modestly successful, frequently serve to divert attention from broader social inequities and to locate responsibility for addressing poverty within the areas suffering from its effects.

213. Hamer, Mick. *Wheels within Wheels: A Study of the Road Lobby.* New York: Routledge & Kegan Paul, 1987.

Keywords: transportation, Britain

This is a study of the powerful road lobby in Britain which is allied to the car industry, oil moguls, giant truck operators and, of course, road makers. The main goal of this lobby, suggests the author, is to control the country's transport policy. This book sets out to reveal:

1) the politics behind campaigns for heavier lorries and more motorways,

2) how the road lobby and its allies in the Ministry of Transport have watered down road safety meas ures although fifteen people a day are killed by motor vehicles, and

3) how the road lobby has contributed to a decline in bus and train service in Britain.

The author researched most of this book when he worked for T2000 and other pressure groups in conflict with the road lobby. It is here that he developed the insight that Britain's transport policy puts cars and lorries (trucks) before people. The constituent parts of the road lobby network of vested interests are carefully identified, their relative influence assessed, "and their lines of communication into the Department of Transport laid bare."

This book also charts the emergence and growth of the anti-road lobby despite the boost given to the road lobby by the Thatcher government, the huge disparity in resources, and their short-sighted policies. A growing number of people are recognizing the flaws of prevailing policies, says the author, and the role of this book is to further expose incoherent transport policy.

214. Hamer, Mick. "City Planners Against Global Warming." *New Scientist*, 24 July 1993, 12-13.

Keywords: air pollution, greenhouse effect, land use, traffic, transportation

This article summarizes initiatives that are being taken by many different organizations and governments to reduce carbon dioxide emissions. Most of these initiatives focus on reducing car use. It also explains why traffic is increasing by examining land use and planning strategies that promote urban sprawl.

215. Hamlin, Roger E., and Thomas S. Lyons. *Economy Without Walls: Managing Local Development in a Restructuring World.* Westport, Conn.: Praeger, 1996.

Keywords: current, case studies, community, economics, neighborhood

The term "economy without walls" refers to the new global, mixed (public and private sector) economy whose impact on urban development is increasingly crucial. These intersectoral partnerships, the authors assume, are beneficial for urban and regional development planning. The theoretical portion of the book supplies background information regarding public, private, and nonprofit sector interactions. Why and how the simultaneous pursuit of private profit and public purpose works and what diminishes its success are also discussed. The implications of the trend toward mixed economies for decision theory, ethics, urban planning, urban development, municipal management, and information systems are explored and found to be far-reaching.

The case studies outline these partnerships, their philosophical foundations, the activities used to implement them, and the organizational and legal structures that allow for such interactions. The first case studies chapter features Housing and Neighborhood Development Strategies (HANDS), a neighborhood revitalization program in Louisville, Kentucky, which is one of the most comprehensive and successful American intersectoral examples. Small business development is of great significance as a tool for economic and urban redevelopment, as espoused by the case studies of the Arizona Technology Incubator, southwestern Michigan, and Hungary's transition to a free market economy. The third case studies chapter researches examples of collaborative capitalism for urban redevelopment in Inch'on, Korea, and the Tokyo region. A reflection on lessons learned and trends in local community management conclude the book.

216. Hancock, Trevor, and Leonard Duhl. *Promoting Health in the Urban Context.* Vol.

1. World Health Organisation Healthy Cities Project. Copenhagen: FADL, 1988.

Keywords: community, health, health care, quality of life, sustainability, urban planning, classic

This is considered a classic document in the healthy cities literature. The authors take a comprehensive view of the relationship between health and urban civilization, noting that complex interactions of people with each other and their physical and social environments come into play between the two.

Acknowledging the differences of opinion regarding what constitutes a healthy city, the authors suggest that one can nevertheless find some common parameters. These they identify as "a clean, safe, high quality physical environment and a sustainable ecosystem; a strong, supportive and participatory community; provision of basic needs; access to a wide variety of experiences and resources; a diverse, vital and innovative economy; a sense of historical, biological and cultural connectedness; a city form that makes all of these possible and a high health status with appropriate, high quality and accessible public health and sick care services." Assessment of all these features, they warn, must take into account qualitative as well as quantitative indicators.

The achievement of a healthy city depends on a process that the authors liken to "family therapy" for the city. For this reason they place great importance on citizen involvement and participation in this process toward health.

217. Hancock, Trevor. *Reporting on Sustainable Development: The Municipal and Household Level*. Ottawa: NRTEE, 1993.

Keywords: sustainability

This is a study done for the "Reporting on Sustainable Development" task force of the National Round Table on Environment and Economy (NRTEE). The report provides a review of some of the issues and challenges involved in reporting on sustainable development at the local level. It is assumed that since the household and municipal levels form the building blocks for national reporting, information systems should be built up from these local levels. Information is to be provided on the current state of sustainability and the processes in place towards making it more viable.

The study includes, first, a survey of literature on sustainable development available at local bookstores. Then interviews were done with key people from local to international levels, with emphasis on Toronto and Victoria. Lastly, interviews with the general public through a small telephone survey were performed to assess household information requirements. Conclusions drawn from the study suggest that there is a crucial need to make more information about sustainability issues available to the general public.

218. Hanson, Susan. *The Geography of Urban Transportation*. New York: Guilford Press, 1986.

Keywords: energy, land use, transportation

Aimed primarily at graduate students, this book is a valuable introduction to various analytical techniques from the field of geography that can be applied to solve transportation problems. The first three chapters give a succinct account of the contexts of urban transportation and the role it plays in shaping cities as well as planning processes. This is followed by an introduction to the analytical techniques themselves. The third and final section of the book looks at various transportation policies that result from an application of these techniques. Issues surrounding land use strategies, public transportation, and energy use are also discussed in this section.

219. Hanten, Edward W., and Mark J. Kasoff, eds. *New Directions for the Mature Metropolis*. Cambridge, Mass.: Schenkman Publishing Co., 1980.

Keywords: democracy, economics, quality of life

Two conferences—"Alternate Futures for Older Metropolitan Regions" and "Managing Mature Cities"—in 1978 were the impetus for the writing of the essays in this collection. They deal with the consequences and issues related to aging cities, such as: development without growth, low public participation, depopulation, low civic morale, and managing for quality of life. Collectively, the essays suggest that "growing older need not be synonymous with decline," if the management suggestions described are followed.

220. Harris, C. M., ed. *Handbook of Noise Control*. 2nd ed. New York: McGraw-Hill, 1979.

Keywords: transformation, noise—physiological effects, noise—psychosocial effects

In the past few decades, the control of noise has become a matter of great social and economic importance. Noise (defined as unwanted sound) is annoying, interferes with communication, affects behavior, produces hearing loss, and is costly to control. This book thoroughly examines noise control in its forty-five chapters written by a number of respected experts in their fields. This work is in the form of a handbook and may be used as a detailed guide or reference. It is written with the realization that noise control is of interest to experts in a wide range of fields including city planners, government policymakers, health officials, psychologists, engineers, architects, business executives, and environmentalists. The range of topics examined include properties of sound, methods of noise measurement, a study of hearing, effects of noise (communication, human performance, physiology, annoyance), noise control, community noise, and the law.

221. Harrison, G. A., and J. B. Gibson, eds. *Man in Urban Environments*. Oxford: Oxford University Press, 1976.

Keywords: urban metabolism, air pollution, built environment, crowding, emotional needs, design, epidemiology, health, nutrition, psychological health

This volume, while a little dated, provides an excellent and comprehensive treatment of many issues related to human health and the built environment. This book has a primarily biological-medical focus. Methodological and theoretical material is also included.
Topics discussed include:
-the biological effects of urbanization

-urban geography and demography
-buildings and architecture in relation to environmental design
-human adaptive capacity
-effects of traffic on human life in cities
-effects of crowding
-nutrition
-effects of air pollution on health
-emotional stress in cities
-social disturbances affecting young people in urban centers
-biochemical responses to environmental stress

222. Hart, John Fraser, ed. *Our Changing Cities*. Baltimore: Johns Hopkins University Press, 1991.

Keywords: support, inner cities, sociology, technology, urban planning

This book concentrates on the various ways in which technology has contributed to the transformation of urban centers. Social, economic, and political implications are discussed. The urban geographers invited to contribute to this volume write about various changes that American cities have gone through. There is considerable discussion on the consequences of urban sprawl and the resulting concentration of poor citizens in inner cities.

223. Hart, Roger D., ed. *A Nation Reconstructed: A Quest for the Cities That Can Be*. Milwaukee: ASQC Quality Press, 1997.

Keywords: social fabric, community, economics, inner cities, public policy, quality of life

There does not seem to be any disagreement over the fact that improvements can be made to our cities, but there is debate as to what these should be and how they are to be implemented. The purpose of this book is to make the reader aware of the value of adopting formal "quality" strategies alongside urban reform and the benefits that come with making quality the foundation on which related programs can be built. The working definition of "quality" moves beyond standard engineering criteria to include social and environmental factors as well. Part 1 covers the issues and concerns of urban revitalization and looks more closely at the need to develop partnerships (private/public, community/government) for urban revitalization, the crisis in human capital development, the lack of focus in urban education, and the difficulties faced by the inner-city family. Part 2 examines how the challenges faced by the inner-city family can be met, and delves into financial debt restructuring, education, crime, economic development, political gridlock, instances of revitalization success, and principles and practices outlined to show how quality techniques have been put into practice. Specific quality solutions are described in part 3, in terms of its application to capital projects, the roles and responsibilities of key players during the first 100 days of program implementation, and quality-effecting techniques that can be employed in physical rebuilding projects and social programs. In the epilogue, the future of cities is explored through a description of worldwide trends and global quality scenarios. The target audience for this book is the "person who seeks to make a difference."

224. Harvey, L. D. Danny. "Tackling Urban CO_2 Emissions in Toronto." *Environment* 35, 7 (September 1993): 16-20, 38-44.

Keywords: urban metabolism, air pollution, energy, energy efficiency, greenhouse effect

In 1991, the city of Toronto was joined by twelve other European and North American cities and by Metro Toronto to form the Urban CO_2 Project, through which participating cities are developing inventories of energy use and CO_2 emissions, exchanging information on successful programs to use energy more efficiently, and developing strategies to reduce their carbon dioxide emissions by 15 to 25 percent by 2005. After explaining why reducing CO_2 emissions is important, the article lists strategies adopted or under consideration by the member cities. The section "Toronto's Strategies" deals with the following topics:
  -the history of CO_2 emissions control
  -results of data collection and analysis
  -community-based retrofitting (a "key element")
  -energy systems such as cogeneration and district heating and their potential savings
  -how to reduce energy used for transportation through better land planning
The article concludes by stating the initial steps that have been taken since the project began, as well as future plans.

225. Haughton, Graham, and Colin Hunter. *Sustainable Cities*. Vol. 7. Regional Policy and Development Series. London: Jessica Kingsley Publishers, 1994.

Keywords: current, air pollution, environmental pollution, public policy, sustainability, urban planning, water pollution

Sustainability issues and problems of the structure of cities are probed in part A. Part B takes a detailed look at pollution. Urban climate, air pollution, fresh water resources, and water pollution are studied to demonstrate current unsustainable practices in cities. Part C outlines guiding principles and policy instruments to bring about sustainable urban development. A superb and comprehensive overview of healthy cities issues (with more of an emphasis on metabolism than sociocultural aspects) is provided.

226. Hawley, Amos H. *Urban Society: An Ecological Approach*. 2nd ed. New York: John Wiley & Sons, 1981.

Keywords: telecommunications, transportation, urban sociology

This book remains a much discussed work in urban sociology. Hawley systematizes various urban phenomena around the "guiding principle" or "hypothesis" that the form and content of collective human life are a function of the efficiency of the means of communication and transportation available to them. Any attempt toward a general theory of urbanization, Hawley suggests, must take into account the groundwork his own efforts have built regarding the relationship between the development of urban institutions and the ability of societies to overcome the friction of distance. He explores various historic societies in an attempt to delineate the linkages between the two in a clearer manner. Hawley's own words succinctly indicate the nature of the book: "This textbook presents in systematic form the concepts, theories, and research findings on urban phenomena. In so doing it explores the interrelations among the many kinds of urban knowledge, organizes them in an intelligible unity, and reveals the relevance of this synthesis for an understanding of society as a whole.

"Organizing the material on urbanization calls for a guiding principle or an hypothesis which can illuminate existing data and reveal their meaning. The position taken in this volume is that the form and content of man's collective life is a function of the efficiency of his means of transportation and communication. The tendency—noticeable in every historic society—for an urban organization to arise and flourish has been decisively influenced by man's progress in overcoming the frictions of space. Thus, far from being a static thing, urban organization is a process, a development, a transformation of the entire society.

"As a concept urbanization tends to become identified with a general theory of societal change and growth. At this time it would be presumptuous to present a mature theory of that nature, but I have indicated in this book what the outline of such a theory might be."

227. Hayden, Dolores. *Redesigning the American Dream: The Future of Housing, Work and Family Life*. New York: Norton, 1984.

Keywords: social fabric, case studies, home environment, housing, neighborhood, urban planning, United States

This is a study of American public and private life and how it relates to housing and city living issues. The author advocates the design of the home as part of a well-thought-out neighborhood and as a support for women in the labor force, not merely as a haven for the white male worker and his dependents.

The author claims that "Americans chose the [latter] model for housing in the late 1940s; we have mass-produced the home as haven and transformed our cities to fit this model and its particular social, economic, and environmental shortcomings. This choice is at the heart of the housing problem of the 1980s. Americans cannot solve their current housing problems without reexamining its history, and the ideals of family, gender, and society it embodies, as well as its design and financing." The first part of this book ("The Evolution of American Housing") provides this reexamination.

The second part, "Rethinking Private Life," seeks to identify the deepest needs and desires associated with the ideal of home. What are the most basic attachments to home, and how are they expressed in modern, urban, industrial societies?

The third part, "Rethinking Public Life," probes for solutions in the planning and design of better housing, social services, and public space. It deals with rehabilitation as well as new construction. Case studies are cited to support the analysis of possible solutions.

228. Hendler, Sue, and Ray Tomalty. "Green Planning: Striving Towards Sustainable Development in Ontario's Municipalities." *Plan Canada* (May 1991): 27-32.

Keywords: environmental planning, sustainability

This short article presents the results of a survey of six Ontario municipalities for evidence that the four principles of sustainability are being incorporated in policy-making. These principles were originally established by the World Conservation Strategy and the Brundtland Report.

They are: (1) improved coordination of environmental policy between government departments and changes to increase the influence of conservation principles on government; (2) a greater integration of environmental concerns in development decisions and policy-making; (3) greater use of environmental planning methods; and (4) increased coordination between government and non-government conservation efforts, along with greater public participation. In the study of the six regions (Ottawa, Ottawa-Carleton, Sudbury, Hamilton-Wentworth, Peterborough and Waterloo), six "concrete mechanisms" were discovered through which sustainable development principles were being incorporated into policy-making. With the exception of a few isolated changes, however, progress was limited to study and public activity with little concrete change in policy. The obstacles to sustainable development as reported by city planners of these municipalities include: the presence of a development lobby, the externalization of environmental effects of development decisions, the resistance to change by city bureaucracies, and the lack of local government departments or agencies dedicated to environmental protection. Local initiatives to resolve these problems are outlined. These include greater public pressure, the unification of the efforts of sustainable development advisory committees and healthy communities projects, and several recommendations for local governments.

229. Herbert, David T., and Colin Thomas. *Urban Geography: A First Approach*. New York: John Wiley & Sons, 1982.

Keywords: current, housing, infrastructure, public policy

This book is designed to provide an introduction to the subdiscipline of urban geography as part of the wider geography curriculum and also to demonstrate ways in which geographers are contributing to the more general, interdisciplinary field of urban studies. Chapter 1 provides an introduction to modern urban geography. Then paradigms, theories, concepts, and history regarding urban geography are presented in chapters 2 to 5. Chapters 6 to 10 deal with more specific issues such as spatial infrastructure, residential patterns, the social world, urban problems, urban trends, and urban policies.

230. Herbert, David, and Colin Thomas. *Cities in Space: City as Place*. Savage, Md.: Barnes & Noble, 1990.

Keywords: current, housing, infrastructure, public policy

This is a revised and updated version of *Urban Geography: A First Approach*, by the same authors (see above). This edition contains new theoretical perspectives, and examples in the latter part of the book have been updated as well.

231. Hijazi, Nasral, and Trevor Smith. *Transportation and the Canadian Environment*. Ottawa: Transport Canada, 1993.

Keywords: air pollution, automobiles, environmental pollution, sustainability, transportation, Canada

The objective of this report (prepared for Transportation Development Center, Policy and Coordination, Transport Canada) is to assess the environmental impact of transportation and to propose research and development activities with the purpose of reducing this impact. The formation of a national workshop to link public and private organizations that wish to assist in funding these R&D activities is also encouraged. The initiatives suggested in this work are based on interviews conducted by Transport Canada as well as literature surveys. It was found that 65.4 percent of the refined petroleum products used in Canada were consumed in transportation, of which 69.6 percent was for automobile use. The emission of nitrogen oxides, volatile organic compounds, carbon dioxide, and carbon monoxide are primary causes of the greenhouse effect and urban smog, and constitute the greatest environmental impact of transportation. The report suggests that the present R&D programs and resources allocated to reduce the environmental impact of transportation are inadequate. Furthermore, the use of environmentally harmful modes of transport, such as private cars, is increasing while the use of environmentally friendly transport, such as transit, is decreasing. Strategies are proposed to alleviate these problems, so as to reduce the environmental impact of transport systems. These include the use of regulating instruments to establish fuel efficiency and emission standards and economic instruments to apply national tradable permits to car manufacturers and fuel carbon content, and the introduction of a carbon tax. In addition to these initiatives, a series of R&D priorities is listed along with potential funding requirements.

232. Hill, Dilys M. *Citizens and Cities: Urban Policy in the 1990s*. London: Harvester Wheatsheaf, 1994.

Keywords: social fabric, democracy, housing, inner cities, public policy, Britain

"How can the individual exercise meaningful choices and benefit from efficient services at the local level?" Using Britain as an example, this study focuses on the concepts of citizenship and community with regard to the urban arena and how this arena has changed in the 1990s especially with regard to significant decision-making. It goes on to explore issues of civic achievement and civic pathologies along with an analysis of the changing role and management of local authorities, the delivery of services, and the emphasis on market solutions. The issues of civil disorder and unrest, urban regeneration and the inner city, education, housing, and community care are also explored.

233. Hinkle, Lawrence E., and William C. Loring, eds. *The Effect of the Man-Made Environment on Health and Behavior*. Atlanta, Ga.: Center for Disease Control-Public Health Service, U.S. Department of Health, Education, and Welfare, 1977.

Keywords: support, built environment, epidemiology, health, housing, safety

"These papers represent an endeavor by the Public Health Service to gain better understanding of the factors in the residential environment which may offer alternative points for intervention to gain reduction of disease and injury. The strategy of controlling disease and injury by environmental changes made under the guidance of the local public health officer has long been accepted practice in community hygiene. The research reviewed and presented by the authors, however, points out that the traditional definition of environment, relating only to the physical surroundings, is too narrow for today in a mobile, impersonal urban community. Their recommendations for further research and for practice of preventive programs may be of interest to epidemiologists; other health professionals; practitioners of design, development and management of residential environments; and professionals in public recreation and social work."

After stating the background and purpose of the book, cited above, topics such as community health and the urban environment, the effects of the residential environment on health and behavior, an assessment of the built environment for safety, the measurement of the effects of the environment on health and behavior, and the problems faced by the elderly are addressed.

234. Hirsch, Arnold R., and Raymond A. Mohl, eds. *Urban Policy in Twentieth-Century America*. New Brunswick, N. J.: Rutgers University Press, 1993.

Keywords: support, public policy, urban planning, United States

The book addresses various urban issues such as race, housing, transportation, poverty, environment, and the effects of the global economy in a historical context. Chapter 7 (Eco-urbanism and Past Choices for Urban Living) is of particular interest because it deals with the impacts of global economic development and the environmental implications of policies of the past.

235. Hiss, Tony. *The Experience of Place*. New York: Knopf, 1990.

Keywords: social fabric, built environment, experience of place, public space, urban design, urban planning

This wonderfully informative and interesting work is about "a new way of dealing with our radically changing cities and countryside." In the introduction, Tony Hiss suggests that we need to make sure of three things when changing a place in order to avoid damaging it. The change should: nurture our growth as capable and responsible people; protect the natural environment; and develop jobs and homes enough for all. He believes our ally for achieving this is "simultaneous perception"—our ability to experience places directly via a conscious or unconscious broad focus which keeps us linked to our surroundings.

Part 1 ("Experiencing Cities") first describes ways in which physical characteristics of places such as the color of walls, the amount of light, and the size of steps affect us. Drawing heavily on his personal experience, especially of New York City, the author discusses at length the psychological aspects of place and the subjective meaning of place. He draws on works by Alexander, Whyte, the Kaplans, Mumford, and others to suggest how to better take care of cities. To use Jane Jacobs' words, "Tony Hiss . . . describes subtle but practical ways to improve mediocre places and transform even some unpleasant ones." Part 2 ("Encountering the Countryside") provides a similar treatment of the countryside.

236. Holcombe, Randall G. *Public Policy and the Quality of Life: Market Incentive Versus Government Planning*. Westport, Conn.: Greenwood Press, 1995.

Keywords: environmental pollution, health care, housing, land use, public policy, urban planning

Market economies provide the best way to enhance the quality of life in the same way as they have been successful at producing goods and services. This argument is leveled against those who would suggest that, while market forces are good at producing goods and services, the quality of life can only be enhanced through government intervention. The book concludes with observations that government intervention, no matter how well meant, may in fact have negative impacts on the quality of life.

237. Holdgate, Martin W. "Caring for the Earth: A Strategy for Sustainable Living." *Scientific World* 1992, 8-13.

Keywords: sustainability

The article summarizes a strategy for sustainable living, based on respect and care for others and the Earth. Concepts of equality, both intra- and intergenerational, survival of species, and resource use versus conservation are among the topics discussed. To implement sustainable living, four actions are outlined:
1) We must develop a universally accepted ethic for sustainable living.
2) The United States should adopt a covenant on sustainability, incorporating it into the constitution and legislation.
3) All people must incorporate ethics into personal and professional behavior.
4) A new organization to implement the world ethic should be conceived.
Economic growth must not be the goal of development. Contexts like health, education, freedom, and the like should also be considered. Development should be conservative and based on protecting the world's natural systems. Pollution prevention, integrity of ecosystems, biological diversity, sustainable use of biological resources, carrying capacity, community involvement, and the user-pays principle are also outlined. The environment must also be properly valued in national accounting. The author declares that the greatest barriers to sustainable living are the attitudes and practices of people. Society must discourage activity incompatible with sustainability. From the perspective of sustainability, new goals are given for different issues. General methods to advance toward sustainable living are defined, but the author says that its implementation will depend on public attitudes.

238. Hommann, Mary. *City Planning in America: Between Promise and Despair*. Westport, Conn.: Praeger, 1993.

Keywords: support, transportation, urban planning

Contrary to popular conceptions, urban planning to the present day (and including the so-called heyday period of planning between 1949 and 1973) has been largely ineffectual in the United States A number of reasons are forwarded to support this thesis: the power and greed of developers; the fact that urban planning has not been legally organized to make a difference; that, at best, local planners are exposed daily to the fiction of their involvement in developmental decisions; that many city planners, finding themselves professionally impotent, engage in alternate or deviant pursuits. This book also "sets out to show that greed settled this country, accompanied by cruelty, disregard, and callous misjudgment."

239. Hough, Michael. *Out of Place—Restoring Identity to the Regional Landscape*. New Haven, Conn.: Yale University Press, 1990.

Keywords: social fabric, community, experience of place, identity, utopia

How can insights derived from natural and cultural processes provide us with ways of re-establishing the identity and uniqueness of places in the contemporary landscape? This is the central question of the book. Michael Hough first identifies the key ingredients of regional identity. Natural and cultural processes that form the basis for regional identity and the dimensions of the regional imperative are explored, and conclusions are drawn about its essential nature. Next, the book deals with how values and the way landscapes are understood have influenced attitudes toward the environment. Contemporary issues and the patterns of change that are shaping our landscape are also examined. Finally, Hough discusses design principles that can create healthy and clearly identifiable contemporary environments.

240. Hough, Michael. *Cities and Natural Processes*. New York: Routledge, 1995.

Keywords: urban metabolism, sustainability, urban design, urban ecology, urban planning

Traditional urban design of the physical landscape is based on values that are inimical to environmental and social health. Hough sets out to remedy this defect by seeking an understanding of, and incorporating, environmental and social processes into urban design.
The author begins with an analysis of how economic and technical values have led to the elimination of a sense of nature from the city, effectively sealing it off from the countryside and its resource bases. The technological permeation of society contributes to resource waste and creates a built form that is not compatible with nature or society. He goes on to discuss the many ways in which attention to nature can make practical improvements in cities, improvements that are increasingly becoming necessary in the face of urban malaise. Chapters on water, plants, wildlife, and city farming and the role each can (and should) play are informative and well argued. Chapter 6 discusses the role of the climate in a persistently intelligent manner. Overall, this is an essential guide for anyone wanting to find out some of the ways in which cities can be made environmentally and socially sustainable.

241. Hough Woodland Naylor Dance Limited and Gore & Storrie Ltd. *Restoring Natural Habitats: A Manual for Habitat Restoration in the Greater Toronto Bioregion*. Toronto: Waterfront Regeneration Trust, 1995.

Keywords: transformation, ecology, environmental pollution, green space, sustainability, Canada

Healthy natural habitats are important components of sustainable cities. Restoring degraded natural habitats is therefore a necessary part of creating a healthy city, but how exactly does one go about executing the restoration? This manual answers this question by focussing on waterfront land in the Greater Toronto Bioregion. It is intended as a guide for those planning, carrying out, or reviewing restoration projects as well as for others seeking reference and educational material on the subject.

The introduction summarizes the seven principles of landscape restoration (1) respect regional identity, (2) recognize the unique ecological character of each site, (3) protect significant natural features, (4) establish priorities for restoration efforts, (5) create low-maintenance, ecologically self-sustaining solutions, (6) use native species, and (7) use the five-step restoration plan:

-determine regional contexts
-inventory and evaluate site conditions
-set restoration objectives
-draw up the restoration plan
-implement, manage, and monitor the restoration

Sections 3 to 6 apply this strategy to the most common habitat types of wetlands, meadows, grasslands, woodlands, and riparian zones. Even pits, quarries, and stormwater ponds may be restored to provide wildlife habitat, as described in sections 7 and 8.

242. Hughes, Peter. *Personal Transport and the Greenhouse Effect: A Strategy for Sustainability.* London: Earthscan, 1993.

Keywords: automobiles, energy, greenhouse effect, public policy, sustainability, technology, transportation

Car use makes a significant contribution to the greenhouse effect. This is examined in detail by the author. He next turns to an analysis of the many technological fixes for greenhouse emissions, from cleaner fuels to more efficient engines. Most of these solutions are seen as being quite inadequate. Only a radical shift away from personal automobiles will have a salutary effect. The behavioral and policy changes that need to be made conclude the book.

243. Hume, Christopher. "Enviro-costs Being Added to the Architectural Balance." *Toronto Star*, April 23 1994.

Keywords: transformation, architecture, energy efficiency, urban planning

The fact that the 1980s involved spending while the 1990s involved paying the costs that often exceed the value of the artifacts produced is used as an introduction to the promotion of eco-friendly architecture. It is argued that the real cost of architecture should be determined by its environmental impact rather than by a dollar amount. Efforts towards this movement started in 1992 when the Ontario Association of Architecture formed a committee on the environment. This new approach to architecture is presented as one that will save the profession. However, there have been attitudinal obstacles, especially during the recession, which dictate that we "cannot afford" the change. It is argued, however, that we cannot afford *not* to make changes. After all, the more energy-efficient buildings are cheaper to operate. Room for improvement is noted in lighting design, and in low-tech solutions such as orientation design strategies, natural ventilation, the use of solar energy, and biotic filtering systems for water. An environmentally friendly rating system not only for materials, but for buildings as well, is expected in the future.

244. International Association for People-Environment Studies. *The Urban Experience: A People-Environment Perspective.* 13th Conference of the International Association for People-Environment Studies. Manchester, edited by S. J. Nearsy, M. S. Symes, and F. E. Brown, London: E & FN Spon, 1994.

Keywords: support, alienation, case studies, community, crowding, democracy, housing, public space, urban design

This book consists of a selection of papers prepared for and presented at the IAPS (International Association for People-Environment Studies) conference on the topic of "Urban Experience." The three parts of the book deal with Participation and Urban Design, User Needs and Evaluation, and Environmental Education and Urban Theory. Within these categories, a wide variety of topics are covered, including alienation, crowding, changing urban values, teenagers' use of public space, multiculturalism in cities, citizen participation, housing, community action, and environmental psychology.

245. International Institute for the Urban Environment. *The Ecological Footprint of Cities.* Amsterdam: International Institute for the Urban Environment, 1997.

Keywords: urban metabolism, sustainability, land use, water pollution

The concept of the ecological footprint was instrumental in allowing us to see just how vast the ecological impact of modern cities actually is. An ecological footprint is merely a means of roughly estimating the environmental impact of an entire city and the people in it. Specifically, it refers to the total amount of productive land and water that a city requires on a continuous basis for the goods that it consumes and the wastes that it produces and must dispose off. London, by this estimate, had an ecological footprint that was over 125 times its surface area in 1995. The current book is organized as a series of debates between scholars and urban planners from around the world. The problems facing cities in the developing world are clearly articulated, as are problems that are expected to arise in the future. It is replete with ideas about how different cities around the world are trying to reduce their ecological footprint.

246. Jacobs, Allan B. *Great Streets.* Cambridge, Mass.: MIT Press, 1993.

Keywords: urban metabolism, social fabric, case studies, pedestrians, streets, urban planning

This book is about some of the best streets in the world. In particular, it is about the physical, designable characteristics of these streets and about street patterns as the physical contexts for urban living. A major purpose of this book is to provide comparable information about the physical qualities of the best streets—plans, cross-sections, dimensions, details, patterns, urban contexts—for designers and urban decision-makers.

247. Jacobs, Brian David. *Fractured Cities: Capitalism, Community and Empowerment*

in Britain and America. London: Routledge, 1992.

Keywords: current, economics, public policy, Britain, United States

Jacobs gives a critical, often scathing appraisal of the impact of the "conservative years" of the 1980s on cities in the United States and Britain. His assessment is that the impact of policies was, in the main, negative and brought about many urban crises. His themes are not restricted to cities alone and, of necessity, roam widely over a comparative analysis of national characteristics, political cultures and government organization.

248. Jacobs, Jane. *The Death and Life of Great American Cities.* New York: Random House, 1961.

Keywords: classic, community, economics, neighborhood, urban planning

Jane Jacobs criticizes the abstract 1960s approach to urban planning in a lively, captivating, often polemical, but always sensible, style in this classic book. Her diagnosis of why American inner cities have "died" because of poor planning is still the best. She suggests a completely different approach that is based on common sense, is empirical in nature, and pays heed to economic evidence. Her ideas deal with reducing crime on the streets, improving the economy of a district, reducing traffic flows, building community, and achieving healthy districts. This is one of the most influential books on healthy cities and considered by many to have been the book that jogged urban planners (to use a Kantian phrase) "out of their dogmatic slumber."

249. Janicke, M., and H. Weidner, eds. *National Environmental Policies: A Comparative Study of Capacity-Building.* Berlin: Springer-Verlag, 1997.

Keywords: current, case studies, environmental pollution, public policy, sustainability

Despite its controversial nature, capacity-building has produced some remarkable results around the world in the past few decades. Capacity for environmental policy and management has been defined by the OECD as a society's "ability to devise and implement solutions to environmental issues as part of a wider effort to achieve sustainable development." Presented here is a collection of case studies describing the environmental policy of thirteen countries in terms of capacity-building. The countries used in the case studies are: the United States, Sweden, Japan, the United Kingdom, the Netherlands, Germany, Denmark, Switzerland, Korea, Chile, China, Nigeria, and Russia. The first chapter presents the conceptual framework that underlies the national case studies. Each following chapter begins with an assessment of the main environmental problems of the country in question, focusing on changes in important problem areas. The development and main characteristics of environmental policy, its instruments, institutions, and policy style are described. The main actors in environmental policy, their strength, strategies, and resources are analyzed, and the qualitative aspects of capacity-building are discussed. Finally, the national process of capacity-building in environmental policy is evaluated. In the final chapter, the findings from the national case studies are summarized. The comparative policies and initiatives discussed have direct relevance to sustainable/healthy cities.

250. Jenks, Mike, Elizabeth Burton, and Katie Williams, eds. *The Compact City: A Sustainable Urban Form?* London: E & FN Spon, 1996.

Keywords: current, built environment, land use, quality of life, sustainability, transportation, urban design, urban planning

Many authors have argued that the compact city is the most sustainable urban form. But is this really the case? The book debates this complex issue from many angles. Although it is clear that there is a strong link between urban form and sustainable development, the relationship is not straightforward. This comprehensive book brings together sometimes conflicting viewpoints and concludes that the compact city is not the one and only route to sustainable cities.

The first part of the book consists of theoretical work. Some predict that compact cities would mean concentration and centralization, while others believe they would be decentralized with some degree of autonomy. Still others suggest a compromise of intensification in cities along with green field suburban development. Although it is clear that compact cities would bring benefits, it must be remembered that the intensified area will be affected by negative impacts as well. Social and economic issues of compact cities are studied in part 2. It reminds the reader that high-density, mixed-use environments may provide a high quality of life for some but not all citizens. Intensification must not only be appealing to citizens, but must also be economically viable. The willingness and unwillingness of developers to invest in intensification projects are examined. Part 3 seeks to understand whether the claimed environmental benefits would actually result from building compact cities. Although compact cities would experience less automobile dependency, some writers argue that less dense, more self-sufficient settlements would be more sustainable, and that perhaps changing travel behavior would accomplish more than intensification would. Part 4, "Measuring and Monitoring," suggests better methodological approaches for the future. Part 5 gives practical advice on implementation issues for agencies, local authorities, and the planning system.

251. Joder, Timothy E., and Anthony J. Mumphrey. *Urban Revitalization: Policies and Programs.* Thousand Oaks, Calif.: Sage Publications, 1995.

Keywords: support, case studies, economics, public policy, urban planning

This volume contains case studies collected by the National Center for the Revitalization of Central Cities under the auspices of the Department of Housing and Urban Development in the United States. The center cooperated with leading urban scholars to research and develop the revitalization program for urban centers.

The focus is on examining revitalization programs over the past fifteen to twenty years and analyzing the reasons for their success and failure. Among the cities discussed are Atlanta, Portland (Oregan), New York, New Orleans, and Minneapolis. The importance of the case studies lies not only in their recognition of which initiatives worked but in discovering which factors of the solution led to success. Strong public leadership, well-focussed planning concepts, the ability to respond quickly to difficulties, and community characteristics such as affluence and education seem to be common to virtually all successful initiatives.

The case studies are structured in terms of city context, policy programs and project

description, impact assessment, and policy implications. The information in this book
will be of help to those concerned with urban management, economic development, and
urban policy.

252. John, De Witt. *Civic Environmentalism: Alternatives to Regulation in States and
Communities.* Washington, D.C.: CQ Press, 1994.

Keywords: community, policy

As we enter into a new era of environmental policy-making, there is a need to understand new issues and address them with new tools through a new political system.
Through discussions of alternative directions for environmental policy, the author evaluates ways to move beyond regulation as a means of protecting the environment. Despite
the American focus, this book's support of bottom-up policy development will help those
committed to reducing environmental impact in communities.

253. Johnston, R. J., and P. Knox, eds. *"World Cities Series."* London: Belhaven Press,
various dates.

Keywords: current

This is a valuable series that analyzes the history, culture, politics, problems, and
strengths of various cities around the world. The cities on which books have already been
published are the following:
Mexico City by Peter Ward (1998)
Lagos by Margaret Peil (1991)
Tokyo by Roman Cybriwsky (1991)
Budapest by Gyorgy Enyedi and Viktoria Szirmai (1992)
Hong Kong by C. P. Lo (1992)
Dublin by Andrew MacLaran (1993)
Vienna by Elizabeth Lichtenberger (1994)
Birmingham by Gordon E. Cherry (1994)
Taipei by Roger Mark Seyla (1995)
Rome by John Agnew (1995)
Beijing by Victor F. S. Sit (1995)
Glasgow by Michael Pacione (1995)

254. Jones, Dylan M., ed. *Noise and Society.* New York: John Wiley & Sons, 1984.

Keywords: support, health, noise—physiological effects, noise—psychosocial effects

This volume concentrates on the psychosocial as well as the more heavily researched
physiological aspects of noise. More specifically, the perception of sound, the description
and measurement of sound, noise-induced hearing loss, the effects of noise on health, and
individual and group differences in the response to noise constitute the study of physiological effects. The psychosocial effects are covered under the following chapter headings: Performance Effects, Noise and Communication, and The Social Psychology of
Noise.

255. Jones, Emrys. *Metropolis*. Oxford: Oxford University Press, 1990.

Keywords: current, population, land use, urban design

Great cities over time have always contributed in various ways to human progress and represent some of the greatest achievements of different cultures. With large size and dense populations, however, come problems such as congestion, poverty, inequality, and squalor. A brief account of the metropolis in proto-history and in European history is followed by an examination of the metropolis in modern times and the contemporary metropolis, with examples from the developing world. Changes and trends that may affect the shape and function of the metropolis of the future are studied, as well as the problems of the great city, shared by those in the past, in the present, and between developed and developing nations of the world. Although there is an emphasis on individual cities, this does not mean that they should be separated from the system of cities of which they are a part. In fact, the author suggests, that they are part of a worldwide urban system with a certain amount of interaction, and even interdependence. This has resulted in part from the improvement of the communication system and from globalization.

256. Jones, Robin Russell, and Tom Wigley, eds. *Ozone Depletion: Health and Environmental Consequences*. New York: John Wiley & Sons, 1989.

Keywords: greenhouse effect, ozone, public policy

This is the edited proceedings of an International Conference on the Health and Environmental Consequences of Stratospheric Ozone Depletion held at the Royal Institute of British Architects, London, from November 28th to 29th, 1988. Descriptions of the problems of ozone depletion, including global warming and ultraviolet-induced carcinogenesis, are followed by a discussion of international controls, global consequences, and the politics of the problem.

257. Kaplan, Rachel, and Stephen Kaplan. *The Experience of Nature: A Psychological Perspective*. New York: Cambridge University Press, 1989.

Keywords: emotional needs, green cities, green space, psychological health

This volume attempts to establish a basic understanding of nature and experiences of nature, with particular emphasis on how urban inhabitants are affected emotionally and psychologically by such experiences. It includes a theoretical framework and methodological strategy for studying the effects of nature on people. The data presented is a synthesis of findings from landscape architects, horticulturists, foresters, nature interpreters, planners, resource managers, psychologists, and others. This deals with a relatively new area of research and has profound implications for the planning and design of healthier urban environments. Major research questions include:
   1. Is it real? Is the effect of nature on people as powerful as it intuitively seems to be?
   2. How does it work? What lies behind the power of environments that not only attract and are appreciated by people but are apparently able to restore "hassled" individuals to healthy and effective functioning?
   3. Are some natural patterns better than others? Is there a way to design, to manage,

to interpret natural environments so as to enhance these beneficial influences?

258. Karp, David A., Gregory P. Stone, and William C. Yoels. *Being Urban: A Sociology of City Life*. 2nd ed. New York: Praeger, 1991.

Keywords: community, urban sociology

This is an examination of the dynamic interplay between what theoretical perceptions tell us about urban life and how ordinary people interpret and respond to the actual experience of living in cities. Major focuses are the primacy of social interaction for an understanding of urban life and the strategies people use to create "community" in environments that, many theorists believe, promote only alienation and social disintegration. This new edition incorporates a strong interdisciplinary perspective and includes new chapters on significant topics (women in the city, for example) that have received little critical attention in the field.

The first two chapters discuss "Classical Conceptions of Urban Life" and "Classical Observations of Urban Life." "The Rediscovery of Community" theorizes about the above-mentioned strategies used to create "community." After this, the following subjects are tackled: "The Social Organization of Everyday City Life," "Lifestyle Diversity and Urban Tolerance," "Women in Cities," "Power, Politics, and Problems," "Sports and Urban Life," and "Urbanism, Suburbanism, and Cultural Change."

259. Katz, Peter, ed. *The New Urbanism: Towards an Architecture of Community*. New York: McGraw-Hill, 1994.

Keywords: new urbanism, urban design, current, sustainability, community, built environment, suburbs

A beautifully illustrated and comprehensive introduction to the principles and concepts of the New Urbanism. Most of its chief practitioners, such as Vincent Scully, Peter Calthorpe, Andres Duany, and Elizabeth Plater-Zyberk, have contributed to this volume. A central section provides an illustrated analysis of towns and villages designed according to New Urbanist principles, followed by a similar analysis of urban reconstruction projects. A must for anyone interested in the New Urbanism.

260. Katznelson, Ira. *Marxism and the City*. New York: Oxford University Press, 1992.

Keywords: community, economics, sociology

In this discussion of Marxism and the city, the author seeks to explore the meaning of cities, urbanism, and space. He shows how the application of Marxist ideas to the spatial dimension of cities provides solutions to urban problems. This book also includes a discussion of the limits of applicability of Marxist theory to cities. Chapter 1 examines Marxism and the city. Chapter 2 discusses themes in Marxist social theory. Chapter 3 is entitled "Towards a respatialized Marxism: Lefebvre, Harvey, and Castells." Chapter 4 looks at capitalism, city space, and class formation through Engels' perspective. Chapter 5 examines the changing "place of the city" from feudalism to capitalism. How working classes "map the city" is the topic of chapter 6. Finally, chapter 7 looks at "remapping the city."

261. Kay, Jane Holtz. *Asphalt Nation: How the Automobile Took Over America, and How We Can Take It Back.* Toronto: Random House, 1997.

Keywords: automobiles

This book provides a thorough discussion of how, over time, we have allowed ourselves to degrade our cities and the natural environment through overreliance on the automobile. Moving beyond diagnosis, Kay is prescriptive in her call for future action. The "real-world" examples in this book offer ideas for those interested in moving beyond automobile addiction.

262. Keating, W. Dennis, Norman Krumholz, and Philip Star, eds. *Revitalizing Urban Neighborhoods.* Lawrence: University Press of Kansas, 1996.

Keywords: social fabric, case studies, community, neighborhood, public policy

Neighborhood-based initiatives for healthier communities have long been a part of the urban discourse. In this comprehensive study of neighborhood revitalization programs in America, their ability to bring about significant change is assessed. The book points out concrete ways for neighborhood residents to take things into their own hands and effect positive change. Part 1, "The Growth and Evolution of Urban Neighborhoods," takes an historical look at federal policies and immigrant and minority neighborhoods in Cleveland. Part 2 chronicles several attempts at revitalization such as those in Boston, Chicago, Minneapolis, Los Angeles, and African-American neighborhoods. The Community Development Movement is the focus of the third section, which studies various actors in the struggle for healthy communities such as community development corporations, community-based housing organizations, and leading neighborhood figures. The book concludes with a section on metropolitan development policies.

263. Keil, Roger, Gerda R. Wekerle, and David V. J. Bell, eds. *Local Places in the Age of the Global City.* Montreal: Black Rose Books, 1996.

Keywords: current, developing countries, ecology, food, housing, interdisciplinary studies, public policy, sustainability, urban planning

Cities should be considered as part of the solution to the problem of urban sprawl instead of being blamed for it. This is the position advocated by this collection of articles which analyze the problem and propose solutions to it. The question of how to sustain local places is addressed from the perspective of the larger political context. The articles are multidisciplinary in nature and cover a wide range of topics such as nature in the city, politics, urban farming, city planning, urban growth, ecopolitics, social movements, women, homelessness, poverty, welfare, food, and trade. A fair portion of the content is Torontonian, owing to the fact that many of the contributors are affiliated with York University. In fact, the book is based on a series of seminars and discussions held at York University on urban sustainability in the age of the global city. There is also a considerable "developing world" focus, as is apparent from studies of cities in Uganda, Colombia,

Guyana, and South Africa.

264. Kelbaugh, Douglas. *Common Place: Toward Neighborhood and Regional Design*. Seattle: University of Washington Press, 1997.

Keywords: new urbanism, urban design, urban planning, community, transportation, environmental planning, classic

Kelbaugh is one of the pioneers of New Urbanism, Pedestrian Pockets, Urban Villages, and Transport-Oriented Development. All of these are strategically deployed in this book to show how we can develop community and create convivial and sustainable places. All the theoretical elements are firmly grounded in practice through the summaries of eight design charrettes—some of these design workshops being led by luminaries such as Andres Duany, Peter Calthorpe, Richard Haag, and Kelbaugh himself. The charrettes apply design concepts to many real problems such as housing, transportation, and sprawl in the Seattle region, but the solutions are pertinent for other regions as well.

This is an extremely important work and will greatly aid designers, planners, municipal officials, developers, environmentalists, and citizen activists.

265. Kemmis, Daniel. *The Good City and the Good Life*. New York: Houghton Mifflin, 1995.

Keywords: community, urban planning

What engenders community? What kind of policies make cities healthier? What makes better citizens? These are the questions that exercise Kemmis as he ruminates over his days as mayor of Missoula, Montana. Ultimately, Kemmis suggests that it is through policies and actions that respect the "wholeness" of things that the good city and the good life can come about. This means an understanding of how cities are linked to their regions and the biosphere, how they are connected to the cycles of the earth and the economies of other cities around the globe. Anyone interested in the day-to-day observations of a practicing, thoughtful mayor will find this a fascinating book. Students of political culture will also find it useful.

266. Kendrick, Martyn, and Linda Moore. *Re-inventing Our Common Future: An Exploration into Community Sustainability*. Hamilton, Ontario: Eco Gateway Group, 1995.

Keywords: current, sociocultural, community, sustainability, urban ecology, urban planning, work

"In 1992, the United Nations International Council for Local Environmental Initiatives (ICLEI) designated Hamilton-Wentworth as their Canadian representative (one of 21 world-wide) to implement the United Nations Agenda 21 recommendations. In 1993, Canada awarded this industrial region the Canadian Environmental Achievement Award in recognition of its outstanding contribution to sustainable development. This book profiles the people behind the extraordinary transformation of this industrial region guided by sustainable development principles."

This volume is a record of a successful attempt to involve sustainable development principles in the day-to-day functions of Hamilton-Wentworth in Ontario. Sustainable development is achieved by cities whose inhabitants are concerned with goals such as the quality of life, social equity, the well-being of the planet, and economic well-being. These goals are met in part by facilitating public awareness, redesigning industry, and providing meaningful work.

267. Kenworthy, Jeffrey R., and Peter W. G. Newman. "Gasoline Consumption and Cities: A Comparison of U.S. Cities with a Global Survey." *APA Journal* (Winter 1989): 24-37.

Keywords: automobiles, energy, fossil fuels, transportation, urban planning

This article is a summary of a study funded by the Australian government, which compares gasoline use in thirty-two cities around the world to evaluate the effect of current physical planning policies on energy expended in transportation. The study involves cities in North America, Australia, Europe, and Asia. The data collected involves land use, automobile use, transit, parking facilities, and road length. The data can be used to examine issues other than gasoline use, for example, air pollution and accidents. It is suggested that reducing gasoline use through planning will provide economic, social, and environmental benefits. The study reveals that gasoline consumption varied by 40 percent amongst ten cities in the United States, primarily due to land use and transportation planning rather than price or income level. It was found that gasoline consumption in U.S. cities was four times that of European cities. Variations in gasoline price, vehicle efficiency, and income explain only half of the difference. Physical planning policies such as reorganization and a reorientation of transportation priorities are recommended as an effective approach for reducing automobile dependence and gasoline consumption.

268. King, Anthony D. *Urbanism, Colonialism, and the World Economy: Cultural and Spatial Foundations of the World Urban System.* International Library of Sociology. London: Routledge, 1989.

Keywords: economics, urban planning

This book is concerned with understanding the "social production" of the built environment and how built environments both represent and condition economies, societies and cultures. Forces that have created contemporary societies and environments, especially those operating on a global scale (such as colonialism) are also considered. The accompanying volume by the same author, entitled *Global Cities: Post-Imperialism and the Internationalization of London,* is also listed in this bibliography.

269. King, Anthony D. *Global Cities: Post-Imperialism and the Internationalization of London.* London: Routledge, 1989.

Keywords: economics, urban planning

The author begins by describing trends in urban studies, with an emphasis on cities as part of the global economy. He goes on to describe the formation of global cities such as Los Angeles, New York, Tokyo/Osaka/Nagoya, Sao Paulo, and London. Part 2 provides a detailed analysis of London's role in the world economy. See also the accompanying volume by the same author entitled *Urbanism, Colonialism and the World Economy*.

270. Kivell, Philip. *Land and the City: Patterns and Processes of Urban Change*. Geography and Environment Series. London: Routledge, 1993.

Keywords: land use, urban planning

Land and the City presents a broad but concise analysis of land-use patterns and processes in urban areas in the developed world. In the rapidly changing sphere of urban development, land is shown to provide the basic morphological structure of the city and, closely connected with environmental questions, to be a source of economic and social power and the key to successful planning.

271. Klarer, Jürg, and Bedrich Moldan, eds. *The Environmental Challenge for Central European Economies in Transition*. Toronto: John Wiley & Sons, 1997.

Keywords: biosphere, case studies, environmental pollution, public policy, sustainability

In contrast to the environmental devastation wrought by communist governments, the democratic revolutions in Central and Eastern Europe brought with them high expectations for a more viable environment. But what exactly are the advances in environmental protection that have been achieved? These achievements and what stands in the way of them are analyzed in this volume. Programs such as "Environment for Europe" at the European and international level are studied along with their implications for environmental policy. Sandwiched between the introductory and concluding chapters are six chapters on the following countries: Bulgaria, the Czech Republic, Hungary, Latvia, Poland, and the Slovak Republic. They present studies into the state of the environment, environmental policy, and key actors such as the public, NGOs, the business sector, and government.

272. Klein & Sears, Environics Research Group, Clayton Research Associates, Lewinberg Consultants, Walker, Poole, and Milligan. *Study of Residential Intensification and Rental Housing Conservation Part 1: Detailed Study of Findings and Recommendations, vol. 1 of 11*. Ontario: Ministry of Municipal Affairs and Housing and Association of Municipalities of Ontario, 1983.

Keywords: support, housing, Canada

This volume of the report contains a summary of all of the other sections. The two objectives of this study are: (1) "To examine the opportunities and constraints that exist for meeting some of the future additional housing needs in Ontario during the 80s and 90s through the intensification of existing residential neighborhoods," and (2) "To examine some of the major forces at work that have and could threaten the conservation of the existing stock of rental housing and the tenants that occupy this stock."

In order to achieve these objectives, the authors first study economic and demographic trends related to housing and then explain what residential intensification is, how it can be achieved, and what the existing constraints are. Following this, the physical and economic conditions are discussed. Tenant demand, neighborhood impact and resistance, and how to conserve the existing rental stock are also addressed. This study is the result of the Ontario government's 1982 decision to investigate the potential for creating new housing through intensification. Since its publication in 1983, it has become the basis for provincial and many municipal housing initiatives.

273. Knox, Paul L., ed. *The Restless Urban Landscape*. Englewood Cliffs, N. J.: Prentice-Hall, 1993.

Keywords: current, built environment, consumerism, economics, megastructures, postmodernism

"The built environment is a good place to begin in order to make sense of the new geographies that are being inscribed onto the old framework of urbanization. New forms of urban development, new architectural styles, and new cityscapes are important elements of these new geographies in their own right. . . . More compelling, though, is their significance as a *text* that can be 'read' in order to reflect the imperatives of economic, social, cultural and political forces at particular times, to reveal the relationships between the social and spatial dimensions of urbanization, to interpret the ideological content of socially-created space and to suggest the conflicts, tensions and contradictions involved in the process of urban development.

"The built environment, then, must be seen as simultaneously dependent and conditioning, outcome and mechanism of the dynamics of investment, production and consumption. . . . Changes in the built environment must be situated not only in terms of the structural transformation of economies and societies but also in terms of the behavior of particular agents of change and groups of individuals in particular localities at particular times."

The table of contents reveals the variety of topics that form this study of the built environment:
1. Capital, Material Culture and Socio-Spatial Differentiation
2. Cycles and Trends in the Globalization of Real Estate
3. The Turbulence of Housing Markets
4. Identity and Difference: The Internationalization of Capital and the Globalization of Culture
5. The City of Illusion: New York's Public Places
6. Megastructures and Urban Change: Aesthetics, Ideology, and Design
7. Social Reproduction in the City: Restructuring in Time and Space
8. The Postmodern Urban Matrix
9. Berlin's Second Modernity
10. Can There Be a Postmodernism of Resistance in the Urban Landscape?

274. Knox, Paul L., and Peter J. Taylor. *World Cities in a World System*. Cambridge: Cambridge University Press, 1995.

Keywords: current, air pollution, case studies, megacities, telecommunications, transportation

The present global economy is propelled by cities like New York, Tokyo, and London, which are the centers of transnational corporate headquarters, international finance, transnational institutions, and telecommunications. Seventeen leading researchers came together to take part in the making of this book, each by contributing an essay on either the theoretical or the practical issues involved in the study of the impact of world cities. Explored are the natures of world cities and their need for specific urban policies, the relationship between world cities within global networks of economic flows, and the relationship between world city research and world systems analysis and other theoretical frameworks.

275. Koren, Herman. *Handbook of Environmental Health and Safety: Principles and Practices*. 2nd ed. Vol. 1. New York: Lewis Publishers, 1991.

Keywords: transformation, air pollution, energy, epidemiology, food, health, health care, indoor pollution, risk assessment, occupational health, toxins, waste, water, water pollution

This handbook is designed to provide a comprehensive, concise discussion of each of the important environmental health areas, including energy, ecology and people, environmental epidemiology, risk assessment and risk management, environmental law, air quality management, food protection, insect control, rodent control, pesticides, the chemical environment, environmental economics, human disease and injury, occupational health and safety, noise, radiation, recreational environment, indoor environments, medical care institutions, schools and universities, prisons, solid and hazardous waste management, water supply, plumbing, swimming areas, sewage disposal, soils, water pollution control, environmental health emergencies, and nuisance complaints.

The book is neither an engineering text nor comprehensive text in any one area. Rather, the purpose of the book is to provide a solid working knowledge of each environmental health area with sufficient detail for general practitioners.

276. Kreimer, Alcira, Theresa Lobo, Braz Menezies, Mohan Munasinghe, and Ronald Parker, eds. *Toward a Sustainable Urban Environment: The Rio de Janeiro Study*. Washington, D.C.: The World Bank, 1993.

Keywords: case study, sustainability

This is a detailed analysis of the city of Rio de Janeiro and the steps that must be taken to rehabilitate those parts of it that are deteriorated and to ensure that all future development is sustainable. The scope of the study is quite comprehensive and includes environmental as well as social sustainability issues. It also examines institutional issues and assesses the ability of various government and non-governmental agencies (NGOs) to deliver sustainability-related services at the best of times, as well as when unexpected disasters have occurred. The financial implications of disaster mitigation and the economic value of the beauty of the region are also discussed. This is a valuable resource for anyone who wants to do a similar analysis of other cities in the South.

277. Krieger, Alex, and William Lennertz, eds. *Andres Duany and Elizabeth Plater-Zyberk: Towns and Town-Making Principles*. New York: Rizzoli, 1991.

Keywords: new urbanism, urban design, urban planning

This is a compendium of village and town designs by Andres Duany and Elizabeth Plater-Zyberk with accompanying essays. Krieger places Duany and Plater-Zyberk's work into a perceptive urban design framework, while Vincent Scully provides a further explanation of New Urbanism principles.

Lennertz and Patrick Pinnell offer the perspective of collaborators and a useful afterword by Leon Krier concentrates on the codes through which the town planning principles of New Urbanism are realized and put into action. Handsomely illustrated.

278. Krieps, Robert, ed. *Environment and Health: A Holistic Approach.* Aldershot, England: Avebury Books, 1989.

Keywords: ecology, electromagnetic fields and health, environmental pollution, greenhouse effect, health, housing, nutrition, ozone, psychological health, toxins

The editor of these proceedings describes the work as follows: "The contributors to this book are specialists in a wide variety of fields: ecotoxicology, immunology, medicine, nutrition, biochemistry, physics, psychiatry, education, politics, international government, architecture, the fine arts, and philosophy.

"The scientists try to explain the ecosystem and its interrelationships, and relate how the science of ecotoxicology was born. They trace the development of the environmental crisis, point out the linkages, and identify the damage that has been recognized. Then they show us how, aided by precise tools created with modern technology, the environmental sciences are beginning to invent ways to assess risks to nature and to human health before action is taken: before chemicals are manufactured and transported, before pesticides are sold and applied, before medicines and food additives are prescribed and imbibed."

The book is based on the conference "Man, Health, and Environment" hosted by the Luxembourg Government from March 3rd to 5th in 1988. The chapter titles listed below indicate the range of topics covered.

1. The spirit of Rene Dubos, or the dangers of a fragmentary approach to ecology
2. Ecology and man: biosphere, noosphere
3. A survey of the dangers of the chemical era: impacts on human and environmental health
4. Evaluating persistent pollutants in the environment
5. The effects of environmental pollutants on the immune system
6. Pollution and forest die-back
7. Environment and skin aging
8. Electromagnetic pollution of the environment
9. Electromagnetic and ideological pollution of the brain
10. The model of the human operator system: a heuristic aid against modern society
11. The whole is greater than the sum of its parts
12. Civilization diseases, time and space
13. Nutrition and health: there is a future
14. The biology of cerebral aging
15. Mental health and the urban environment
16. Housing and the home after 150 years of industrial society

17. Ecological principles in town planning: the impact of vegetation on the quality of life in the city

18. The crisis in industrial societies at the dawn of the twenty-first century

19. Environmental protection: a labor of ethics

20. Scientific commitment and the crisis in the environment

21. Radioactivity with regard to the production and use of nuclear weapons: its impact on health

22. Understanding our concept of nature

23. The ozone layer and climatic change

24. Environment and health in the light of WHO's mandate

25. Environment policy in the European Communities

26. Modern art and the psychology of an age

27. Efficiency and the pursuit of humanism

28. The psychological roots of the environmental crisis

279. Kromer, John. *Neighborhood Recovery: Reinvestment Policy for the New Hometown*. New Brunswick, N. J.: Rutgers University Press, 2000.

Keywords: urban planning, housing, community

John Kromer is Philadelphia's housing director and his experience of actual work in the field is readily apparent in this perceptive study of urban renewal. Kromer describes how a blending of public-sector leadership and community initiative can produce successful results. Other topics addressed include: ways to foster home ownership; housing for the homeless or those with special needs; the role of community-based organizations; and the importance of advocacy in advancing neighborhood reinvestment policy.

280. Krupat, Edward. *People and Cities: The Urban Environment and its Effects*. Vol. 6. Cambridge Series in Environment and Behavior, ed. Daniel Stokols and Irwin Altman. Cambridge: Cambridge University Press, 1985.

Keywords: social fabric, sociocultural, psychological health, environmental psychology, crowding, noise, density, alienation, experience of place

In recent decades, the relationship between human behavior and the physical environment has attracted researchers from the social sciences—psychology, sociology, geography, and anthropology—and from the environmental-design disciplines—architecture, urban and regional planning, and interior design. This series offers a common meeting ground for those who analyze various aspects of environment-behavior links. It is good on issues pertaining to urban crowding and stress, as well as on methodological and theoretical concerns relating to the urban environment.

Part 1, "The Idea of the City," introduces and studies the city as an environment, its specific characteristics, and its perception by city dwellers. Part 2, "Living in the City," addresses the problems of crowding, noise, stress, and isolation. Discussions of social relations in the city, the impact of the physical environment, and the question "Can the City be a Livable Place?" can also be found in this section.

281. Kryter, K. D. *The Effects of Noise on Man*. New York: Academic Press, 1970.

Keywords: support, health, noise—physiological effects, noise—psychosocial effects

This volume represents an attempt "to provide a critical and historical (dating from 1950) analysis of the relevant literature in the field, and, as warranted, to derive new or modify existing techniques for the evaluation of environmental noise in terms of its effects on man. In Parts 1 and 2 of this book, fundamental definitions of sound, its measurement, and concepts of the basic functioning and attributes of the auditory system are provided. These chapters also present, along with their experimental basis, procedures for estimating from physical measures of noise its effect on man's auditory system and speech communications. Part 3 is devoted to man's nonauditory system responses and includes information about the effects of noise on such things as work performance, sleep, feelings of pain, vision, and blood circulation. It is clear that some of the more complex, and perhaps more important from a health viewpoint, effects of noise have to do with these somewhat second-order reactions. Tolerable limits of noise with respect to its effects on man's auditory and nonauditory systems are suggested at various places."

282. Kryter, K. D. *The Handbook of Hearing and the Effects of Noise*. San Diego: Academic Press, Inc., 1994.

Keywords: support, urban metabolism, noise, noise—physiological effects, noise—psychological effects

The author's own words describe this volume succinctly: "*The Handbook of Hearing and the Effects of Noise* presents the methods and the results of research for quantitatively describing the major attributes of hearing and the effects of sound and noise on people. . . Chapters 1-3 cover the basic nature and measurement of sound, the structure and functioning of the ear, and auditory sensations and perceptions. Chapters 4-7 are devoted to research methods and findings pertaining to noise-induced hearing loss, speech communications in noise, assessments of hearing handicaps, compensation for hearing loss, and the conservation of hearing. Chapters 8-10 review and evaluate research findings and theoretical concepts related to: (1) mental and psychomotor work performance in noise, (2) nonauditory system physiological reactions, and sensations in nonauditory sense modalities, from exposure to sound and noise, and (3) psychological reactions and stress-related health disorders in noisy work and residential areas." The implications of the last few chapters for healthy cities are obvious.

283. Kubiski, Walter S. *Citizen Participation in the '90's: Realities, Challenges and Opportunities*. Winnipeg: Institute of Urban Studies, 1992.

Keywords: social fabric, case studies, community, democracy, urban planning

This short paper concentrates on a number of related themes: the need for community empowerment and citizen participation; the need for innovative responses from cities in the face of economic decline and economic restructuring; the necessity of making hard choices and trade-offs to ensure an acceptable quality of urban life; the quest for urban sustainability; and an orientation towards the future. The emphasis here is on the need for urban planners, politicians, policy-makers, and citizens to work together to develop new models of sustainable urban life.

284. Kulp, G., and M. C. Holcomb. *Transportation Energy Data Book*. 6th ed. Park Ridge, N. J.: Noyes Data Corp., 1982.

Keywords: automobiles, energy, transportation

"This document is the sixth edition of the *Transportation Energy Data Book*, a statistical compendium published by Oak Ridge National Laboratory (ORNL) under contract with the Office of Vehicle Engine Research and Development in the [U.S.] Department of Energy (DOE)." This useful desktop reference book contains data in tables that characterize transportation activity and transportation energy use. Topics such as price per barrel of crude oil, car sales, transportation energy use by mode, total vehicle miles, and many more are covered. Chapter 1 contains data regarding energy use and supply, by sector and by mode. Chapter 2 focuses on the highway mode because it is by far the largest consumer of energy. The chapter is divided into characteristics of vehicle stock, household sector, and non-household sector. Chapter 3 deals with non-highway modes, namely air, water, rail, and pipeline. Trends in vehicle and engine characteristics are presented in the fourth and final chapter.

285. Kumar, Ranjit, and Barbara Murck. *On Common Ground: Managing Human-Planet Relationships*. Toronto: John Wiley & Sons, 1992.

Keywords: biosphere, ecology, environmental pollution, public policy, sustainability, urban design

This book is an ideal introductory learning package on sustainability. Straightforwardly written yet comprehensive, it stresses the importance of learning about how natural systems work. The complex inter-relatedness of natural processes as well as the need to consider them in a broad context are also emphasized. The book, written for the Foundation for International Training, addresses questions such as: Can we actually conceive and realize sustainable futures? Is it possible to find or design pathways to healthy, productive human-planet relationships by taking specific actions and setting definite goals? Why, and in what specific ways, should the issues and constraints of sustainability influence decision-making in the public and private sectors? How are managers and policy-makers to achieve the level of expertise that they require in order to incorporate all these concerns into the decision-making process? And what are the human dimensions of such a vision and a process?

Part 1, "Managing the Planet: Challenge for Our Future," reveals the necessity of a fundamental shift in perspective regarding human-planet relationships. The section discusses why current natural resource utilization and apportionment practices are not sustainable. Part 2, "Decision Making and the Environment: A Conceptual Framework," is an edited version of a chapter from Dr. Donella Meadows' book, *Harvesting One Hundredfold: Key Concepts and Case Studies in Environmental Education*. It briefly introduces the eight Earth Systems so that the reader may gain a basic understanding of natural processes underlying environmental problems. "System 5: Human Settlements and Urbanization" is of particular significance to Healthy Cities work. It considers the city as a metabolic system and an ecosystem and points out the environmental implications of urban growth, waste, and pollution and of altering the natural physical environment. As well, "System 8: Earth Materials, Energy, and Waste" provides basic information on minerals, the energy cycle, traditional and alternative energy sources, and the main concerns regarding waste management. A two-page description of industrial ecosystems is also included. Finally, in part 4, "Creating Sustainable Futures: The Human Dimension," the fact that human needs and interests are intertwined with the natural systems of Earth is reiterated. How to integrate the new sustainable futures perspective into daily life and governmental decision-making is the focus of this section.

286. Kunstler, James Howard. *The Geography of Nowhere: The Rise and Decline of America's Man-Made Landscape*. New York: Simon & Schuster, 1993.

Keywords: social fabric, architecture, built environment, experience of place, new urbanism, classic

Written from the perspective of a crusading concerned citizen, *The Geography of Nowhere* is a literary event. In a style that ranges from being pungent and satirical to lyrical (but always elegant), Kunstler laments the loss of great American cities and towns. He harshly criticizes the "joyless junk habitat," the "landscape of scary places" that has replaced formerly vibrant communities.

The Geography of Nowhere was instrumental in bringing the disaster of suburbia and the evisceration of city centers to the attention of the general public and making the attendant problems a part of general public discourse. For this reason alone, it belongs in the rarefied heights of Jane Jacob's *Death and Life of Great American Cities*.

The book is also a splendid guided tour of the best and worst in American cities, delighting in demonstrating what works and why, remorseless in exposing what is ugly and spiritually degrading. Kunstler is not shy about criticizing who and what is to be blamed for the current fiasco; the influence of Modernism, the evolution of car culture, and policies that made the suburb inevitable are all targeted. The closing chapter suggests ways through which we can build better places. For anyone interested in the work of Christopher Alexander, Andres Duany, and Randall Arendt, this is the best place to start.

This is an invaluable book for anyone interested in any aspect of the built habitat, but like all good literature it transcends the genre of writings about the city.

287. Kunstler, James Howard. *Home From Nowhere: Remaking Our Everyday World for the 21st Century*. New York: Simon & Schuster, 1996.

Keywords: built environment, experience of place, social fabric, new urbanism

Home from Nowhere continues the crusade against unsightly and soulless suburban sprawl begun in *The Geography of Nowhere*. Kunstler's critiques are as caustic as ever and his prose remains scintillating. The great advantage of this work is that it distils all the wisdom of the New Urbanism in which Kunstler has thoroughly schooled himself. The work thus quickly moves beyond criticism to practical examples of what has been done, and what can be done, to remedy conventional development. This is, without doubt, the finest and most comprehensive discussion of New Urbanist principles, the rationale behind them, and how they can be put into practice. Once again, an indispensable book for anyone interested in the sustainability of the built habitat, from planning professionals to citizen activists and students.

288. Kunstler, James Howard, ed. *The City: Lost and Found.* Special Issue of *The Bulletin of Science, Technology, & Society.* Vol. 20, No. 4. Thousand Oaks, Calif.: Sage Press, August 2000.

Keywords: new urbanism, architecture, sustainability, urban planning, urban design, public spaces, experience of place

With contributions from Norman Crowe, Andres Duany, Douglas Kelbaugh, Kunstler, and more, this is an outstanding collection of articles on healthy/sustainable cities. A unifying theme is the contribution that the New Urbanism can make toward environmental and social sustainability. This is an indispensable collection for anyone engaged in healthy city research.

289. Labov, William. "The Logic of Nonstandard English: Studies in the Black English Vernacular." In *Language in the Inner City*, pp. 201-40. Philadelphia: University of Pennsylvania Press, 1972.

Keywords: children

Experts have attempted to discover the problems of ghetto children that underlie their poor school performance. Black ghetto children are said to receive little verbal stimulation so that they are not able to form concepts or convey logical thoughts. This is known as the deficit theory, via which the blame is put on the children or their parents instead of the education system. This paper examines the faulty studies supporting the deficit theory and attempts to discover the mechanism that is preventing black children from learning to read. It is shown that the language used by ghetto children is not nonlogical but is a concise and logical dialect of the English language. Test situations threaten children, and it is concluded that social situations are the most powerful key in verbal behavior. A teacher must enter the correct social relationship with a student to determine his or her language abilities. Examples of conversations with children are given to emphasize this. A teacher's attitude towards a student has been shown as an important element in the child's performance and, if a student speaks in a way deemed illogical by many, the teacher's attitude will reflect this. The student will become hostile towards school and look for comfort in his peers. The poor education of ghetto youth is a failure of the education system and not of the child.

290. Laguerre, Michel S. *The Informal City.* London: Macmillan, 1994.

Keywords: community, economics

"The informal arena provides a hidden space where one can stand to read the city as a social laboratory of everyday practice. The intent of this book is to identify, describe and explain the grammatical, syntactical and morphological rules and structures of that informal reality as they are inscribed, but hidden, in the textual map of the American City." The author uses the San Francisco-Oakland Metropolitan Area to construct the model of informality and then explore ideas such as informal space, economy, urban politics, medical practices, and inter-ethnic relations.

291. Landreth, Robert E., and Paul A. Rebers, eds. *Municipal Solid Wastes: Problems and Solutions.* Boca Raton, Fla.: CRC Press, 1997.

Keywords: transformation, case studies, hazardous waste, waste

Creative new ways of dealing with municipal solid wastes are necessary in order to achieve sustainable cities along with the need for drastic waste reduction. Some chapters deal with end-of-pipe technologies such as technical improvements in recycling facilities and incinerators. Other articles provide insight into the policy, implementation, and legal issues. For example, the chapter on composting discusses programs and systems currently in use, related laws, utilization, and marketing strategies. Also included is a case study of The Strawberry Creek Recycling Center in Harpswell, Maine, and its program to reduce air emissions and increase reuse of materials. Another chapter estimates the extent of human exposure to mercury and dioxin. The legal issues surrounding the disposal of hazardous chemicals are illustrated through the description of Jacksonville's collection and disposal program.

292. Lane, Barbara. "Health and Wellness in the City." In *Perspectives on Urban Health*, ed. Brijesh Mathur, pp. 5-12. Winnipeg: Institute of Urban Studies, 1991.

Keywords: support, health, health care

This article presents an overview of the changing concept of health in the twentieth century. It notes all major changes including those initiated by Sigerist, Payne, and the World Health Organization. The sick care system is criticized, and current health promotion initiatives in Canada are discussed. The article then considers the many factors affecting health in a city, from air quality to recreational facilities.

293. Lang, Jon T. *Urban Design: The American Experience.* New York: Van Nostrand Reinhold, 1994.

Keywords: architecture, buildings—social aspects, emotional needs, urban design

"*Urban Design: The American Experience* places social and environmental concerns within the context of American history. It returns the focus of urban design to the creation of a better world. It evaluates the efforts of designers who apply knowledge about the environment and people to the creation of livable, enjoyable, and even inspiring built worlds." *Urban Design: The American Experience* emphasizes that urban design must take a user-oriented approach to achieve a higher quality of life in human settlements. The keys to this approach are spelled out in chapters that address:
 - urban design as both a product and process of communal decision-making
 - types of knowledge required as a base for urban design action
 - how to apply recent environmental and behavioral research to professional design
 - how human needs are fulfilled through design
 - the true role of functionalism in design

294. Langdon, Philip. *A Better Place to Live: Reshaping the American Suburb.* Amherst: The University of Massachusetts Press, 1994.

Keywords: support, community, housing, land use, neighborhood, public space, suburbs, transportation

Although others, such as Peter Calthorpe, James Howard Kunstler, Andres Duany, and Elizabeth Plater-Zyberk, have written about the ills of modern suburbs, Philip Langdon also makes a significant contribution to the literature of North American suburbs and the history of suburbanization. While on a search for better places to live, Langdon visited many suburbs and towns throughout the United States. He found that places which followed older design principles had more community spirit and more enjoyable public spaces, were more compact and more walkable, and generally provided a more satisfying individual and family life. Langdon contrasts this with modern suburb planning which ignores the wealth of older knowledge available on building healthier, more convivial places. As a result, postwar North American suburb designers are more concerned with the buildings themselves than with the community layout and the pattern of daily life that it defines. Instead of suburbs that foster walking and cycling, the newer suburbs require extensive use of automobiles. This is largely due to the segregation of land use among residential, industrial, retail, and office space. Even the houses contribute to segregation by economic status because different types of housing are located in different areas.

The book begins by noting these failures of postwar suburbs in terms of streets, the marketing of suburban housing developments, and the strict control imposed by some homeowners' associations. Next, the book turns to investigating how suburban design can and should be changed by building suburbs more like towns, rethinking work, shopping and transportation, and suggests what governments can do. The final two chapters discuss further the necessary changes, how they can be brought about, and the obstacles to this new vision. Langdon does not address the problem of how sprawl is unsustainable and thrives at the expense of the inner city.

295. Lave, Lester B., and Eugene Seskin. *Air Pollution and Human Health.* Baltimore: Johns Hopkins University Press, 1977.

Keywords: quality of life, air pollution, health, public policy

The primary goal of this text is to quantify the health benefits that would result from the abatement of air pollution. The authors assert that: "The work of many investigators will enter into this quantification. While we cannot estimate the total benefits with certainty, we arrive at a number of specific conclusions regarding the net benefits to society (benefits minus the associated costs) of imposing stringent emission standards to control each compound. Estimates of total benefits (not only health benefits) and total costs will be presented . . . but our investigation will focus on the association between air pollution and health."

Many of the effects of air pollution, though evident, are difficult to quantify or evaluate. What is the effect of air pollution on one's "lifestyle"? What is the value of enhanced "quality of life" as a result of air pollution abatement? These are two of the fundamental questions examined by the investigators.

296. Lave, Lester B. *Toxic Chemicals, Health, and the Environment.* Baltimore: Johns Hopkins University Press, 1987.

Keywords: environmental pollution, health, toxins

This volume presents state-of-the-art information on the relationship of toxic chemicals to human health and to the environment. The control and monitoring of toxic chemicals in the environment and in biological matter are also considered. Important issues relating to the toxicity of chemicals discussed in the book include:
-the right of the public to have proprietary data
-the role for risk assessment in risk management
-the need for improved toxicological data
-communication of data and decisions to the various communities involved

297. Lea, Chris. "Urban Visions." *City Magazine* 12, 3 (1991): 13-21.

Keywords: current, community, democracy, energy, green cities, public policy, quality of life, transportation, urban planning

The three articles in this collection visualize humane, healthy, and ecological cities. An image of a green city is given by Toronto architect Chris Lea. He emphasizes the need to reduce private automobile use through urban planning and the need to increase population density to facilitate mass transit. Special consideration is given to the need for reducing energy use in Canada. Energy alternatives such as liquid biomass fuels, solar and wind energy, and hydroelectric power are suggested, with a view to becoming self-reliant in energy. Restructuring the economy in order to become economically self-reliant is also suggested as a step toward sustainable, healthy, and ecological cities. The suggestions made are not city-specific, but Toronto is often used as an example.

The second article presents two visions for the city of Vancouver—the Executive City and the People's City. The trickle-down benefits and short-term productivity offered by the elitist Executive City vision are criticized. The alternative vision offers a livable city that is considerate of individual needs such as security, comfort, and companionship, establishing the human as something more than a money-spending consumer. The lack of public participation in the planning process of Vancouver is also criticized, and visions of local planning committees are presented as a solution. In a postscript by Kent Gerecke, current politics emphasizing the Executive City are criticized, as are their philosophies voiced by Michael Goldburg.

The third article is concerned with an urban vision arising from a citizens' inner-city inquiry in Winnipeg. Great concern for the inner-city was expressed in light of government cuts to the finances necessary to support inner-city needs. The author, Sheldon Gee, summarizes seventeen recommendations made by the citizens into the three major elements of the vision: empowerment, self-sufficiency, and a focus on fundamental problems. The future of Winnipeg's inner city remains uncertain, however, due to a lack of government support. Nevertheless, the development of urban visions that visualize healthy, ecological cities is an essential step in the movement towards urban regeneration.

298. Leavitt, Helen. *Superhighway-Superhoax*. Garden City, N. Y.: Doubleday, 1970.

Keywords: classic, automobiles, transportation

Highway construction and transportation based on autos and trucks rather than light rail are due to an implicit agreement/conspiracy among state highway officials, contractors, auto manufacturers, engineers, congressmen, state legislators, newspaper publishers, and representatives of road user groups. Whether this argument is true or not, no one has been able to disprove Leavitt's finding that as the number of highways increases, congestion increases.

Leavitt criticizes the building of highways through cities because it isolates people without cars, destroys valuable land and communities, and results in even more car traffic. As a result, bus operation is frustrated and room must be made for more and more parking spaces. Leavitt outlines these and other far-reaching implications of urban highway construction: economic problems, suburban stores with parking lots that take away business from stores in the city, less room for playing and strolling, and decreased social interaction. To put it simply, "This book is about the men and institutions who promote highways and how they destroy our churches, schools, homes, and parks."

This is a classic book about Healthy Cities, second only to Jane Jacob's *The Death and Life of Great American Cities*.

299. Lefebvre, Henri. *Writings on Cities*. Cambridge, Mass.: Blackwell, 1996.

Keywords: current, community, urban design

Lefebvre is widely regarded as France's only postwar intellectual to consider the nature of cities and urban life. His writings raise questions about the "nature of urban reality, the production of space and modernity." Topics covered include: industrialization and urbanization; philosophy and the city; town and country; urban form; and continuities and discontinuities.

300. Lennard, Suzanne, and Henry L. Lennard. *Livable Cities: People and Places—Social and Design Principles for the Future of the City*. New York: Gondolier Press, 1987.

Keywords: current, case studies, community, health, public space, quality of life, transportation, urban design, urban planning

"The idea of the livable city, as developed in this book, conceives of the restoration of the core, or heart of the city not only for commercial activity but equally for the renewal of vital social processes—reviving the social, moral and cultural life of the community. Livable cities enable diverse groups of people to live in the city again; most importantly, families with children, by offering an infrastructure of services and work opportunities in the vicinity. They provide for a variety of places for social life, communication and dialogue, and for meaningful community occasions.

"Livable cities pay attention to the creation of architecture, streetscape and public space design that facilitate the presence of city dwellers in the public domain and in the heart of the city. Such cities are also committed to reducing traffic, and to resolving problems of safety, pollution and noise by utilizing a variety of mechanisms." The specific issues addressed in this excellent overview of healthy communities are urban space design principles, markets, social life, festivals and street entertainment, criteria for public art, transportation, and pedestrians, as well as some case studies.

301. Leo, Christopher, and Robert Fenton. "'Mediated Enforcement' and the Evolution of

the State: Development Corporations in Canadian City Centers." *International Journal of Urban and Regional Research* 14, 2 (1990): 185-206.

Keywords: economics

Downtown redevelopment reflects the official thinking of the 1980s—partly a reaction against ideas of the 1960s and an attempt to improve long-neglected facilities in the downtown core and reverse damage done by car-dominated suburban development. Although downtown redevelopment is clearly a major phenomenon, little attention has been given to it in political academic literature. The author notes that a reader who wants to understand the politics of downtown redevelopment, as well as its role in the evolution of the modern state, will find little in the current literature. Downtown redevelopment has immediate economic and political significance in cities and is part of wider economic and political forces. This paper looks at urban development corporations chosen by governments as the major vehicle for downtown redevelopment since, from the government's point of view, they are more effective than government departments at dealing with private sector organizations. The author states that by observing these corporations, one can learn about the evolving relationship between state and private capital, as well as how relations between levels of government are changing, since many urban development schemes are joint initiatives.

The article concludes that the state is not as pictured by Ofte, Winkler, and others: a monolith whose details are uninteresting. To explain the creation of urban development corporations, the Canadian federal government is pictured as being pulled by three forces: the growing power of a better educated electorate that demands more, the growing power of capital, and the government's financial limitations. This view of the state is closely examined and tested against the realities of downtown Vancouver, Winnipeg, and Toronto. Ofte and Winkler's theories are criticized for not being focused enough.

302. Leslie, George B., and F. W. Lunau, eds. *Indoor Air Pollution: Problems and Priorities*. Cambridge: Cambridge University Press, 1992.

Keywords: air pollution, health, indoor pollution, occupational health

"This volume addresses the problems arising from pollutants that all too commonly contaminate the indoor environment, including biological sources such as bacteria, fungi and moulds, common combustion products, radon and other sources of radiation, solvents used in industry, offices and the home, asbestos and dust pollution. The aim is to provide a balanced account of the health risks associated with these major pollutants and to quantify the scale of the problem on a pollutant-by-pollutant basis. Each chapter covers exposure levels, sources of pollution and routes of uptake, health effects, control measures, and regulatory guidelines. The volume provides a valuable source of reference and information for all those working in the areas of environmental toxicology, pollution control, industrial and occupational hygiene, and for health and safety personnel."

303. Leung, Hok Lin. *Land Use Planning Made Plain*. Kingston, Ontario: Ronald P. Frye, 1989.

Keywords: classic, land use, built environment

This book provides an excellent introduction to making and implementing land use decisions. It seeks to develop a set of coherent planning principles by drawing out useful and generally applicable elements from a variety of systems and approaches. It makes assumptions about what land use planning is supposed to do and what elements in existing theories and practices can be useful in this pursuit. The purpose of this book is not to report or critique but to serve as a guide for practice.

The target audience is city planners who make and implement plans; politicians or the administrators who legitimize and supervise the planner; developers and property owners whose actions are affected by these plans; and the general public whose welfare and quality of life are affected by all of the above. This book seeks to promote shared understanding so that "both the planner and the planned may become more responsible and responsive" in land use planning.

304. LeVine, Duane G., and Arthur C. Upton, eds. *The City as a Human Environment.* Only One Earth Series. Westport, Conn.: Praeger, 1994.

Keywords: current, urban metabolism, automobiles, built environment, green space, pedestrians, transportation, urban planning

This is an important book for healthy city research. It is comprehensive, and persistently preventive in orientation. Both environmental and social sustainability are discussed. Sustainable land-use patterns, preservation of green spaces, environmental planning, energy efficiency, and sustainable transport policies receive close attention.

305. Levy, John M., ed. *Contemporary Urban Planning.* 4th ed. Upper Saddle River, N. J.: Prentice-Hall, 1997.

Keywords: current, environmental planning, urban design, urban planning

Despite being an urban planning textbook, this volume contains good sections on neighborhood development, neotraditional planning, urban renewal, community development, housing, transportation, environmental planning, and energy planning. Aside from the above-mentioned material which is not often covered by textbooks, the book presents a history of planning, the legal basis of planning, the politics of planning, and a guide to comprehensive planning. The fields of planning discussed include urban design and capital facilities, transportation, economic development, growth management, environment and energy, and metropolitan region planning. Throughout the book, the author comes back to the question of who benefits and who loses as a result of various decisions. He introduces students to American state, metropolitan, and local planning, focussing mostly on the latter.

The chapter on urban design provides a useful overview of the major movements in urban design by people such as Le Corbusier, Wright, Duany, Calthorpe, Whyte, and Jacobs. It emphasizes the importance of pedestrian-oriented design, the concept of a neighborhood, and social interaction. The chapter also provides a clear explanation of what urban design is and what is involved in the process. Similarly, the chapter entitled "Urban Renewal and Community Development" first explains what the Urban Renewal program in the 1950s and '60s was and suggests that a lot can be learned from its failures. The Community Development movement which takes a "preserve and improve" approach rather than a "clear and rebuild" attitude of urban renewal is then analyzed.

306. Lewis, Charles A. "Healing in the Urban Environment." *APA (American Planning Association) Journal* (Summer 1979): 330-38.

Keywords: green space, psychological health

Urban stress may be caused by the fact that urban living is very new relative to human evolution, most of which occurred in natural environments. A variety of human needs thus cannot be satisfied by the urban technological environment.

The author suggests that "Strategies for achieving a better fit of man in the built environment might be found in urban activities and settings involving nature which are life-enhancing, and create a sense of tranquility and well-being." Gardening projects in low income areas of New York, Philadelphia, Chicago, and Vancouver, B.C., are shown to provide human benefits and satisfactions of enhanced self-esteem, increased sociability, reduction in vandalism, cleaner streets, painted buildings, and revitalized neighborhoods.

Another area of benefit is delineated by current psychological research which identifies landscape configurations that people consistently prefer and find satisfying, and sees them as the kinds of settings that would have provided survival information for primitive man. Researchers theorize that, today, the preferred landscape configurations satisfy sign stimuli that man learned to prefer during evolution. Architects, planners, psychologists, and sociologists are challenged to recognize these person/plant relationships, to study them to understand their human benefits, and to use them for relieving stress in existing situations and preventing stress in environments yet to be built.

307. Lewis, Philip H., Jr. *Tomorrow By Design: A Regional Design Process for Sustainability*. New York: John Wiley & Sons, 1996.

Keywords: current, architecture, case studies, ecology, experience of place, green cities, green space, interdisciplinary studies, land use, sustainability, urban ecology

The details of the Regional Design Process, as applied to the American upper midwest, are presented here. The author emphasizes the importance of first understanding the impact a development will have on natural and cultural systems. Therefore, the first step in the Regional Design Process should be to take inventory of landscape resources and patterns. Part 1 presents a way of looking at the natural environment to recognize possible threats from humans. It is argued that an integrated land/social ethic is needed in order to protect and enhance the natural and cultural qualities of design. Broad guidelines for restorative efforts are given. Part 2 contains the basic principles and an example of a resource value inventory, creative analysis, a synthesis of two- and three-dimensional design options and educational efforts involved in the Regional Design Process. Plenty of maps and diagrams make it clear what exactly is meant by patterns. Here, the author builds upon Christopher Alexander's classic *A Pattern Language* in describing various landscape patterns. Alexander's theory is actually put to work in Part 2 where the Regional Design Process is applied to Circle City in the upper midwest. Included is a design proposal for a higher density locality along a rail corridor which will, it is hoped, avert urban sprawl in all directions.

All of the work involved in the design process should be done by interdisciplinary teams. How to operate in these teams and how to make use of interdisciplinary expertise is also discussed. All in all, the book provides many examples, at various scales, that have put into practice the principles behind the Regional Design Process, which seeks to create a more sustainable natural and cultural landscape.

308. Ley, David. *A Social Geography of the City*. New York: Harper & Row, 1983.

Keywords: current, ecology, economics, urban sociology

This book attempts an integration of new traditions in human geography (including behavioral, humanistic, and radical perspectives) with conventional urban geography (which emphasizes spatial form) to create a distinctive social geography of the city. As such, the book contains a number of current and novel emphases. These include a treatment of the geography of everyday life in the city and the role of culture and values, not only in defining our experience of the urban environment but also in molding the pattern of urban land use. Social groups in the city, both informal groups and urban institutions, are examined systematically, and their interactions through urban politics and the urban land market are assessed. The quality of life experienced by urban residents is given special emphasis, and various explanations for its geographic variation are considered. The book begins and ends with an analysis of the broader historical contexts that surround the development of urban land use patterns and the quality of urban life. In chapter 2, the distinctive contexts of the emergence of the industrial city, the prototype for so much urban analysis, are considered; in chapter 11, the contemporary contexts of urbanism are laid out, and the prospects for attaining a truly livable city are assessed.

309. Liggett, Helen, and David C. Perry, eds. *Spatial Practices: Critical Explorations in Social/Spatial Theory*. Thousand Oaks, Calif.: Sage Publications, 1995.

Keywords: current, urban planning, United States

Representing the City was the theme for this collection of essays prepared for a lecture series. The lectures "raised questions about the politics embedded in familiar narratives of American city life and most particularly about the political, economic, and physical relations that constitute the city. Issues of the spatiality of these relations figured in each presentation."

310. Lightbody, James, ed. *Canadian Metropolitics: Governing Our Cities*. Toronto: Copp Clark, 1995.

Keywords: democracy, public policy, Canada

What makes this urban politics textbook relevant to healthy cities is the fact that it goes beyond presenting the usual chapters on historical, legal, and political-economy contexts of Canadian city government. Rather, the text also contains chapters that illustrate the significance of urban politics through issue discussions. In particular, chapter 4 focuses on women and cities. It studies data on women's participation in local politics and attempts to explain why women are represented more in local than in provincial, territorial and federal governments. Chapter 5, "When 'They' is 'We': Movements, Municipal Parties, and Participatory Politics," studies urban reform movements in Vancouver, Winnipeg, and Montreal that sought to bring municipal government "closer to the people." The author concludes that political parties are an inadequate vehicle for expanding public participation. The political structure and role of citizens in local public schooling is the subject of chapter 10. Another chapter examines the conflict between environmental and economic agendas and the difficulty of "green" politics.

311. Lin, James C. *Electromagnetic Interaction with Biological Systems*. New York: Plenum Press, 1989.

Keywords: electromagnetic fields and health, health

The purpose of the book is to present a succinct summary of the interaction of electromagnetic fields and waves with biological systems as they are now known. The subject matter is interdisciplinary and focuses on three major areas: medical diagnostics and therapy, biological effects and mechanisms, and safety guides and rationales.

312. Lincoln Institute of Land Policy *Alternatives to Sprawl*. Dwight Young, ed. Cambridge, Mass.: Lincoln Institute of Land Policy, 1996.

Keywords: current, built environment, sustainability, urban design

This easy-to-read report looks at the factors contributing to urban sprawl, the impacts of urban sprawl, and provides a variety of ways to combat the problem. For developers, architects, and engineers who are unfamiliar with non-sprawl options, the report is an excellent primer.

313. Linden, Eugene. "Mega Cities." *Time (Canada)*, January 11, 1993, pp. 30-40.

Keywords: developing countries, megacities

The article asks the questions "Does the growth of megacities portend an apocalypse of global epidemics and pollution? Or will the remarkable stirrings of self-reliance that can be found in some of them point the way to their salvation?" Kinshasa, Zaire, plagued by violence, starvation, epidemics, and severe poverty is the example used to show the desperate state of cities on the verge of an "apocalypse." Curitiba, Brazil, with its creative vision, an outstanding public transit system, many parks, and extremely high recycling rates, is used to exemplify cities' hope for "salvation."

After contrasting these two cities, the section entitled "The Dawning Age of Megacities" discusses the tremendous rate of population growth in many cities of the developing countries. Here again, the author discusses both the misery such a population boom will bring about and the role of cities as "the cradle of civilization's creativity and ambition."

In the next section, "Cities and Civilization," the seemingly unalterable cycle of urban boom and decline throughout history is documented. The following section documents "The Medical and Environmental Toll" of megacities, such as epidemics that spring up in crowded, unsanitary settlements, the burden of garbage, and air pollution so severe that breathing outside is a serious health hazard. "Will Cities Lose Their Allure?" again discusses the negative aspects of megacities, while "The Revival of Self-Reliance" examines various efforts that have been undertaken to provide citizens with the power to improve their communities.

314. Lippmann, Morton, ed. *Environmental Toxicants: Human Exposures and their Health Effects*. New York: Van Nostrand Reinhold, 1992.
Keywords: buildings—health aspects, health, toxins, water

This useful volume provides a comprehensive knowledge base on human exposure to critical environmental toxicants and the effects of such exposures on human health. The chemicals and physical agents discussed are of current concern in the field of environmental health. Specific topics address asbestos, benzene, carbon monoxide, diesel exhaust, dioxin and related compounds, food contaminants, formaldehyde, indoor bioaerosol contaminants, lead compounds, microwaves, and electromagnetic fields. Attention is also given to the sick building syndrome.

315. Little, Jo, Linda Peake, and Pat Richardson, eds. *Women in Cities: Gender and the Urban Environment*. London: Macmillan, 1988.

Keywords: social fabric, feminism, community

"The aim of this book is to elaborate the particular contribution that feminist geography can make to the analysis of women's activities and experience and the nature of their oppression in urban areas, and to indicate the kind of research agenda to which it gives rise. . . . Feminist geography can be defined as the examination of the ways in which socio-economic, political and environmental processes create, reproduce and transform not only the places in which we live, but also the social relations between men and women in these places and how, in turn, gender relations also have an impact on these processes and their manifestations. . . . To summarize, the particular contribution of this book to the literature on women in urban environments is to illustrate that an understanding of the nature of women's oppression is greatly enhanced by examining how women's lives and activity patterns—that is, their active use of space and time—affect, and are affected by, spatial structure and environmental change."

316. Loeb, Michel. *Noise and Human Efficiency*. New York: John Wiley & Sons, 1986.

Keywords: transformation, health, noise—health effects

This volume provides some background information on the nature of sound, the anatomy and physiology of the ear, and the psychophysiology of hearing. However, the bulk of material focuses on the physiological effects and subjective reactions to noise, as well as the influence that noise has on the performance of work tasks. Some material on policy and safety guidelines is included.

317. Logan, Michael F. *Fighting Sprawl and City Hall: Resistance to Urban Growth in the Southwest*. Tucson: University of Arizona Press, 1995.

Keywords: current, case studies, land use, public policy, urban planning, suburbs

Unlike most reporters who assume that environmental activism originated in the 1960s, Logan investigates the opposition to urban sprawl in Tucson and Albuquerque which began in the late 1940s. He traces the origins of antigrowth activism in these two cities. The story of continued urbanization despite conflict between developers, environmentalists, and citizen groups is told here. For each city, an overview of development prior to World War II is provided. Then, the booster and governmental efforts at urban development are presented. Political, ethnic, and environmental resistance patterns are explored in detail. The book is helpful in providing insights into the workings of government-citizen group disputes.

318. Long, Marybeth, and Alastair Iles. *Assessing Climate Change: Co-evolution of Knowledge, Communities, and Methodologies.* International Institute for Applied Systems Analysis, 1997. Stockholm: Interim Report. IR-97-036.

Keywords: greenhouse effect

This report reviews climate change impact assessment methods. Its usefulness is twofold. First, for those who work in this field directly, the paper is an excellent resource with its historical overview of impact assessment and case studies of sea level rise and health impact sectors. For those whose work is related to environmental impact assessment generally, this paper raises important questions about assessment methods and the relationship between science and policy.

319. Low, Nicholas, Brendan Gleeson, Ingemar Elander, and Rolf Lidskog. *Consuming Cities: The Urban Environment in the Global Economy after the Rio Declaration.* London: Routledge, 2000.

Keywords: urban metabolism, sustainability, case studies

Cities are the dominant engines of consumption of the world's environment. The Rio Agreement and Agenda 21 led to a spate of national policies to achieve environmental sustainability. The impact of these policies was mainly felt by cities. This book examines the effectiveness and impact of various policies around the world.

The first part of the book conceptually sets up the metabolic dimension of cites that allows them to be engines of consumption. The second, core part is a collection of separately authored national studies "under the rubric of ecological sustainability and environmental justice." The countries examined are the United States, Japan, Germany, Britain, China, India, Sweden, Poland, Australia, and Indonesia.

This is a useful comparative analysis of the effectiveness of various environmental policies and the possible direction these will have to take in the future.

320. Lowe, Marcia D. "Shaping Cities." In *State of the World: A Worldwatch Institute Report on Progress Toward a Sustainable Society*, ed. Lester R. Brown. pp. 119-37. New York: Norton, 1992.

Keywords: crowding, developing countries, energy, green cities, land use

Eliminating threats to our future requires an end to the fossil fuel age, efficient solar-based energy, convenient transportation networks that lessen automobile use, the elimination of inequality in all cultures, and a shift to smaller families. These are some of the themes of this book. The various articles suggest that the knowledge and technology for this evolution exists; all that is required is commitment and social change along with political will. *State of the World* examines options to solve problems of sustainability for the economy, our cities, and our planet.

Chapter 8, "Shaping Cities," which is most relevant for research on healthy cities, focuses on population trends and their relationship to sustainability, crowding, pollution, land use, patterns in the "developing world" and transportation. Strategies for greening the city and strategies for achieving energy efficiency are also examined. The article discusses the contours of a planning method that takes environmental and human concerns into consideration with greater forethought. It concludes with a discussion of ways in which urban growth can occur without cities spreading into forests or farms.

321. Lowry, Stella. *Housing and Health*. Plymouth: Latimer Trend & Company, 1991.

Keywords: transformation, buildings—health aspects, electromagnetic fields and health, housing, indoor pollution, noise—physiological effects

"The connection between health and the dwellings of the population is one of the most important that exists," declared Florence Nightingale. But what is actually known about the connection? The author looks at some of the more important influences on housing and health in Britain today.

After offering a brief historical background, Lowry discusses specific factors that affect human health in a building such as temperature, humidity, indoor air quality, sanitation, noise, space, light, electromagnetic radiation, and the possibility of accidents. Following this is a discussion of the impact of housing (or lack thereof) on groups such as families, people with special needs, and the homeless. Public policy measures to promote more healthy housing are also suggested.

322. Lozano, Eduardo E. *Community Design and the Culture of Cities: The Crossroad and the Wall*. Cambridge: Cambridge University Press, 1990.

Keywords: current, architecture, interdisciplinary studies, urban design, urban planning

This is an excellent and comprehensive analysis of all aspects of urban design, form, and planning—from historical and contemporary perspectives. Having identified the roots of widespread urban problems and the recurrent shortcomings of most community-scale plans, Eduardo E. Lozano has created a large and humane vision for community design, geared toward urban planners and designers, as well as those concerned with the communities of the future. The author strives to unify theory and practice by calling for an awareness of the systemic nature of urban design. He highlights relevant lessons from historical examples in order to rediscover the community design metier forgotten after the Industrial Revolution. Lozano relies on interdisciplinary studies: he draws from biology, ecology, and political science, as well as from history. Throughout the book there is an emphasis on the interrelationship of design and culture—society, technology, institutions, and values. Attention is also given to the need for an agenda for political and cultural change.

323. Luccarelli, Mark. *Lewis Mumford and the Ecological Region: The Politics of Planning*. New York: Guilford Press, 1995.

Keywords: ecology, urban planning

This book represents an in-depth look at the concept of regional development advocated by Lewis Mumford. The topics of part 1, "Developing a Sense of Place," trace the intellectual sources of Mumford's vision of the "ecological region." This vision includes a criticism of "possessive individualism" and a call for cultural renewal through experience which allows us to explore the ecology of place. Mumford also advanced the notion of regional planning—planning to adapt technology to natural patterns and to respect limits and diversity.

Part 2, "Undertaking a Vision," outlines Mumford and the Regional Planning Association of America's (RPAA) struggle to make their ideas a guiding principle in urban development. Luccarelli argues that the new urban form for which the RPAA stood, the garden city, was a good solution to mass suburbanization. He also argues that the reasons the RPAA's ideas were not put into practice was due to "a moral shortcoming within the country," as well as Mumford's over-optimistic attitude.

Part 3, "Ecological Regionalism: Challenges and Prospects" discusses three of Mumford's major conclusions that are still relevant today. He recognized the need (1) "to develop a public discourse and civic consciousness as a means not of dissolving but of redirecting the professionalization of knowledge"; (2) for "the ability to find a medium to make aesthetic concerns public issues and therefore make discourse about beauty a criterion of public life"; and (3) "to democratize economic and political power as an accompaniment to any attempt to reconfigure the built environment."

324. Lundin, Lena. *On Building-Related Causes of the Sick Building Syndrome*. Stockholm, Sweden: Almqvist and Wiksell International, 1991.

Keywords: transformation, health, indoor pollution, sick building syndrome

This volume examines the phenomenon of the sick building syndrome through a longitudinal field study. Technical and sensory aspects of air quality were assessed simultaneously over a fall-winter-spring period. Instrument observations gave conditions for specific aspects of the climate for variables such as humidity, temperature, carbon dioxide, air flow, volatile organic compounds, and proportion of return air. Research methodology and results provide useful data for the diagnosis and amelioration of the syndrome.

325. Lynch, Kevin. *Growing Up in Cities: Studies of the Spatial Environment of Adolescence*. 1st ed. Cambridge, Mass.: MIT Press and UNESCO, 1977.

Keywords: growing up, built environment, children, community, experience of place, identity

Urban lifestyles are a major concern for planners and those members of the public and administration whose work impinges on the quality of life available in cities, towns, and villages. The point of departure for this book is the subjective perception of children, something that is often overlooked in planning. The author asks, "How do children and adolescents themselves feel about growing up in cities?" and goes on to correctly suggest that the perception of children "of the environment they live in, just as, in a wider perspective, that of all dwellers in cities, has to be assessed as an important factor in attempts to make a better quality of life a reality for all."

326. Lynch, Kevin. *A Theory of Good City Form*. Cambridge, Mass.: MIT Press, 1981.

Keywords: current, neighborhood, urban design, urban planning, utopia, classic

Lynch reviews the history of normative theories in relation to urban form and design in his quest to answer the question "What makes a good city?" The purpose of the study is identified as the development of a general statement about the features of a good settlement: a statement that remains responsive and relevant to any human context and that further serves to connect general values to specific actions. Lynch restricts his analysis to the connection between human values and the spatial, physical city. The ensuing discussion is nevertheless wide-ranging enough to encompass notions of vitality, access, control, justice, efficiency, city size, and neighborhoods as well as city design and models. All in all, this is an excellent contribution to the literature on healthy cities.

327. Lynch, Kevin. *Wasting Away*. San Francisco: Sierra Club Books, 1990.

Keywords: output, community, efficiency, waste, urban metabolism

Historically, urban planning has not been particularly concerned with natural systems, focusing instead on man-made changes to the environment. The assumption seems to have been that technology and planning could solve all problems and could overcome natural constraints. But the limitations of technology have become all too evident as we struggle to provide water to cities in arid climates, to clean up toxic wastes that contaminate urban water supplies, or to rebuild cities destroyed by natural disasters. This book focuses on the sociocultural aspects of waste in the urban-industrial environment. The appropriate management of waste is essential to achieving a life-enhancing environment.

Some of the basic values underlying urban planning, in fact, relate directly to waste management. One value is to maintain and provide for the health and safety of human settlements. A second value is achieving efficiency, one that implies that land and other resources should be put to their best use, without wasting them. A third waste-related value, the need for adaptability, requires that instead of wasting resources that are no longer useful, they should be recycled. Much planning is occupied with doing just this: finding new uses for old military bases, dying city centers, or industrial areas, to name a few. It is as important for planners to help places decline or even die gracefully as it is to promote development and growth. Increasingly, planners will be called upon to manage waste processes and the consequences of waste-related disasters.

328. Lyon, Larry. *The Community in Urban Society*. Philadelphia: Temple University Press, 1987.

Keywords: social fabric, built environment, community, neighborhood, quality of life

The concept of community is one that is difficult to define. In this text, the community is a place where theory and the "real" world come together, a means of improving the world without taking on everything at once. It becomes a starting point for improvements to our physical surroundings where theory can be put into practice a little at a time, and in a realistic manner. The community thus becomes and represents a microcosm for the world. The author believes that the community is more than an abstract object of theoretical inquiry; it is a place where we live and a place we can study and improve. Some of the important questions being asked about communities are explored, such as: What is a community? How does a community differ from a city? How have communities changed and why? What are the best ways to conceptualize and study communities? In the first chapter, many definitions of community are looked at. Chapters 2 through 5 delve into different approaches to the community: community on a rural-urban continuum; the ecological approach; community as a spatial phenomenon; the community as a social system; and the conflict approach. In section 2, the quality of life is the central theme as the three chapters (7, 8, and 9) look at the loss of and quest for community, community development, and planned communities. Section 3 is more detailed and specific, presenting research skills and research findings. Chapter 10 covers the securing and interpretation indicators of the quality of community life. Chapter 11 explores designing community surveys and questionnaires, choosing samples, and administering the surveys and analyzing the results. Chapter 12 discusses community power, while chapter 13 looks at measuring local power. In chapter 14, field research is done in terms of holistic studies and methods, and lastly, chapter 15 explores the quality of life and the quality of communities.

329. MacKenzie, James J. *The Keys to the Car: Electric and Hydrogen Vehicles for the 21st Century*. Washington, D.C.: World Resources Institute, 1994.

Keywords: air pollution, automobiles, energy, technology, transportation

Author James J. Mackenzie argues that it is not necessary to sacrifice human mobility and convenience in order to alleviate environmental crises that are associated with automobile use (such as the greenhouse effect). Instead, he proposes the widespread commercial development and use of zero-emission vehicles.

A cost-benefit survey of the environmental and economic consequences of the use of alternative fuels such as ethanol, methanol, and natural gas is performed. Although such fuels are cleaner, they do not substantially eliminate carbon dioxide emissions or reduce the dependence on imported resources. Thus, it is concluded that these fuels should be used only during the transition phase towards zero-emission electric vehicles. Electric vehicles fuelled by natural gas (in which the natural gas runs an engine at peak efficiency, which in turn powers a dynamo or battery) would cut carbon dioxide emissions in half. If fuelled by a photovoltaic cell, wind, or other renewable resources, emissions would be reduced to zero and fossil fuel imports would be drastically reduced. The status of current electric vehicle technology is explored. It is emphasized that a move towards electric vehicles is vital to the international competitiveness of the U.S. automakers, considering the advances that have been made in Japan and Europe.

The following policy shifts are recommended:

1) Fuel prices should be reformulated to reflect the environmental and social impacts of automobiles.

2) Government financial assistance should be provided for research and development.

3) The development of infrastructure such as battery recharging facilities and hydrogen production systems is needed.

4) Market stimulation through incentives is also required.

James J. Mackenzie is a senior associate in the World Resources Institute's Climate, Energy and Pollution program. This work is part of WRI's effort to promote sustainable development.

330. Maclaren, Virginia. "Sustainable Urban Development in Canada From Concept to Practice (Volume III: A Compendium of Initiatives)." Department of Geography and Program in Planning, University of Toronto, 1992.

Keywords: current, public policy, sustainability, Canada

This volume provides information on the responses to a Sustainable Urban Development questionnaire. It is a useful summary of sustainable urban development projects undertaken in Canada in 1992. One section presents results from city government offices or departmental units that have significant responsibilities for sustainable development initiatives or that are themselves initiatives. Another section consists of a description of city government external/public advisory committees with relevant sustainable development initiatives. The last section describes a selected number of initiatives that were felt to be particularly innovative or relevant for sustainable development. Volume 1 (the actual analysis of these questionnaire responses) is also listed in this bibliography.

331. Maclaren, Virginia W. *Sustainable Urban Development in Canada From Concept to Practice (Volume I: Summary Report).* Department of Geography and Program in Planning, University of Toronto, 1992.

Keywords: public policy, sustainability, Canada

This report attempts to fill the gap in the "analysis of the methods for and implications of adopting sustainable development practices at the local level." The lack of such research leaves municipalities without the guidance and tools through which they might be able to resolve the pressures on the urban environment and undertake other sustainable initiatives. The present study addresses this research gap "by investigating how some of Canada's large municipalities are seeking to operationalize the concept of sustainable urban development."

The goal of this volume is to bring to attention the necessity of giving local officials the tools to better understand what they can do with regard to sustainable development. Interdepartmental cooperation and coordination are shown to be of key importance, and the author suggests that local economic and social concerns affecting environmental problems have not been given enough attention. Larger municipalities in Canada are investigated in terms of how they seek to operationalize the concept of sustainable development, and their most innovative and effective efforts are outlined.

Volume 3 (responses to the questionnaire on which the report is based) can also be found in this bibliography.

332. MacNeill, Jim, Peter Winsemiris, and Taizo Yakushiji. *Beyond Interdependence.* New York: Oxford University Press, 1991.

Keywords: ecology, sustainability

The authors of this book maintain that the world has now moved beyond economic interdependence to ecological interdependence. This work was prepared at the request of the Trilateral Commission and builds on, and extends, the argument of the Brundtland Commission's *Our Common Future*. A meshing of the world's economy with the earth's ecology is a new reality with profound implications for government, national and international institutions. Human activity's impact on the biosphere has, in many instances, outstripped that of natural processes. The authors point out that it must be understood that environmental risks pose the greatest threat to our safety, making a widening of the concept of natural security necessary. Key options related to climate changes, forestry, and biodiversity are discussed in detail, along with probable costs of remediation. How industrialized nations can take "unilateral and regional action" to address environmental threats, while improving microeconomic efficiency and international competitiveness, is also addressed.

333. Makower, Joel. *The Green Commuter*. Bethesda, Md.: Tilden Press, 1992.

Keywords: automobiles

The goal of this "consumer guide" type of book is to provide readers with information regarding selecting driving patterns and vehicles that are least harmful to the Earth. The first chapter acknowledges that no matter how or what one drives, it will have a negative impact on the environment. The impacts of automobiles on air pollution, acid rain, global warming, ozone depletion, water pollution, solid waste, land use, health and safety, and national security are outlined. Chapter 2 lists what consumers should look for when buying a car. How to drive, maintain, and dispose of cars in an environmentally responsible manner are the topics of the next three chapters. "Don't Drive" is the title of chapter 6, which lists the benefits of walking, bicycling, carpools, vanpools, taxes, telecommuting, mass transit, and other incentives to reduce driving. Chapter 7 takes a look at emerging technologies and "what's inevitable, what's possible, and what's still some time off." Methanol, ethanol, natural gas, and reformulated gasoline fuelled cars are considered, as are electric cars, solar-powered cars, recycled cars, engine controllers, smart tires, smart highways, greener manufacturing processes, and increased use of plastics. Possibilities for "green" policies are summarized. The handbook concludes by stating how consumers can press manufacturers and government for "greener" cars.

334. Mantell, Michael A., Stephen F. Harper, and Luther Propst. *Creating Successful Communities: A Guidebook to Growth Management Strategies*. Washington, D.C.: Island Press, 1990.

Keywords: current, case studies, community, environmental planning, public space, public policy

Are the aesthetics of your neighborhood being degraded by an onslaught of billboards? Is a local wetland facing undesired development? Want to become involved in neighborhood initiatives but don't know how? This guide by The Conservation Foundation is full of practical advice regarding the above-mentioned situations. The guide was

written in response to the need for concerned citizens to have information on how to preserve important natural and cultural resources. This informative and useful guide presents
step-by-step instructions on how to contact the appropriate politicians, how to inform
yourself of the relevant laws and policies, how to join a nonprofit corporation, and much
more.

The first five chapters deal with specific resources to be conserved or preserved such
as agricultural land, rivers, wetlands, open space, and historic, cultural, and aesthetic resources. Each chapter contains four to six profiles of communities that have worked together to achieve their goal of preservation of open space or a historical site, for example.
How they achieved their goals is outlined in detail. The last two chapters deal with starting and managing a nonprofit corporation and how to work your way into a decision-
making position, again with profiles of community organizations.

335. Marlin, John Tepper. *The Livable Cities Almanac*. New York: HarperCollins, 1992.

Keywords: support, health, health care, quality of life, United States

This book shows people who have the option of choosing their city or neighborhood
how to make the best choice from the perspective of health. It compares the environment
(air and water quality), the disease and mortality rates, the availability of health services,
and other criteria for the major cities in the United States It advises people with particular
ailments which cities to avoid. The primary focus here is on health and quality of life in
specific American urban centers.

336. Masser, Ian, Ove Sviden, and Michael Wegener. *The Geography of Europe's Futures*. London: Belhaven Press, 1992.

Keywords: democracy, economics, environmental pollution, public policy, technology,
telecommunications, transportation

This book was written as part of the work for the Europe 2020 group of the Network
for European Communications and Transport Activities Research (NECTAR). It discusses the possible state of Europe in the year 2020. These predictions are presented as
scenarios that depend on different policies that may be enacted. Three scenarios are presented.

1) in the growth scenario, economic growth is the primary objective of policies.

2) in the equity scenario, policies try to reduce inequalities in society.

3) in the environmental scenario: the quality of life and of the environment are the
primary concerns of policies.

In each scenario, the changes in transport and communication technologies are heavily
emphasized.

The predicted population, lifestyles, economy, environment, regional development,
urban and rural form, goods transport, passenger transport, and communications of each
scenario are presented—first in a one-paragraph summary of each scenario, then in a detailed description. Some of the questions addressed in the scenarios include "Will the
creation of the Single European Market lead to a further concentration of activities in the
core belt stretching from London to Milan?," "What will be the impact on urban and rural
form of the decentralization of economic activities from large urban centers?," "What

will be the socio-economic impacts if the use of the automobile is drastically curtailed for environmental reasons?" and "Will the introduction of fiber optics technology in communications reduce regional disparities within Europe by 2020?"

337. Mathur, Brijesh, ed. *Perspectives on Urban Health.* Winnipeg: Institute of Urban Studies, 1991.

Keywords: support, health

This work is composed of a collection of five papers, a sample of the material presented at the Canadian Urban and Housing Studies Conference, which was hosted by the Institute of Urban Studies in February 1988. These papers share the goal of promoting urban health via public health practices and urban planning.

In the paper "Health and Wellness in the City," Barbara Lane redefines health as a state of well-being, instead of just an absence of disease. The importance of designing new indicators with which to measure health based on this new definition is also emphasized.

In his paper "Health Promotion Approaches," Dexter Harvey describes three approaches to health promotion. Regardless of the approach, it is emphasized that public involvement in the context of life and action directed towards determinants of health are essential components of health promotion.

In "Issues and Problems in Urban Health," Chris Greensmith discusses the health problems associated with an urban environment, especially amongst low-income groups such as Urban Aboriginals. Health is discussed in the context of the urban social environment and emphasis is placed on increasing interpersonal relationships and support networks. The importance of clean air, water, and land to health promotion is also stressed.

Suzanne Jackson focuses on the World Health Organization's European Healthy Cities Project in "The Concept of Healthy Cities." The new view of health, defined by Lane, is premised on the existence of Healthy Cities and health promotion. A list of indicators for measuring Healthy Cities is also provided.

In the final paper, "Healthy Cities: Implications for Urban Planning," Brijesh Mathur discusses the impact of the Healthy Cities Project on urban planning in Canada. The need to incorporate new tools and ideas in planning practice is stressed.

338. McClintock, Hugh, ed. *The Bicycle and City Traffic: Principle and Practice.* London: Belhaven Press, 1992.

Keywords: case studies, transportation

This book assesses current bicycle usage in developed countries as well as the potential for increasing it. Part 1, "Principles" begins by determining the significance of bicycles in city traffic and concludes that it is often underestimated. It is also argues that transport and planning policies have eroded the position of the bicycle. Chapter 2 analyzes bicycle promotion policy in relation to general transportation policies. Opportunities for bicycle promotion through highway planning, traffic management, and town planning policies are the subject of chapter 3. The next chapter contemplates the relationship between public transport and cycling. The need for a balance between planning and engineering measures, as well as road safety education and traffic law measures, is argued for in chapter 5. Part 2, "Practice" consists of seven case studies of bicycle use promotion. Five of the case studies are of cities: Nottingham, Cambridge, London, Groningen (Netherlands), and Odense. The other two studies are of national programs in Germany and the United States.

339. McDowell, Michael E. *The Identification of Man-Made Environmental Hazards to Health: A Manual of Epidemiology.* London: Macmillan, 1987.

Keywords: environmental pollution, epidemiology

This book consists of the collection, analysis, and interpretation of evidence on possible health hazards of anthropogenic environmental pollution. The range and number of possible environmental hazards that have been identified in recent years are unlikely to abate as public awareness of potential dangers increases and the number of harmful substances in the environment also rises.

After the introduction, McDowall first discusses the types of potential environmental health hazards, their biological mechanisms and impacts on human health. Then, epidemiological methods and data for the identification of environmental hazards and their expected levels and statistical significance are analyzed. The problems of establishing causality and providing proof in order to enact policies regarding the substances are also addressed.

340. McGee, T. G. *The Southeast Asian City: A Social Geography of the Primate Cities of Southeast Asia.* New York: Praeger, 1967.

Keywords: developing countries, economics, housing, population, case studies

The growth, characteristics, and roles of the great cities of Southeast Asia are examined in the hope of using the findings to shed light on all of the developing world's cities. The author claims that Southeast Asia is a microcosm of the developing world and thus an ideal region to study.

Much of the material for this study was obtained by the author firsthand on his travels through Southeast Asia. Many of his points are illustrated with case studies of Southeast Asian cities. The phase of primary urbanization, the impact of the West, the colonial city, cult centers, demographics, economics, residential patterns, and slums and squatters are considered in some detail.

McGee, an Australian geographer, states that, unlike European countries' "true urban revolution," developing world countries are undergoing "a phase of pseudo-urbanization." By this, he means that there is little economic development to match the enormous population growth in these cities. There is little expansion in the secondary manufacturing job sector as well. The tremendous increase in low-paying tertiary sector jobs such as street hawkers, pedi-cab drivers, and domestic servants, he argues, is due to the inability of politicians to deal effectively with rural development policies.

341. McGrath, James J., and Charles D. Barnes, ed. *Air Pollution: Physiological Effects.* New York: Academic Press, 1982.

Keywords: air pollution, health

In this volume, investigators from industry, government, and academia review their studies of physiological responses to air pollutants. The authors present the historical basis and theory from which their interest evolved, the current status of their specialized area, and directions for future research. Toxins discussed in detail include sulfur dioxide, carbon monoxide, aerosols, diesel fumes, and lead.

342. Mega, Voula. "Improving the Urban Environment: European Challenges." *Ambio* 23, 7 (1994): 451-54

Keywords: case studies, democracy, green cities, transportation, urban ecology

"The paper presents the first results of a European overview of urban innovations, undertaken by the European Foundation for the Improvement of Living and Working Conditions. Projects have been chosen which improve urban metabolism; have a collective aim; resist time; favor local democracy and participation at the conception, decision and execution phase; and produce models that are transferable to different places. Projects concerned with urban environmental auditing or social justice in cities are extremely important as they can lead to new planning to achieve the European sustainable city." The case studies are interesting but brief. The three main areas examined are ecological factors, transportation, and social innovations.

343. Meyer, William B. *Human Impact on the Earth*. Cambridge: Cambridge University Press, 1996.

Keywords: air pollution, ground pollution, population, water pollution

At a conference in October of 1987, a large group of scientists and scholars gathered to discuss "The Earth as Transformed by Human Action." The major forms of human impact on the earth over the past 300 years, the many human activities that are principally responsible for global environmental transformation, and the environmental history of selected regions around the world were examined in the many presentations by experts. These conference papers led to the publication of a large volume, on which this smaller one is based. Changes made from the larger volume included the updating of information, the amplification of important issues, and the interpretation or clarification of certain points made by the authors in the larger text. This book offers an inventory of human impacts in their varied forms, ranging from long-standing to new and surprising ones that have emerged in recent years. Genuine environmental disasters, and false alarms, as well as success stories of environmental management are also discussed. In looking into the likely fate of the planet, the chapters cover topics such as changes in population and society, land, biota, water, chemical flows, oceans, atmosphere, climate, and three centuries of industrialization "that shook the earth."

344. Michelson, William, Saul V. Levine, and Ellen Michelson. *The Child in the City: Today and Tomorrow*. Vol. 1. Toronto: University of Toronto Press, 1979.

Keywords: support, growing up, children, health, psychological health, sociology

This volume's focus is on the influences of the built environment on children's psychological and physical health—from sociological, psychiatric, and medical perspectives. It includes material on urban planning and spatial design relevant to children's needs, social services, industrialization, daycare and more. Both theoretical and applied research elements are included.

345. Michelson, William, Saul V. Levine, and Anna-Rose Spina. *The Child in the City: Changes and Challenges*. Vol. 2. Toronto: University of Toronto Press, 1979.

Keywords: support, growing up, children, environmental pollution, health, housing, psychological health, sociology, traffic, urban design

This is a companion volume to *The Child in the City: Today and Tomorrow*. Topics include families, community services, childrearing systems, the law, adolescents and ethnic diversity. Chapter 7 (Children and the Urban Physical Environment) is of particular interest to healthy city researchers. It contains material related to scale of environments, pollution, traffic, housing conditions, land-use, children's control over space, and other topics.

346. Middleton, Michael. *Cities in Transition: The Regeneration of Britain's Inner Cities*. London: Michael Joseph, 1991.

Keywords: social fabric, case studies, community, inner cities, quality of life

Cities are always in a state of transition. During the past thirty years, however, British inner cities have succumbed to decay and decline. How has a new interest in urban regeneration that arose in the late 1970s, influenced British cities? What exactly is being done to regenerate cities? A brief look at the current state of affairs—the problems, policies, and programs—makes up part 1. Based on visits to each of the major British conurbations, Michael Middleton provides a study of the following urban regeneration projects in part 2, London's Docklands, Merseyside, Glasgow, South Wales (Swansea-Cardiff-the Valleys), the North East (Tyne and Wear-Teesside, Leeds, Sheffield, Bristol), the West Midlands (Birmingham-the Black Country), Greater Manchester (Manchester-Trafford-Salford), and West Yorkshire (Bradford-Calderdale). Part 3 focuses on specific aspects of regeneration common to many projects such as what to do with derelict land, the power of community initiatives, the role of the arts, and how successful regeneration projects are for improving the quality of life. The lessons learned from these case studies reveal an optimistic outlook without forgetting the chronic deprivation that still exists.

347. Mier, Robert. *Social Justice and Local Development Policy*. Newbury Park, Calif.: Sage Publications, 1993.

Keywords: case studies, community, democracy, economics, public policy

Following a narrative form of storytelling, this book is a compilation of true stories, most reported by the author's mentors, colleagues, and friends. The stories chosen were selected in order to build a broad and deep case for the place of a social justice agenda in local economic development practice. They are both social scientific and phenomenological, and topics vary from shaping policy to implementation and management. Chapter 1 examines the issue of working poverty, and forces any conception of social justice in a work ethic society to confront the structural inadequacies of work. In chapter 2, social justice and public policy are addressed. Chapter 3 builds on the first two by dealing with job generation as a road to recovery. In chapter 4, a shorter version of a longer work entitled "Harold Washington and the Neighborhoods" is given which discusses the political experience of campaigning for, and then forming, the municipal government in Chicago. Chapter 5 entitled "Strategic Planning and the Pursuit of Reform, Economic Development, and Equity" focuses on two features of the campaign plan in chapter 4: its emphasis on a small number of goals and policies and its redistributive thrust. The discussion of implementation continues in chapter 5, "Managing Planned Change." Chapter 7, "Decentralization of Policy Making," looks at how the goals and objectives of the Chicago Works Together plan were reflected in the work of community organizations. The story of a municipal lawsuit to prevent the closing of a toy manufacturing plant at Christmas time is told in chapter 8. Chapter 9, "Spatial Change and Social Justice," continues the story of trying to build toward a national industrial and employment policy through local action. In chapter 10, the Washington experience is summed up by looking at the nature and the role of progressive leadership. The last chapter, "Community Development and Diversity" tries to draw some personal conclusions from the experience of helping formulate and deliver an alternative development agenda.

348. Miller, E. Willard, and Ruby M. Miller. *Environmental Hazards: Toxic Waste and Hazardous Material—A Reference Handbook.* Santa Barbara, Calif.: ABC-CLIO, 1991.

Keywords: environmental pollution, hazardous waste, toxins

The Introduction to this book provides various definitions of wastes and identifies their sources. A description and analysis of the evolution of the awareness of toxic waste and hazardous material in the environment are provided here as well. The introductory chapter concludes with a discussion of some environmental toxic chemicals, waste control technology developments, the transportation of hazardous wastes, and a review of petroleum-based environmental pollution and asbestos control. Chapter 2 has a useful chronology listing some of the critical dates for pesticide control, the identification of major toxic waste sites, chemical accidents, major oil spills, and the enactment of various laws and regulations. Chapter 3 provides an overview of key legislation relating to toxic waste and hazardous material. Chapter 4 provides a directory of organizations that have been established to consider environmental problems. Chapter 5 lists a number of recently published reference manuals, books, journal articles, and government documents on the subject.

349. Mingione, Enzo. ed. *Urban Poverty and the Underclass: A Reader.* Cambridge, Mass.: Blackwell Publishers, 1996.

Keywords: alienation, inner cities, poverty, sociology

"Factories of heightened social privation" is what the editor calls big cities of the North. This collection of articles, which grew out of a UCLA roundtable on urban poverty, explores urban poverty in the North from many angles while trying to define the relationship between urban poverty, discriminated social groups, and decaying areas. Most of all, how urban poverty affects and is affected by sociopolitical systems is contemplated. Part 1, "What is Urban Poverty?" presents various theoretical and analytical frameworks to study urban poverty as a form of social exclusion. Part 2 contains debates regarding the term "underclass" and what it means in terms of ethnicity, class, and culture. Here, most of the cities studied are American. European cities take center stage in part 3, which analyzes empirical data to determine whether economic and social transformations in Europe are exerting pressures to turn urban poverty into social exclusion, as in American cities.

350. Mitchell, William J. *City of Bits: Space, Place and the Infobahn*. Cambridge, Mass.: MIT Press, 1995.

Keywords: architecture, community, economics, telecommunications

In the age of the Internet and apparently ubiquitous digital telecommunication networks, what cities are, what they are for, and how they can be made may have to be rethought. Mitchell reimagines urbanism in this new age characterized by a transition from spatial to antispatial, corporeal to incorporeal, focused to fragmented, synchronous to asynchronous, narrowband to broadband, and contiguous to connected. He comments upon the effect of this new age on the meaning of place, citizens, architecture, cities, business, transport, and communication. He argues that, by understanding the enormous implications of these changes, we can better assist in ensuring that the new digitally mediated environment is conducive to the kinds of cities and communities we want to have.

351. Moeller, Dade W. *Environmental Health*. Cambridge, Mass.: Harvard University Press, 1992.

Keywords: air pollution, electromagnetic fields and health, energy, environmental pollution, food, occupational health, risk assessment, sewage, waste, water

The author's own words summarize the book accurately: "Many aspects of human well-being are influenced by the environment, and many diseases can be initiated, sustained, or exacerbated by environmental factors. For that reason, understanding and controlling people's interactions with their environment is an important component of public health. In its broadest sense, environmental health is the subfield of public health concerned with assessing and controlling the impacts of people on their environment (including vegetation, other animals, and natural and historic landmarks) and the impacts of the environment on them.

"The field of environmental health is defined more by the problems faced than by the specific approaches used. These problems include the treatment and disposal of liquid and airborne wastes, the elimination or reduction of stresses in the workplace, purification of drinking-water supplies, the impacts of overpopulation and inadequate or unsafe food supplies, and the development and use of measures to protect hospital and other medical workers from being infected with diseases such as acquired immune deficiency syndrome (AIDS). Environmental health professionals also face long-range problems, including the effects of toxic chemicals and radioactive waste, acidic deposition, depletion of the ozone layer, and global warming. The complexity of these issues requires multidisciplinary approaches for their evaluation and control. A team coping with a major environmental health problem may include scientists, physicians, epidemiologists, engineers, economists, lawyers, mathematicians, and managers. Input from all these experts is essential to the development and success of broad strategies that take into account both lifestyles and the environment."

There is some emphasis in this work on a systems approach in terms of methodology. Air, water, sewage, food, solid waste, rodents, and insects are studied as possible carriers of environmental hazards. Other topics examined include the workplace, injury control, electromagnetic radiation, standards, monitoring, energy, and disaster response.

352. Mogridge, Marten J. H. *Travel in Towns*. London: Macmillan, 1990.

Keywords: automobiles, transportation

This book is a summary of a series of research papers on how to improve transportation in towns. It comments on popular misconceptions about transport policy and tries to explain the complexity of behavior that confounds transport planning. What follows is a rigorous discussion of various economic theories to analyze the option costs associated with transport—from road pricing to light rail, commuter terminals to continuous bus lanes. The works of economists Marshall, Pigou, Edgeworth, and others are examined to throw light on this subject.

353. Montanari, Armando, Gerhard Curdes, and Leslie Forsyth, eds. *Urban Landscape Dynamics: A Multi-Level Innovation Process*. Aldershot, England: Avebury, 1993.

Keywords: transformation, case studies, land use, transportation, urban planning

This work is divided into two parts. Part 1 looks at actual innovations in a select urban sample and shows the many transformations that have occurred in response to new technologies, changing economies, and the diffusion of new cultures. Part 2 is a compendium of thematic papers on the development of innovative processes and their impact on land use and urban form. Some of the innovations are in the areas of transportation, town planning, city centers, and waterfronts.

354. Moore, Curtis. "Greenest City in the World!" *International Wildlife* (January/ February 1994): 38-43.

Keywords: transformation, case studies, green cities, transportation, waste

The article outlines the various strategies that have made Curitiba, Brazil "the ultimate human environment." The city's success is attributed to its transportation system and recycling/garbage schemes. Special lanes are reserved for the efficient bus system. Residents can trade bags of garbage for food. This saves money on garbage collection, ensures clean streets and provides local farmers with income (from the government's food purchases). Local children explain garbage separation to adults. As a result, the city has one of the highest recycling rates in the world. The article also contains a short comparison of other cities' strategies for dealing with skyrocketing automobile use.

355. Moore, Terry, and Paul Thorsens. *The Transportation/Land Use Connection: A Framework for Practical Policy*. Chicago: APA, Planning Advisory Service, 1994.

Keywords: land use, public policy, transportation

This report presents a framework for evaluating land-use and transportation policies. Transportation planners are now considering policies that go well beyond more and better highways—the traditional engineering solution to traffic congestion. Most involve complementary changes in land-use and transportation policies coordinated at the regional level. Such policies include:
-improving the quantity and quality of infrastructure that serves pedestrians, bicyclists, and high-occupancy vehicles
  -increasing the price of auto travel relative to other modes of travel
  -regulating more directly the design of new development
  -restricting the spread of urban expansion
  -encouraging or requiring suburban development to be at higher densities
  -creating nodes of new high-intensity development

356. Morris, David. *Self-Reliant Cities: Energy and the Transformation of Urban America*. San Francisco: Sierra Club Books, 1982.

Keywords: current, energy, energy efficiency, sustainability

American cities have been transformed by changing sources and forms of energy. Part 1, "Losing Control" chronicles the development of small, independent, self-sufficient villages into large cities dependent on imported fuels and materials. This part focuses on the period from 1870 to 1970, during which oil prices fell continuously. The cities' increasing dependence on remote corporations and governments and the loss of citizens' economic and political power are emphasized. On the other hand, part 2, "Gaining Autonomy" reports optimistically on cities' attempts at gaining self-reliance in "the age of expensive energy." Technological, institutional, and financial changes that are leading to increased local control and sustainability are considered. Morris predicts and calls for cities with humanly scaled energy systems, completely restructured waste disposal and transportation systems, and financing from the energy utility and the municipal corporation.

357. Moudon, Anne Vernez. *Public Streets for Public Use*. New York: Van Nostrand Reinhold, 1987.

Keywords: social fabric, transportation, democracy, health, pedestrians, safety, streets

The author explains that now "Urban designers have the opportunity to offer a new view of what streets are all about. Traditionally, highway engineering, which until recently dominated the management and design of streets, has tended to support only the travelers who use streets and especially those with motorized vehicles. Urban designers can view streets more broadly; they are for all users and for many more purposes than simply transportation. It is important, though, to understand the full range of groups that participate in streets and, conversely, the full range of opportunities that streets can offer to each individual.

"It is the urban designer's and the highway engineer's task to work out ingenious solutions for the design and the use of street spaces and to optimize the participation and satisfaction of the maximum possible numbers of different people and groups." An excellent addition to the literature on streets.

358. Moughtin, Cliff. *Urban Design: Green Dimensions*. Oxford: Bath Press, 1996.

Keywords: current, architecture, built environment, buildings—social aspects, energy, environmental pollution, transportation, urban design

At a time when we fear the greenhouse effect, when pollution is on the rise, the ozone layer is being destroyed, and natural resources are declining, any discussions of urban form or design must address environmental issues. This stems from the strong links between the physical characteristics of our cities, the ways in which they are designed, and the different levels of negative environmental impact which will result from each individual design decision. The central focus of this book is sustainable city development, which is regarded as development that is nondamaging to the environment and which contributes to the city's ability to sustain its social and economic structures. The problem of defining quality in urban design is explored, and evaluated in terms of its impact on the global environment. This book attempts to come to terms with the phrase "sustainable development" and to outline its place and meaning within society, and then formulates principles of urban design based on the acceptance of this particular environmental outlook. Chapter 2 deals with the development of a building process that minimizes pollution. Chapter 3 delves into the relationship among transport, energy, and pollution. A sustainable transport system is then outlined, and finally, the regional and local political and administrative structures necessary for achieving a sustainable transport system are discussed. The need for public participation in the design, development, and management of the system is also emphasized.

359. Moulaert, Frank, and Allen J. Scott, eds. *Cities, Enterprises and Society on the Eve of the 21st Century*. London: Pinter, 1997.

Keywords: current, economics

This collection of essays by leading scholars provides an up-to-date review and restatement of concepts and analytical insights about the dynamics of the production system and urban society. A number of key questions underline the arrangement of the book and constitute the central debates in the individual chapters:

-How have large cities and city systems developed in the context of economic globalization and the restructuring processes of the international economy?

-What are the restructuring strategies of firms within the urban economy, and how does the urban economy relate to regional, national, and international space?

-How have social and political harmonization and polarization in urban society been affected by entrepreneurial strategies?

-What has been the response of other urban participants, local authorities in particular, to economic restructuring?

Although informative, this book is difficult to read for those readers not well versed in political and economic theory.

360. Mumford, Lewis. *The City in History: Its Origins, Its Transformations, and Its Prospects*. New York: Harcourt, Brace & World, 1961.

Keywords: sociology, technology

At 657 pages, this is an extremely comprehensive treatment of the city's history in western civilization. Mumford notes in the preface that, because of his unfamiliarity with the regions, material on Spain, Latin America, Palestine, Eastern Europe, and Soviet Russia is not included. The purpose of this look back in time is to understand the historic nature of the city in order to be able to improve current urban life and work towards a utopia, rather than the "dreary mechanical caricatures" that today's cities are becoming.

The study of the city's 5000-year history begins with hunting camps, early farming villages, and the first cities of Egypt and Mesopotamia, and continues through to the post-World War II emergence of suburbia. After studying the city's past, the current situation of cities is considered. Mumford states that humanity is now at a crossroad. We can either develop cities by incorporating our deepest humanity or surrender to our dehumanized alter ego, "Post-historic Man," and contribute to the loss of feeling and creativity in the modern city.

361. Munn, Jon. "Sweat and Equity: CoHousing Comes to Langley." *City Magazine* 14, 3 (Summer 1993): 25-7.

Keywords: social fabric, case studies, community, democracy, neighborhood

The author provides an outline of the CoHousing project in Langley, B.C. It is designed by the residents to be pedestrian-friendly, to respect the natural landscape, and to foster a cooperative community atmosphere. The remainder of the article consists of anecdotal evidence of the fully participatory and cooperative nature of the CoHousing planning process.

362. Murphy, D. C. *Industrial Pollution: A Guide to Assessment and Control*. London: Industrial and Commercial Techniques, 1972.

Keywords: transformation, health, industrial pollution, occupational health, work environment

This small book provides a summary of early methods of occupational hygiene and pollution control in industry. Occupational hygiene is defined as the science of the preservation of health and is devoted to the recognition, evaluation, and control of those environmental factors or stressors, arising in or from the workplace, that may cause sickness, impaired health and well-being, or significant discomfort and inefficiency among workers or among citizens of the community. Specific stressors that are studied are air pollutants, noise, radiation, and heat.

363. Myers, Norman, ed. *Gaia: An Atlas of Planet Management*. 2nd ed. New York: Anchor Books, 1993.

Keywords: current, democracy, developing countries, ecology, environmental pollution, population, poverty, sustainability

Every page of this definitive guide to our planet and our problems is filled with colorful and striking charts, maps, graphs, diagrams, and photos that at a glance reveal more than the accompanying text. The book provides a superb and detailed overview of the current state of the environment and projected future states depending on what actions we take now. The book is divided into sections entitled Land, Ocean, Elements, Evolution, Humankind, Civilization, and Management. Within the Humankind section, "Health for All" (pp.190-91) is relevant to healthy cities for it discusses prevention, alternative medicine, barefoot doctors, regional hospitals and the main problems of health care in the North and in the South. Another section of great relevance to healthy cities is "Chaos in the Cities" (pp. 206-207). The exodus of the rich from northern cities and the massive influx of the poor into southern cities is explained here. As well, "Managing Our Civilization" (pp. 218-229) examines the interdependence between the North and South and between cities and the countryside and includes a section on urban regeneration.

364. Nadis, Steve, and Jane J. Mackenzie. *Car Trouble*. Boston: Beacon Press, 1993.

Keywords: automobiles, environmental pollution, social ecology, transportation

As the title suggests, the topic of this book is the problem of excessive reliance on the car. The historical development and reasons for current patterns of car use are probed in some detail before moving on to a review of the critical consequences of this use. Among the primary concerns are oil-dependence on the Persian Gulf, release of CFCs from car air-conditioners, carbon monoxide and carbon dioxide emissions, and ozone emissions. Predictions of a catastrophic future are made unless drastic action is taken to wean society from the car. The problem of why public policy is tilted toward automobile use is cogently discussed. Various solutions are suggested. These range from legislation to mandate changes in transportation policy to energy taxes to make gasoline prices reflect the social, environmental, and defense-related costs of gasoline. Another incentive for fuel-efficient automobiles is increased competitiveness of the American car industry with that of the Japanese. New technologies, "clean fuels," and "smart cars" are also explored. Information and strategies are offered concerning new electric, solar, and "hybrid" cars, policies necessary to eliminate oil use and encourage the use of alternative fuels, and how to rate current car models to assist consumers in choosing the "greenest" option.

365. Nasar, Jack L. *The Evaluative Image of the City*. Thousand Oaks, Calif.: Sage Publications, 1998.

Keywords: urban design, experience of place

How people evaluate the landscape directly influences their feelings and behavior. This thesis has been explored in the works of Kevin Lynch (whom the present author follows) and Christopher Alexander. The present work extends the ideas of Lynch by further exploring the role of human evaluations of the cityscape. Nasar's perceptive analysis provides a useful guide to how one can improve the image of one's surroundings to make them more pleasing. Designers and planners will find the book particularly valuable since Nasar gives detailed descriptions of how to assess, plan, and design the appearance of cities to make them much more satisfying for their inhabitants.

366. National Research Council. *Environmental Epidemiology: Public Health and Hazardous Wastes*. Washington, D.C.: National Academy Press, 1991.

Keywords: output, biosphere, air pollution, environmental pollution, epidemiology, food, ground pollution, health, hazardous waste, water pollution

Environmental Epidemiology: Public Health and Hazardous Wastes presents the results of studies of hazardous wastes in air, water, soil, and food, reviews the available evidence on the risk of exposure to toxic materials, and makes recommendations for filling gaps in the data on risk and improving health assessments. The volume also explores the results of substantial state and federal programs on hazardous waste sites and the potential uses of biologic markers in health risk assessment. Particular attention is given to the problems associated with exposure monitoring and assessment, air exposures, domestic water consumption, and soil and food as potential sources of exposure at hazardous waste sites.

367. Nelson, Gene C. "Office Building Saves Costs with Free Cooling and Peak Shaving Systems." *ASHRAE Journal* 36, 3 (1994): 32-40.

Keywords: transformation, case studies, energy, energy efficiency

This article is written by an engineer who entered his design for the American Family Insurance National Headquarters Facility in the ASHRAE Technology Awards for energy saving designs. The new building won second place in the commercial buildings category. The office building incorporates a free cooling system, variable volume chilled water pumping, and a mini-supervisor control and data acquisition (MSCADA) system. The article mainly consists of the specifications and descriptions of the cooling and energy systems. It also lists the design features that were included to ensure adequate indoor air quality.

368. Newman, Oscar. *Defensible Space: Crime Prevention through Urban Design*. New York: Macmillan, 1972.

Keywords: built environment, buildings—social aspects, experience of place

This important work examines one aspect of how environment affects behavior. Specifically, the book examines how the built form can encourage criminal behavior by disempowering its inhabitants, or prevent it by giving them a sense of "defensible space." The book is aimed at a wide readership: from architects, police, city planners and housing developers, to academics and the general public. It backs up its assertions with a significant empirical component. The findings of this book are now an accepted part of the vocabulary of new housing developments and urban renewal projects.

369. Newman, Peter and Jeffrey Kenworthy. *Cities and Automobile Dependence: An International Sourcebook*. Aldershot, England: Gower Publishing, 1989.

Keywords: automobiles, transportation

How can we reduce automobile dependence in cities? This is the main question addressed in this valuable book. The authors realize that a deep understanding of the relationship between a city's social, economic, and environmental aspects is essential. They traveled to thirty-two world cities to collect data on approximately 100 parameters for the years 1960, 1970, and 1980. After the introductory chapter, the authors discuss the methodology used in their research. Chapter 3 contains the main findings of the study using data from 1980. The data reveal that patterns in gasoline use are related to many urban form parameters. The characteristics of both high gasoline/high car use cities and low gasoline/low car use cities are defined using factor and cluster analysis.

Other parameters that explain urban transport patterns are the focus of chapter 4. Geographic, economic, political, technological, and demographic factors are carefully analyzed. This analysis provides some suggestions for policies that would reduce urban automobile dependence. These policies are presented under the following two main headings in the fifth chapter: reurbanization (focus on the central city and focus on urban density) and reorientation of transport priorities (focus on congestion). Following this, all of the collected data are presented in two sections. The first one contains raw data on urban transport and land use. The second one consists of standardized data deduced from the raw data, such as urban density.

370. Newman, Peter, and Jeffrey Kenworthy. *The City and Automobile Dependence.* Aldershot, England: Avebury, 1989.

Keywords: automobiles, energy, transportation, urban planning

This volume is a rich source of data on the links among urban land use, transport, and energy for cities in North America, Asia, Europe, and Australia. The interpretation of the data suggests that transport and planning agencies can play a much greater role in reducing automobile and gas dependence. The authors' analysis of the data is a valuable contribution to transport policy and helps to articulate many feasible goals. Their discussion of various policies for reurbanization and the reorganization of transportation priorities reveals strategies that can reduce dependence on the automobile with attendant economic and environmental benefits. Useful descriptions of city forms that reduce car use enhance the value of this book.

371. Newson, Malcolm, ed. *Managing the Human Impact on the Natural Environment: Patterns and Processes.* London: Belhaven Press, 1992.

Keywords: biosphere, ecology, energy, environmental pollution, sustainability, waste

The contributors bring a holistic geographical perspective to environmental pollution. The first part of the textbook focuses on how people affect the biosphere by presenting an historical overview of the changing attitudes toward the natural environment. Then, the geography of pollution and the geography of conservation are introduced. Environmental law and environmental economics as means of promoting a more sustainable relationship with the Earth are also studied. Practices are the focus of the second part of the text. Management and monitoring of air, water, and land pollution as well as emergency planning issues are covered. In the last section, entitled "Futures," an attempt is made to assess present and future trends in environmental management. The management of radiation in the environment and implications of future energy supply and use are two aspects of this assessment. How does the Gaia hypothesis influence our concept of environmental management? Stevenson and Newson contend that optimistic scenarios of recovery and restoration are realistic for some natural systems. A holistic approach to environmental management is sketched out in the final chapter, in terms of controlling pollution, environmental planning, and data collection. Although the text does not adopt an urban perspective, the general background on the state of the biosphere and the strategies for management are useful for healthy cities studies.

372. Nicholson-Lord, David. *The Greening of the Cities*. London: Routledge & Kegan Paul, 1987.

Keywords: current, case studies, ecology, green cities, land use, urban ecology

During the past thirty years, cities have undergone great demographic, technological, and cultural changes. At the same time, the environmental movement has emerged as a significant force for change. So how can the environmental movement be applied to improving cities? This is the central question asked in this work. It traces the historical roots of urbanism, nature, and wilderness and how these ideas were expressed in English landscaping. Then, current "greening" initiatives in England are described and analyzed. Many of the ideas presented are similar to the Garden Cities movement. British cities, especially London, are the focus of this study which reminds readers of the inextricable links between a city and its hinterland.

373. Nieuwenhuis, Paul, and Peter Wells, eds. *Motor Vehicles in the Environment: Principles and Practice*. Chichester, West Sussex: John Wiley & Sons, 1994.

Keywords: automobiles, public policy, transportation

"Although public opinion in much of the industrialized world has turned 'green,' confusion still remains as to the implications for the motor industry. Will the car survive, and if so in what form? Can we afford to do without the motor industry, and can we distribute our goods without tracks? *Motor Vehicles in the Environment* highlights a number of issues which form the basis of future legislation affecting the motor industry. It offers a series of perspectives ranging from 'green,' governmental, economic and marketing issues, to the impact on a specific sector of the industry . . . experts analyze the implications of the green revolution for their specialist fields and areas of interest."

The book offers an analysis of a wide range of issues that result from the "greening" of the transportation industry. Bicycle and light rail transport is considered. The implications of "greening" are considered for the truck and automotive presswork industry. The book also contains a chapter on the seldom-addressed topics of the long-life car and car disposal.

374. Nijkamp, P., and S. Reichman. *Transportation Planning in a Changing World*. Aldershot, England: Gower Publishing, 1987.

Keywords: interdisciplinary studies, transportation

This volume is the outcome of a series of three international workshops on transportation sponsored by the European Science Foundation. The main theme of this book is that transportation issues are not merely technical in nature, but have complex social and economic dimensions as well. This necessarily calls for a contextual interdisciplinary approach to problem solving, and this text makes an admirable contribution in this regard. There is a persistent attempt to bridge the gap between technological and social perspectives throughout the book, and insights are imported from economics, geography, sociology, and ecology to shed light on transportation problems.

The book is divided into the following four sections:
1) Identifying main transportation concerns presently faced
2) Transportation as an industrialized procedure
3) Methodological considerations
4) Policy making

375. Nijkamp, Peter, ed. *Sustainability of Urban Systems: A Cross-National Evolutionary Analysis of Urban Innovation.* Aldershot, England: Avebury, 1990.

Keywords: case studies, sustainability

This publication contains international, comparative, urban research prepared by the Urban Innovation Network and focuses on sustainability in the urban context. Sustainability in this book refers to the resilience of various natural and social systems in the face of dynamic urban changes. The Introduction clarifies the notion of sustainability and subsequent chapters contain case studies. Research and innovative contributions from different countries are brought together, as are comparative methodology/theory. Response to difficulties and the learning process required to analyze changing multidimensional urban systems at the international level are also outlined. Structural urban evolution is dealt with from the viewpoint of innovation (the change of all activities, lifestyles, or institutions brought into being to solve problems related to city life) as the main mechanism. The book ends with a discussion of various practical considerations in implementing sustainability.

376. Norquist, John O. *The Wealth of Cities: Revitalizing the Centers of American Life.* Reading, Mass.: Addison-Wesley, 1998.

Keywords: economics, urban planning, suburbs, inner cities

Many federal and state policies—some designed to help cities—have deeply harmed American cities, mainly by encouraging suburban sprawl. Sprawl, in turn, has eviscerated once thriving urban centers, turning them into pathological entities. Norquist discusses the steps that must be taken, mainly by cities themselves, through which they may once again thrive, both naturally and organically. Budgeting, management, public safety, and design principles are outlined in this regard. Federal and state policies are criticized for making large parts of the United States into a sprawling collection of faceless places, neither rural nor urban, and with no lasting value. What new policies must replace these are then outlined. *The Wealth of Cities* is for taxpayers, mayors, bureaucrats, scholars, investors, developers, and homeowners. It is meant to speak for those who love cities but have forgotten why, and it seeks to persuade those who have never loved cities that they are worthy, if not of love, at least of respect, and to realize that cities add value to the nation.

377. Nozick, Marcia. *No Place Like Home: Building Sustainable Communities*. Ottawa: Canadian Council on Social Development, 1992.

Keywords: social fabric, community, democracy, sustainability

After arguing for the desperate need for sustainable communities, Marcia Nozick sets out to instruct citizens how to go about developing them. Self-reliance, the local economy, ecological design, culture, and social and material needs are the areas addressed with an emphasis on grassroots and community action. This readable account is full of common-sense arguments and simple workable schemes.

378. O'Loughlin, John, and Jürgen Friedrichs, eds. *Social Polarization in Post-Industrial Metropolises*. Berlin: Walter de Gruyter, 1996.

Keywords: support, case studies, economics, social ecology

Global economic restructuring is a major influence on the demographics, economics, and social structure of cities. This collection studies the impact of global economic restructuring on polarization. The global trends are clearly discernible, for example, in the trend of deindustrialization through a reduction in Fordist production and labor unions, but impacts vary from city to city. This is the main thesis that is developed in this book, which consists of case studies of eleven post-industrial cities. These case studies address the following four questions:
   1) Why does the city fit the "post-industrial restructuring" profile?
   2) What economic, demographic, and social changes have taken place between 1960 and 1991?
   3) What is the relationship between the changes mentioned in (1) and (2) and what are the spatial implications?
   4) What are the relationships between international, national, regional, and household analyses of the above?

379. O'Riordan, Tim, ed. *Ecotaxation*. London: Earthscan, 1997.

Keywords: economics

This book considers two approaches to placing a monetary value on pollution. The first is the "polluter pays" approach—one that forces those who contribute to bear the financial burden of their behavior. The second is a new approach to environmental taxation. It involves a shift from taxing income and labor to taxing activities with negative environmental impact. It is an interesting approach to one of the challenges of sustainable development: linking the economy with the environment.

380. Oberlander, H. Peter, ed. *Improving Human Settlements: Up with People*. Vancou-

ver: University of British Columbia Press, 1976.

Keywords: current, architecture, developing countries, housing, inner cities, population

The authors of the articles in this volume are from both developed and developing nations and are all actively engaged in their respective countries in determining how best to cope with the problems of rapid population growth and widespread urbanization. The papers range from discussions of overcrowding in India and other areas of extremely dense population, to the effect of settlement on previously sparsely populated areas such as Canada's north and the tendency even in such environments for the population to concentrate in urban centers rather than remain scattered in smaller communities. A discussion of the ethical and moral principles that must govern our response to accelerating population growth in order that humankind survive is also included. These papers were presented at the University of British Columbia between February and May 1976 in preparation for the UN Conference on Human Settlements: Habitat '76.

381. Organization for Economic Cooperation and Development (OECD), Group on Urban Affairs. *Environmental Policies for Cities in the 1990s*. Paris: OECD, 1990.

Keywords: current, case studies, green cities, public policy, sustainability, urban design

Individually and collectively, cities must contribute to sustainable development through short-term policies within a long-term perspective. What policies are effective and how can they be implemented? This report is the result of a three-year inquiry into twenty cities that asked this question. The case studies investigate existing urban environmental improvement policies. Chapter 1, "The Nature of the Challenge," reviews the state of urban environments, their problems, and the contributing factors such as changing economic structures, changing societal values, intervention failures, and market failures. Why are urban initiatives for environmental problems necessary? What are the present approaches? What future policy directions are desirable? These three questions are addressed in the second chapter. Certain organizational and institutional mechanisms are required to integrate urban sustainability projects into government agendas. These are outlined in chapter 3, along with available policy instruments that internalize environmental costs into urban development strategies. Financing, short and long term impacts, and feasibility of urban rehabilitation, transport, and energy are the focus of the fourth and final chapter. The case studies are presented as brief insets throughout the report.

382. Organization for Economic Cooperation and Development (OECD). *The World in 2020: Toward a New Global Age*. Paris: OECD, 1997.

Keywords: sustainability, economics

This publication sets out a vision of the world economy in the year 2020 where governments and societies seize the challenge of realizing a new age of global prosperity. This will not happen automatically. Firm policies to guide the economy, the built habitat, and energy use will be required. Innovative policy responses to make future development sustainable are examined here in some detail.

383. Organization for Economic Cooperation and Development (OECD). *Urban Energy Handbook, Good Local Practice*. Paris: OECD, 1995.

Keywords: transformation, case studies, energy, energy efficiency, sustainability, transportation

"This handbook describes some of the more significant forms of innovation which are now being used in OECD cities to improve the effectiveness and efficiency of urban energy management and their implications for wider questions of urban sustainability. In particular, this handbook assesses managerial, technical, and institutional options which can be used to deal with energy-related environmental problems in cities. It also proposes ways and means to improve the co-ordination of energy policies and the integration of environmental considerations in policy-making." This collection includes case studies material relating to initiatives such as energy conservation, energy efficiency, and co-generation in several countries, including Canada.

384. Outerbridge, Thomas. "The Big Backyard: Composting Strategies in New York City." *The Ecologist* 24, 3 (May/June 1994): 106-9.

Keywords: output, case studies, waste

"Massive quantities of organic waste are produced every day in New York City, a high percentage of which could be safely and economically composted. Pilot schemes have shown that composting is technically feasible, but there are difficulties in sorting, collection and transport. Nevertheless, New Yorkers are moving ahead on several fronts to find creative solutions to these obstacles so as to develop a comprehensive composting system that might enhance the local, national and even global environment." The article provides an interesting look at New York's pilot project.

385. Owen, Stephen. *Planning Settlements Naturally*. Chichester: Packard Publishing Limited, 1991.

Keywords: current, ecology, green space, land use, urban planning

Planners must sensitively and carefully integrate the natural environment into their work. This is the position put forth and clearly defended in this useful book. It is true that natural environments are not usually considered in the planning of cities and towns, although doing so can contribute to a preventively oriented design of healthy cities. The author seeks to provide the enduring principles of healthy settlements that come out of studying the relationship among nature, settlements, and planning. He shows how landforms, sunshine, wind, water, vegetation, and wildlife habitats can influence the planning process and how their consideration leads to more pleasant communities. Guidelines for improved local planning practice are presented through examples.

386. Owens, Susan. *Energy, Planning and Urban Form*. London: Pion, 1986.
Keywords: case studies, energy, energy efficiency

The energy crisis of the 1970s forced planners to integrate energy considerations into the planning process. This preventive approach is necessary for healthy cities, so Susan Owens is curious as to whether this idea has been put into practice. She takes stock of energy-integrated planning in Britain, the United States, Denmark and Australia. More specifically, she summarizes what has been learned regarding the energy-land use relationship in theory, and points out policy implications, problems, constraints, and successes. Chapter 2 ponders the possible impact of energy constraints on urban and regional trends. Chapter 3 considers planning to reduce transport energy requirements while the reduction of energy requirements in buildings is the topic of chapter 4. Chapter 5 synthesizes the lessons learned from energy-efficient environments. The case studies are analyzed in the final chapter to yield criteria for successful energy-integrated planning. Owens' book is essential reading for those interested in exploring the link between energy and urban form.

387. Palen, John J. *The Suburbs*. New York: McGraw-Hill, 1995.

Keywords: social fabric, community, suburbs, utopia

Contrary to popular opinion, some suburbs have more office workers and office space than traditional downtowns. They are also multicultural and are not just residential areas but contain significant retail, employment, and administrative opportunities. The author examines the scope and nature of contemporary suburbia and dismisses many misconceptions. The book also contains significant historical content in which the evolution of suburbs is traced from nineteenth-century affluent railroad suburbs to early twentieth century streetcar suburbs, to rapid post-WWII suburbanization and to the more complex and diverse suburbia.

There are four chapters most relevant to healthy cities. The chapter that discusses minorities in suburbia dispels the myth of the all-white suburb. The chapter on women and family posits that the suburban home changed family activity patterns. Chapter 10, "Contemporary Issues and Problems," deals with zoning, growth policies, crime, and political representation. Another chapter focuses on planned suburbs such as romantic/garden suburbs, railroad suburbs, streetcar suburbs, "planned utopias," New Towns, neotraditional developments, and retirement communities, and gives examples of each.

388. Papanek, Victor. *The Green Imperative: Ecology and Ethics in Design & Architecture*. London: Thames and Hudson, 1995.

Keywords: transformation, architecture, sustainability, design

Design and architecture should be spiritual and sustainable. This is the principle that the designer Victor Papanek passionately and convincingly puts forward in this book. Designers and architects, he feels, have a special obligation to ensure that their work will contribute to human and ecological well-being. By using fascinating examples from various cultures and 162 illustrations, Papanek explains his spiritually satisfying approach to design, as well as how objects, places, and buildings affect us.

Chapter 1 outlines the environmental crisis and how responsible design can help to heal the biosphere. Chapter 2 continues to summarize the problems of over-consumption and how green design, re-use, and using less material can combat the problem. The third chapter provides guidelines to designers to include the spiritual in design. They must ask questions such as "Will the design significantly aid the sustainability of the environment? Can it make life easier for some group that has been marginalized by society? Can it ease pain? Will it help those who are poor, disenfranchised or suffering? Will it save energy or—better still—help to gain renewable energies? Can it save irreplaceable resources?"

We sense a dwelling not only through sight, but by the mood, the lighting, the texture beneath our feet and against our skin, smells, sounds and rhythms, body movement, and the organic geometry. Our biogenetic heritage, and how it has influenced us to be more receptive to, and pleased by, certain forms, is emphasized. More directly related to healthy cities is chapter 5, "The Biotechnology of Communities." Here, Papanek once again calls on history and our collective unconscious to assert that certain magic numbers exist for ideal community and meeting place sizes. The importance of having a center, of not focussing on motorized traffic, and of a suitable site is emphasized. The concept of vernacular architecture, its myths, and examples are the focus of the sixth chapter.

Chapter 7, "Form Follows Fun," continues to criticize current design principles based on short-life, trendiness, and fun for the moment. "Is Convenience the Enemy?" is the title of chapter 8. It expresses the author's disgust with design for greed, not need. He notes ten "convenience" traps: too small, too powerful, too many, too much, too complex, too "improved," buying on impulse, too untested, "state of the art," and package as product. Many objects such as lawnmowers, snowblowers, and vacuum cleaners are great candidates for sharing among community members. This "Sharing not Buying" principle is expanded upon in chapter 9.

Chapter 10 addresses the issue of the education of future designers. How can ethical design be made an important part of this education? Who are the best designers in the world? The answer is easy, Papanek says in chapter 11; the Inuit are. Their astounding design skills are revealed through examples. Chapter 12 concludes the book by summarizing the proposed design concepts and restating that we must recognize "the proper place of what we do in terms of the ever-present now as well as the lasting . . . [and] help to ensure a future of fleeting episodes that will form a rich web of permanence through continuity."

389. Park, Robert E., Ernest W. Burgess, and Roderick D. McKenzie. *The City*. 2nd (1967) ed. Chicago: University of Chicago Press, 1925.

Keywords: alienation, psychological health, quality of life, urban sociology

The Chicago school of urban sociology had a strong influence on the study of cities between 1915 and 1940. This book is one of its representative works. The Chicago school's ecological model sought to understand urban processes in terms of the economics of space and land and population movement. Their views of the city were largely negative, probably due to the perceived unhappiness of the large influx of European and rural immigrants at the time. They sought to explain the problems these new urbanites encountered. The Chicago school sociologists argue that competitive and impersonal city life was difficult to adjust to, since these immigrants came from close-knit communities. They explore the issues of integration, marginalization, and the requirements for an urban community.

This book contains theoretical expositions and interpretive essays regarding the cultural patterns of urban life. The authors—along with their fellow Chicago school sociologists—were known for their fascination with discovering patterns in what initially appeared to be urban chaos. Issues addressed in this book include specific ones such as the history of the newspaper, juvenile delinquency, and hobos, as well as more general topics such as mental well-being.

390. Patterson, Jeffrey. "Urban Public Transit and Sustainable Cities." *Sustainable Cities (IUS newsletter supplement)*, 1993, 1-9.

Keywords: environmental pollution, transportation, Canada

Recent trends in public transit use indicate that ridership is declining. This article presents the results of a detailed study of twelve Canadian cities' public transit systems. After establishing an upward trend in ridership between 1965 and 1986 and a downward trend between 1986 and 1991, the researchers attempt to correlate these trends to various city characteristics, particularly density. They find a positive correlation between transit rides per capita and density of urbanized area.

The article also explains the impact of urban transportation on air quality. The effects of sulfur dioxide, nitrogen dioxide, ozone, carbon monoxide, particulate matter, VOCs and greenhouse gases are discussed. The impact of motorized transport on water and soil quality and energy use is cited and it is noted that automobiles also cause or contribute to various social and economic problems. Thus it is concluded that greater use of public transit and reduced reliance on the automobile are requirements for healthier cities.

391. Paustenbach, Dennis J., ed. *The Risk Assessment of Environmental and Human Health Hazards: A Textbook of Case Studies*. New York: John Wiley & Sons, 1989.

Keywords: air pollution, case studies, epidemiology, hazardous waste, occupational health, risk assessment, water pollution

In spite of the importance of risk assessments, the scientist who wishes to learn how to develop an analysis of a potential or alleged health hazard is hard-pressed to know where to begin. Very few environmental assessments describing the likelihood of an adverse effect following repeated low-level exposures to a chemical have been published in the scientific literature, perhaps fewer than a dozen.

The purpose of this text is to help advance the art of risk assessment by sharing high-quality examples prepared by the foremost authorities within the scientific community. Emphasis has been placed on assessments that evaluate the potential health hazards associated with exposure to chemical and physical agents in our environment. This is a very good resource for case studies information on the assessment of water contaminants, hazardous waste sites, air contaminants, occupational hazards, potential hazards to consumers, and the risks to wildlife.

392. Peirce, Neal R., and Robert Guskind. *Breakthroughs: Re-creating the American City*. New Brunswick, N.J.: Center for Urban Policy Research, 1993.

Keywords: community, urban planning, inner cities

The Rudy Bruner Award for Excellence in the Urban Environment was founded in 1986 to recognize positive urban transformations. This book describes six award-winning projects, which came about through the collective action of citizens, bureaucrats, and entire communities. Four of these projects are urban and two rural. The urban projects include New York City's Tenant Interim Lease Program, a landmark housing program that has enabled thousands of America's poorest minority people to become owners of their own apartments. Portland's Downtown Plan of 1972 is next credited for transforming the city's Willamette riverfront from a roaring traffic artery to a park, leading to a handsome bus mall and a successful new light rail system. This plan has helped make Portland a vibrant and appealing city. Boston's southwest corridor is the story of how a fight against freeways culminated in a mass transit line and neighborhood-sensitive development along its every mile. The project is hailed as a landmark testimony to how "officialdom" and citizens, poor and rich, can work together. The story of Lincoln's "Radial Reuse" project reveals how citizen action can correct even the biggest blunder by City Hall. Here, a four-mile corridor that had been devastated so that it could become a road corridor was redeveloped into homes through grassroots actions by the citizens of this Nebraska city. Cabrillo Village is an example of aesthetically appealing low-income housing and also reflects the village's strong native culture. This community was rebuilt by farm workers who decided to take their future into their own hands and thus organized to save their own homes. Finally, Vermont's Stowe Recreation Path is a model of a pedestrian- and bicycle-friendly pathway through a city.

393. Perks, William T., and David R. Van Vliet. "Sustainable Community Design: Restructuring and Demonstration." *Plan Canada* (November 1993): 30-36.

Keywords: social fabric, case studies, community, sustainability, urban design

"Demonstration residential community projects should be part-and-parcel of policies and plans by Canadian cities to restructure for sustainability. The authors argue that demonstration (pilot) projects are necessary ingredients for the urban restructuring process. The authors outline the restructuring phenomenon, then report on their research into sustainability, conducted in Swedish and Danish residential community projects. These Scandinavian projects were planned and designed around novel arrangements in communal organization, with resident and community stewardship roles defined. The sustainability goals can be transformed into nine performance propositions for planning and design. In the second part of the article, a concept design and outline implementation strategy for a demonstration project are presented."

394. Perloff, Harvey S., ed. *The Quality of the Urban Environment*. Washington, D.C.: Resources for the Future, 1969.

Keywords: environmental pollution, land use, urban ecology

This work consists of a collection of essays by different authors concerned with the urban environment and its influence on the quality of life. These papers were originally prepared for a conference sponsored by Resources for the Future Inc. with the theme of urban environments. Their purpose was to review (1) established, evolving, and required concepts in the field, (2) existing and required information to advance study, and (3) policies related to improving the urban environment. Although no attempt was made to unify the papers, they do have common threads. The first common theme is the consideration of the quality of natural urban resources such as air, water, and space. Another common theme is the consideration of problems associated with micro-environments (i.e., indoor air circulation, air-conditioning and heating, etc.) and macro-environments (the outdoors). The final theme involves the development of indicators to be used as measurement tools to assess environmental and social conditions for the purpose of decision-making.

The first paper establishes a framework for studying the urban environment, reporting findings, and making policies. The second deals with the issue of pollution, reveals the interrelated system of urban life and waste production, and suggests disposal methods with the greatest benefits.

Five essays deal with urban space: its value, its uses in different locations, and how people relate to it. Finally, two papers suggest how different contexts within which urban environmental problems may be viewed lead to different solutions.

395. Phillips, E. Barbara. *City Lights: Urban-Suburban Life in the Global Society.* New York: Oxford University Press, 1996.

Keywords: current, built environment, experience of place, housing, inner cities, land use, public space, suburbs, work

This engaging textbook introduces students to cities and how they work. The comprehensive nature of the book is evidenced by the nineteen chapters that deal with everything from urban history to the theories of Marx and Weber to community development. Besides all of the conventional topics, issues relevant to healthy cities such as structural models of cities, the effects of ethnicity on housing patterns, gentrification and economic activity in cities, perception of the built environment, and the experience of place are also explored. The author applies the principles "what you see depends on how you look at it" and "how a problem is defined determines the solution" to all of the material in the textbook.

396. Platt, Rutherford H., Rowan A. Rowntree, and Pamela C. Muick, eds. *The Ecological City: Preserving and Restoring Urban Biodiversity.* 1st ed. Amherst: University of Massachusetts Press, 1994.

Keywords: built environment, ecology, green space, public policy, urban ecology

This outstanding book explores the relationship between cities and their natural environments, that is, the ecology of urban communities. Issues of geography, ecology, landscape architecture, urban forestry, law, and environmental education are addressed. "Contributions include broad overviews of common problems as well as detailed case studies of specific programs, from the reuse of an old urban park in Springfield, Massachusetts, to a wetland restoration program in Illinois . . . the book focuses on matters of public policy and public-private collaboration. The aim is not only to assess the impact of increasing urbanization on biodiversity, but also to propose new ways of preserving and restoring the balance between the natural and the built environment through planning and design."

397. Plotnikoff, Nicholas, et al. *Stress and Immunity.* Boca Raton, Fla.: CRC Press, 1991.

Keywords: support, health, psychological health

This volume introduces and updates the status of research on stress and immunity. Clinical aspects of stress and immunity are presented in the first half of the book and include discussions regarding the influence of depression disorders on immune functions and stress interrelationships with cancer, AIDS, chronic fatigue syndrome, etc. There is also a review of the effects of physical exercise on immunity. This is a rather technical book designed for medical specialists such as psychiatrists, neurologists, psychologists, and immunologists.

398. Porter, Douglas R. "A 50-Year Plan for Metropolitan Portland." *Urban Land* (July 1995): 37-40.

Keywords: case studies, housing, transportation, urban planning, United States

"Portland is a metropolitan area that works, a model for other urban regions seeking a regional solution to difficult growth issues. Its downtown and inner-city neighborhoods are robustly alive. Development is controlled within an urban growth boundary, preserving farmlands, forests, and access to natural resources. The transportation system has shifted determinedly from the dependence on highways to a balance of alternatives. Workable affordable housing programs are in place. And the region operates under an effective metropolitan governance system that is unique in America. In 1992, Metro [Metropolitan Portland, Oregon] . . . embarked on a Region 2040 planning process . . . Metro developed a 'base case' of future development that extended current trends, and postulated three alternatives, Growth Concepts A, B, and C." The article outlines the fifty-year plan (base case and three alternatives) as well as the recommended plan.

399. Proshansky, Harold M., William H. Ittelson, and Leanne G. Rivlin, eds. *Environmental Psychology: Man and His Physical Setting.* New York: Holt, Rinehart, and Winston, 1970.

Keywords: social fabric, urban design, urban planning

This is one of the early compilations of research into the field of environmental psychology, but remains extremely useful because of its comprehensiveness and excellent selection of material. This volume includes articles by all of the well-known professionals in the area of environmental psychology, including: Edward Hall, Christopher Alexander, Kevin Lynch, William Ittelson, John Calhoun, Rene Dubos, Robert Sommer, Jane Jacobs, Daniel Glaser, Herbert Gans and others.

The book is broken down into six major sections:
1. Theoretical Conceptions and Approaches
2. Basic Psychological Processes and the Environment
3. Individual Needs in the Organization of the Environment
4. Social Institutions and Environmental Design
5. Environmental Planning
6. Methods in Environmental Research

400. Pucher, John. "Urban Travel Behavior As The Outcome of Public Policy." *Journal*

of American Planning Association (Autumn 1988): 509-20.

Keywords: automobiles, public policy, transportation

Urban transportation systems and travel behavior are the result of public policy as opposed to independent decisions made by the general public. Since public policy is to an extent a reflection of cultural values, culture plays a role in public policy. But aspects of culture are also partly formed by the result of long-term public policies. The automobile lobby's influence on voters is well documented and it is assumed that these interests are what the population wants as a whole. However, some people argue that the car, oil, rubber industries, and related manufacturers deliberately planned to destroy mass transit, and this article shows there is reason to doubt that public policy genuinely reflects the preferences of citizens. Policies and subsidies promoting suburbanization increase car use. Though many people prefer the independence of cars, this article gives evidence that, if public policy allowed an unbiased choice of the means of transportation, a greater percentage of Americans would choose public transport. The role of public policy in determining urban transportation development and local behavior in the United States, Canada, and the western European countries is outlined. Even though the analysis is historical, it has applications to current policy. Heavy taxation of automobile use and careful land use controls could lead to a higher percentage of people using public transport. The absence of these policies in the United States, as opposed to other countries studied, explains the failure to revise American public transportation.

401. Pugh, Cedric, ed. *Sustainability, the Environment and Urbanization.* London: Earthscan, 1996.

Keywords: current, case studies, developing countries, environmental pollution, green cities, health, poverty, sustainability

The discussion on sustainable development has paid considerable attention to "green" issues such as biodiversity and natural habitats. However, "brown" issues such as poor sanitation, water quality, and housing have not been adequately addressed. The overview of the brown agenda presented in this book has a strong southern focus and includes case studies of healthy city programs. The contributors seek to first understand the broad economic context in order to deal with the problems. Conceptual issues of sustainability, current unsustainable practices, global warming, health, and economics are discussed. Chapter 3 is dedicated to sustainable infrastructure for low-income communities, while chapter 4 focuses on poverty and its significance for healthy cities. A chapter entitled "Urban Sustainability and Social Cohesion" explores the relationship among environmental, economic, and social sustainability. Another chapter presents various methodologies of environmental assessment techniques for cities. The comprehensiveness and the focus on southern countries makes this a valuable reference work.

402. Raglon, Rebecca. "The Bonsai Wilderness: Urban Naturalism and Green City Concepts." *Environments* 21, 2 (1993): 16-21.

Keywords: input, green cities, urban ecology

This paper places recent Green Cities ideas into the context of earlier conservation and wilderness movements. It argues that little about the concept of a Green City is new except for the changed circumstances of city and countryside in the late twentieth century. Although these new circumstances have lead to new efforts at reintegrating wilderness back into the city imperative, the paper also suggests that what will be re-created will not be "wilderness" in the classical sense but a miniature "bonsai" replica.

403. Redclift, Michael. *Wasted: Counting the Costs of Global Consumption*. London: Earthscan, 1996.

Keywords: biosphere, ecology, economics, energy, environmental pollution, sustainability, waste

To live within sustainable limits, we need to know more about present consumption rates and their consequences. This book contemplates what we need to know and what we need to do about consumption. As well, the radical overhaul of economic and social institutions that must take place must be preceded by a paradigm shift in how we think about the environment, consumption, and waste. The book takes a political economy approach, and seeks to build bridges between sociological analysis and an analysis of social commitments and the global political economy that defines consumption. It is a valuable resource for statistics on consumption and waste.

To begin the analysis, Redclift provides a recent background to global environmental management attempts. The second chapter discusses the Earth Summit of 1992 and the frustrations that arise from conflicting agendas and "political blocs." Chapter 3 covers the history of environmental change starting with the Industrial Revolution. The chapter also addresses sustainability indicators and the relationship between cultural evolution and natural systems. Chapter 4 features discussions on the hydrocarbon model of development and the political economy of global environmental change. Chapter 5 studies energy consumption in Europe and Brazil. The economic ideology that sees nature only in terms of resources to be transformed and environmental services to be used for the production of commodities is the subject of the sixth chapter. The next chapter investigates the cultural basis of consumption. Three case studies on employment, waste management, and food policy make up the final chapter. The resistance to sustainable development, it is argued, is embedded in our cultural traditions.

404. Reddy, K. Narayan. *Urban Redevelopment: A Study of High-Rise Buildings*. New Delhi: Concept Publishing Company, 1996.

Keywords: support, buildings—social aspects, case studies, office buildings

The redevelopment of inner cities in India is taking the shape of high-rise construction. The book considers both the advantages (more community space and lower development costs for example) and possible disadvantages of high-rise development. It studies social problems, family relationships, security, and psychological effects in the context of high-rise living. Research on high-rise buildings and high-density living is applied to Indian cities; Hyderabad City is used as a case study. The author first provides the conceptual framework, then the geographical background, followed by the redevelopment process and trends and the process of vertical development. It also examines commercial and business use of high-rise buildings, problems and prospects of residential use, and socioeconomic implications.

405. Reid, Barton. "The Coming of the Postmodern Suburb." *City Magazine* 14, 15 (Fall/Winter 1993): 27-28.

Keywords: social fabric, community, postmodernism, suburbs

The article outlines the "postmodern" approach to planning suburbs. This new breed of suburbs, for which the author cites North York and Mississauga as examples, consist of "Mixed use precincts containing residential and commercial land uses with a pedestrian focus and good transit linkages, rather than a highway focus."

406. Richardson, Nigel. *Land Use Planning and Sustainable Development in Canada.* Ministry of Supply and Services, Canada, 1989.

Keywords: environmental planning, environmental pollution, land use, sustainability, urban planning

This report was commissioned by the Canadian Environment Advisory Council with the following objectives:
1) to explore how land use planning can contribute to sustainable development.
2) to determine and apply land use planning principles to achieve sustainable development in Canada.
3) to examine the role of the government in land use planning in Canada.
The study of land use planning is not limited to the municipal level but includes examples of programs outside the mainstream, such as policies concerning regional economic development, environmental impact assessment, and conservation strategies. Emphasis is placed on the framework of policy, law, and administration related to land use planning. The conclusion drawn is that land use planning is an effective tool for achieving sustainable development. The main obstacle is identified as the perception that land is simply a commodity, instead of a life-support system. Several recommendations are made, primarily for land use planners and the government, that outline an approach to land use planning that will allow the achievement of sustainable development.

407. Roaf, Susan, and Mary Hancock, eds. *Energy Efficient Building: A Design Guide.* Oxford: Blackwell Scientific Publications, 1992.

Keywords: transformation, energy efficiency

The introduction describes the current energy "inefficiency" of buildings and why they should be improved (moral reasons, less environmental damage, lower fuel consumption, lower long-range costs, etc.). The aim of the book is to help civil engineers develop skills in the realm of energy efficiency. The paper "Innovation in the Design of the Working Environment: A Case Study of the Refuge Assurance Building," describes a high-quality, award-winning building in the UK. The book contains excellent progressive views on, and strategies for, worker health and the building's impact on the wider environment and energy efficiency. In a nutshell, it is a simple approach to building that the author calls, "climate-responsive design."

408. Robinson, John B, et al. *Life in 2030: Exploring a Sustainable Future for Canada*. Vancouver: University of British Columbia Press, 1996.

Keywords: current, ecology, quality of life, sustainability

No more urban sprawl, suburbs converted to urban nodes, no commuting, native vegetation, schools that teach environmental management, improved public transit, electric cars, pedestrian and cyclist-oriented streets, and an Environmental Bill of Rights—these are parts of a vision for Canadian cities in the year 2030 described by the authors of this book. But is this vision feasible? The answer is "yes," assuming that many legal and political changes are made and the criteria for a sustainable society are met. Chapter 1 provides background for the Sustainable Society Project. Chapter 2 outlines the purpose, objectives, methods, and organization of the study that sought to develop the sociopolitical and environmental/ecological design criteria for the sustainable future scenario. A definition for and a set of principles of sustainability are offered in chapter 3. The design criteria for a sustainable Canadian society are presented in the subsequent chapter. The sustainability scenario and the changes necessary to achieve it are the subjects of chapters 5 and 6, respectively. Chapter 7, "A Retrospective," draws together the lessons learned by the authors through working on the Sustainable Society Project.

409. Rogers, Richard. *Cities for a Small Planet*. London: Faber and Faber, 1997.

Keywords: architecture, urban design, sustainability

The contemporary city is directly responsible for the unfolding environmental catastrophe, says renowned architect Richard Rogers, and will inevitably lead to civilization's self-destruction unless strong measures are taken to incorporate sustainability into architectural practice and urban planning. Rogers sees sustainable urban planning as being fundamentally guided by the Precautionary Principle as well as being democratic, involving citizens in decision-making at every level. It also uses a holistic approach, combining both social and environmental concerns. This is a finely articulated and passionately argued book about architecture that enhances the public domain, public transport that protects street life, and energy systems that reduce our dependence on nonrenewable resources. Well illustrated, this book is brimming with ideas about how we can become more sustainable while enhancing our respect for people and the environment.

410. Roseland, Mark. *Toward Sustainable Communities: A Resource Book for Municipal and Local Governments*. Ottawa: National Round Table on the Environment and the Economy/Table ronde nationale sur l'environnement et l'économie, 1992.

Keywords: energy efficiency, land use, sustainability, waste

Although environmentalists have striven to protect the biosphere for many generations, they lack the goal of creating healthy, equitable, and sustainable communities. This book is a guide to achieving a sustainable community based on the outcomes of the Habitat, Healthy Cities, and Eco-city movements. It is part of a National Round Table

Series on sustainable development. An exploration is made of human activity and its impact on the environment. The concept of sustainable development is then applied to arrive at practical and tested tools, initiatives, and resources that may be applied to a variety of problem areas in order to achieve a sustainable community. These include economic and community development, air quality, traffic management, land use, energy use, waste production, and water use. The suggestions made can be used by both government officials and citizens who would like to see their communities become sustainable.

411. Roseland, Mark, ed. *Eco-City Dimensions: Healthy Community, Healthy Planet.* Gabriola Island, B.C.: New Society Publishers, 1997.

Keywords: current, case studies, community, economics, energy, green cities, health, sustainability, urban ecology

Building eco-cities is not only a concern for city dwellers and city lovers. Since almost half of the world's population now lives in cities, achieving a sustainable future is inextricably linked to creating sustainable cities. As well, no matter where one lives, in order for the option of a rural lifestyle to exist in the future, cities must be stopped from consuming the countryside. Thus eco-city design is of universal importance, as this book demonstrates.

The introductory chapter provides a working definition for the eco-city concept and an overview of the literature in the field. The first of the two articles regarding eco-city planning identifies three ideas that should be worked into town planning: high density walking-based centers and sub-centers linked by transit, mixed land use, and natural and localized community processes. The second article identifies ten principles for ecosystem planning and suggests five steps for implementing it. The second part, "Healthy Communities, Healthy Planet," begins with Trevor Hancock's article arguing for a holistic and truly democratic approach to decision-making within communities. Next, Local Employment Trading Systems (LETS) are investigated in terms of their impact on people's health. How the city of Berkeley, California, uses economic development as a path to sustainability and London, Ontario's efforts to build community partnerships for a sustainable local economy are the subjects of part 3, "Green Economic Development." Part 4 is concerned with eco-city housing and community development. The first article performs a comparative ecological footprint analysis of various housing types. In the second article, an ecological community designer sets forth ten recommendations for translating ecological community theory into practice. Part 5, "Municipal Eco-city Initiatives," first takes a look at Waitakere City, New Zealand, which has incorporated the Maori concepts of resource management into a "greenprint" for the city. Next, the municipal initiatives for promoting the use of renewable energy in European urban areas are outlined. Finally, part 6, "Assessing Our Progress," considers how the sustainability of a community can be addressed. Elizabeth Kline describes the four factors that should be measured: economic security, ecological integrity, quality of life, and empowerment with responsibility. as how to measure them. Jennie Moore asks the question why many initiatives for sustainability fail to translate into actual healthy communities. She notes that perceptual or behavioral barriers, institutional or structural barriers, and economic or financial barriers are the culprits.

412. Roseman, Curtis C., Hans Dieter Laux, and Günter Thieme, eds. *EthniCity: Geo-*

graphic Perspective on Ethnic Change in Modern Cities. Lanham, Md.: Rowman & Littlefield Publishers, 1996.

Keywords: social fabric, case studies, urban sociology

After defining an EthniCity as urban areas that "contain varieties of peoples having distinctive cultures and origins," the book probes the geographic, socioeconomic and political processes associated with the following cities: Los Angeles, Chicago, Sydney, Melbourne, Paris, London, Amsterdam, the Ruhr Conurbation, Vienna, Milan, Madrid, Singapore, and some South African cities. Each chapter begins by describing the roots of ethnic change from the perspectives of residential segregation, integration, marginalization, discrimination, or xenophobia. Competition for housing, education, employment, and political representation between ethnic groups is a topic that is frequently revisited. Cultural enrichment of the city is another common theme throughout the case studies. The articles demonstrate that ethnic change is an important issue in urban areas around the globe, but that the nature of the change varies considerably. The final chapter integrates the findings of the case studies and suggests that the factors that most affect the process of ethnic change are immigration and welfare policies, immigrant adjustment processes, residential segregation, societal responses to immigrants, and the specific historical and cultural context of the city and the ethnic groups.

413. Rowland, Anthony J., and Paul Cooper. *Environment and Health*. London: Edward Arnold, 1983.

Keywords: support, air pollution, disease, food, health, noise—health effects, occupational health, water pollution, work environment

"The objective of this book is to explore relationships between the environment in which people live and the health that they enjoy. To be healthy is not just to be free of obvious disease—it is a positive state of physical, social and mental well-being, each of these aspects interrelating with and influencing the others. People who are physically unwell will be anxious, if only a little, about their symptoms; mental distress may evidence itself as so-called 'psychosomatic' symptoms or illness; bad social conditions or social disadvantages bring physical and possibly mental ill-health in their train. Indeed, social and behavioral factors are becoming increasingly important as influences on health, so that the social environment is becoming just as important as the physical.

"This book sets out to demonstrate how inextricably environment and well-being are interrelated, to examine in detail some ways in which environment and health interact, and to point to the ways in which we may influence both our own lives and those of others for better or worse. The authors are committed to the view that a comprehensive study of the various components which make up the practice of environmental health is necessary to an understanding of its relevance to everyday life now and, perhaps increasingly, in the future." The specific hazards studied include: communicable diseases; cancer; coronary heart disease; accidents; contaminants in food, air, and water; and noise and radiation created by technology, in housing, and in the environment at various workplaces.

414. Royal Commission on the Future of the Toronto Waterfront. *Regeneration: To-*

ronto's Waterfront and the Sustainable City. Toronto: Queen's Printer of Ontario, 1992.

Keywords: current, case studies, environmental planning, environmental pollution, sustainability, Canada

The city has been described in many different ways: as a pestilence, as a beacon, as a natural phenomenon, as a cancer to Gaia (the earth), and as "the" human invention par excellence, among others. This book is a study of the links between the city and nature in the various regions of Toronto and ways in which to achieve a more positive view of the city through environmental regeneration and economic recovery. The ecosystem approach serves as the foundation for a plan to work towards the sustainability of Toronto in the preservation and improvement of its natural assets and the improvement of the relationship among its people, the economy, health, and the environment. The plan is in three phases, with this as the final report. Part 1 of this volume looks at the regions in question, the nature of the problem, principles, and planning practice. Part 2 addresses environmental imperatives in terms of water, shoreline, greenways, and the winter waterfront, as well as the story of the Don River. In part 3, the regions in question are looked at individually and in greater detail, and these are: Halton, Mississauga, Etobicoke, the Central Waterfront, Scarborough, and Durham. Lastly, in part 4, regeneration and recovery are investigated. Although specifically targeting the GTA, this book's ideas are broadly applicable.

415. Rusk, David. *Cities Without Suburbs.* 2nd ed. Woodrow Wilson Center Special Studies. The Woodrow Wilson Center Press. Baltimore: Johns Hopkins University Press, 1995.

Keywords: current, suburbs, urban planning

America must end the isolation of the central city from its suburbs in order to attack its urban problems, argues the author, a former mayor of Albuquerque. A key reform, he says, is creation of metropolitan area governments—cities without suburbs—or else adoption by state governments of metro-wide requirements for local governments. He coins the term "elastic city" to refer to cities that have both (a) vacant land that can accommodate new inhabitants, and (b) powers to annex neighboring areas. The book is set up so that each chapter states a "lesson" learned from census data from 1950 to 1990 in 320 metropolitan areas of the United States. Listed below are the lessons.
Lesson 1: The real city is the total metropolitan area—city and suburb.
Lesson 2: Most of America's Blacks, Hispanics, and Asians live in urban areas.
Lesson 3: Since World War II, all urban growth has been low-density, suburban style.
Lesson 4: For a city's population to grow, the city must be "elastic."
Lesson 5: Almost all metropolitan areas have grown.
Lesson 6: Some central cities have grown; others have shrunk.
Lesson 7: Low-density cities can grow through in-fill; high-density cities cannot.
Lesson 8: Elastic cities expand their city limits; inelastic cities cannot.
Lesson 9: When a city stops growing, it starts shrinking.
Lesson 10: Elastic cities "capture" suburban growth; inelastic cities "contribute" to suburban growth.
Lesson 11: Bad state laws can hobble cities.

Lesson 12: Neighbors can trap cities.

Lesson 13: Old cities are complacent; young cities are ambitious.

Lesson 14: Racial prejudice has shaped growth patterns.

Lesson 15: Inelastic areas are more segregated than elastic areas.

Lesson 16: Inelastic areas that segregate blacks segregate Hispanics.

Lesson 17: City-suburb income gaps are more critical a problem than overall income levels in metropolitan areas.

Lesson 18: Fragmented local governments foster segregation; unified local governments promote integration.

Lesson 19: Dispersed and fragmented public education is more segregated than centralized and unified public education.

Lesson 20: The global economy sets the rules, but local areas can decide how to play the game.

Lesson 21: The smaller the income gap between city and suburb, the greater the economic progress for the whole metropolitan community.

Lesson 22: Poverty is more concentrated in inelastic cities than in elastic cities.

Lesson 23: Elastic cities have better bond ratings than inelastic cities.

Lesson 24: Rebuilding inner cities from within has not happened.

416. Rybczynski, Witold. *City Life: Urban Expectations in a New World*. New York: Scribner, 1995.

Keywords: support, built environment, consumerism, economics, experience of place, social ecology, suburbs, transportation

In his lively and readable style, Rybczynski (an architect by training) ponders how North American cities came to be the way they are. He compares North American cities to European cities and explains their differences in terms of history, politics, and economics. Cities' evolution and their current state of affairs are analyzed by considering a wide range of topics from malls, civic squares, and public art to consumerism and suburbs. Rybczynski calls upon his experience with a large number of cities, and laments that a willful ignorance of our past has significantly contributed to the "undistinguished record" of post-World War II urban planning and design.

417. Sachs, Wolfgang. "If Wishes Were Horses: Desire and Democracy in the History of Transport." *The Ecologist* 24, 3 (May/June 1994): 94-99.

Keywords: automobiles, transportation

"The history of transport in modern Germany demonstrates how the desire to conquer distance has been confused with desires for social distinction. The automobile was originally promoted as a luxury commodity which, in contrast to the railway, conferred advantages of privacy, autonomy and prestige upon those who could afford it. However, as the number of cars on the roads has increased, these advantages have been superseded by congestion, compulsion and banality. The motor industry sees a way out of this dilemma through 'intelligent highways' and toll roads. But the real solution lies in recognizing that people's perception of the value of distance has been distorted by wayward desires, and that there is fulfillment in the intimate, the slow and a social structure in which short journeys once again become meaningful."

418. Safdie, Moshe, and Wendy Kohn. *The City After the Automobile: An Architect's Vision*. Toronto: Stoddart Books, 1997.

Keywords: automobiles, urban planning

In this book, Safdie, an internationally known architect, presents readers with a choice. We can continue to remain totally dependant on the automobile, with all of its negative impacts on our cities, or we can choose a different way of future city building. This new way of planning will involve a reinforcement of public life, contributions to "cultural richness" and enhancement of physical beauty. The final chapter of the book, "City After the Automobile," is an interesting read.

419. Sagoff, Mark. "Do We Consume Too Much?" *Atlantic Monthly,* June 1997, 80-96.

Keywords: current, consumerism, developing countries, economics, energy, food, population, poverty, quality of life, sustainability, technology

Continued economic growth is unsustainable. This is the basis on which environmentalists often attack standard economic theory. But are the charges valid? Mark Sagoff concludes that the world has enough resources to support a decent quality of life for even 10 billion people—the projected population peak of the next century. He presents four misconceptions on which the faulty premise of resource depletion is based: (1) We are running out of raw materials, (2) We are running out of food and timber, (3) We are running out of energy, and (4) The North exploits the South. Each misconception is clarified using concrete examples and clear explanations. Given that resources are not running out due to technological improvements, is economic growth sustainable? Sagoff convincingly argues that economic growth is necessary for more people to attain a decent standard of living. And for everyone to live more sustainably, decent standards of living are required. However, to get at the heart of the question, the context of the sustainability debate must be reconsidered. If the debate is framed in terms of the physical limits to growth imposed by resources, it is clear that economic growth is sustainable. However, Sagoff posits that a paradigm shift is necessary to look at the debate in terms of moral and social arguments. He proposes that we look at economic growth and consumerism in the following manner: "We consume too much when market relationships displace the bonds of community, compassion, culture, and place. We consume too much when consumption becomes an end in itself and makes us lose affection and reverence for the natural world." The article does not explicitly discuss cities, but since consumerism is currently one of the key obstacles to achieving healthy cities, this article is relevant.

420. Samet, Jonathan M., and John D. Spengler, eds. *Indoor Air Pollution: A Health Perspective*. Johns Hopkins Series in Environmental Toxicology. Baltimore: Johns Hopkins University Press, 1991.

Keywords: transformation, air pollution, health, home environment, indoor pollution, sick building syndrome

"Contributors—including epidemiologists, clinicians, risk assessors, experts in air monitoring, microbiologists, and engineers—discuss methodologies used in measuring exposures to pollution, strategies for improving indoor air quality, and other issues. They also assess the health effects of specific pollutants: tobacco smoke, carbon monoxide, wood smoke, nitrogen dioxide, biological agents, formaldehyde, and radon."

421. Sassen, Saskia. *The Global City: New York, London, Tokyo.* Princeton, N. J.: Princeton University Press, 1991.

Keywords: economics

An examination of the relationship between cities and the global economy is the focus of this book, which has already become something of a classic. The author examines the major changes in global economic activity that have occurred since the 1960s; namely, the dismantling of industrial centers in the United States, UK, and Japan, the industrialization of some developing countries, and the emergence of a worldwide financial industry. It is hypothesized that spatial dispersal and global integration have resulted in a new role for large cities. This new type of cities (which act as command points, locations for finance and specialized service firms, production sites, and markets) Sassen calls global cities. She shows that the global cities of New York, London, and Tokyo have undergone enormous and parallel changes in their economic base, spatial organization, and social structure. In terms of the latter category, Sassen notes that social polarization results from the extreme concentration of financial institutions in cities. This creates a population consisting both of the very wealthy and the very poor. Unemployment rates increase and certain ethnic groups seem to continuously occupy the lowest paying jobs. Sassen asks what the trade-offs between economic dominance and social ills are.

422. Sassen, Saskia. *Cities in a World Economy.* Thousand Oaks, Calif.: Pine Forge Press, 1994.

Keywords: current, economics, policy

According to the author, we can no longer rely upon the standard sociological approaches to studying cities. The examination of the ecology of urban form, economic globalization, and the subsequent development of a global culture are all cause for us to reconsider our former ways of doing. The purpose of this book is to help the reader understand the relationship between cities and global culture. Saskia Sassen illustrates how cities like New York, Tokyo, London, Toronto, and San Paolo have evolved into transnational market "spaces." She emphasizes that there is a greater commonality between cities than between cities and nation-states. Sassen challenges us to reconsider traditionally held views that cities are subunits of nation-states and feels we should look at the organization of labor, income distribution, patterns of consumption, and spatial structure to determine what new patterns of urban social inequity are revealed. Sassen's overall purpose is to provide us with a vocabulary and analytic framework to grasp new urban forms.

423 Savitch, H. V. *Post-Industrial Cities: Politics and Planning in New York, Paris and London.* Princeton: Princeton University Press, 1988.

Keywords: current, built environment, case studies, democracy, urban planning, social ecology

Paris, New York, and London serve as subjects in these case studies of the politics of planning. Information about these cities was used to derive propositions as to city planning. This book about how people plan cities, make decisions, deal with interest groups, and treat their populations is a result of an application and adaptation of what is known as power structure theory. It is also an analysis of the endless threads that connect governmental and social order. The fundamental questions that provide the framework for this work are:

1. What changes have taken place in the demographic and industrial order of New York, Paris, and London over the past twenty years?

2. How have planning and development responded to demographic and industrial change?

3. What kinds of political struggles occur behind planning choices?

4. What kinds of events tell us about the politics of the built environment?

5. How can we understand the relation between politics and planning, once it is cast in comparative perspective?

424. Schipper, Lee, and Stephen Meyers. *Energy Efficiency and Human Activity: Past Trends, Future Prospects.* Cambridge: Cambridge University Press, 1992.

Keywords: energy, energy efficiency

This work is concerned with the forces that influence energy use in formerly planned, developing, and industrial economies. The material presented is based on a decade of research at the Lawrence Berkeley Laboratory.

The book is divided into three sections. The first section contains an analysis of world energy consumption in the manufacturing, transportation, residential, and service sectors over the past twenty years. In the second section, energy demand in the future is considered. Strategies with which to restrain energy consumption in order to meet economic and environmental goals are outlined here as well. The third section emphasizes the benefits of energy efficiency and the policies required to achieve efficiency potentials. The government and private sector are encouraged to participate in promoting energy efficiency.

425. Scitovsky, Tibor. *The Joyless Economy: An Inquiry into Human Satisfaction and Consumer Dissatisfaction.* Oxford: Oxford University Press, 1976.

Keywords: consumerism, economics

Written by an economist, this book considers people's tastes, spending habits, and the way they arrange their lives in relation to money. This economist deems the traditional approach, that the consumer is rational and consumer behavior reflects his or her preferences, as unscientific, and he lays the groundwork for a different theory. An attempt to explain consumer behavior and motivation is made using behavioral psychology. The first chapter reviews the need for economists to change traditional assumptions of behavior. The second, third, and fourth chapters outline how psychologists treat behavior and conclude that behavior is both complex and irrational. Chapter 5 links the psychologists' and economists' approaches. Economic activity and welfare are placed in the psychologists' context. The sixth chapter tries to reconcile the economic and psychological conceptions of "satisfaction," and chapter 7 ends the theoretical part of the book by exploring the lack of correlation between income and happiness.

Part 2 attempts to test the theoretical insights by using them to explain the patterns of consumerism in the United States. The book concludes with a discussion of how specialization has led to the high and rising efficiency of production, while simultaneously leading to a society with members who are for the most part poor "generalists." The American perspective has a low opinion of most generalists—homemakers and politicians for example—but it is this general, interdisciplinary knowledge that is of value.

426. Scott, Allen J., and Edward W. Soja, eds. *The City: Los Angeles and Urban Theory at the End of the Twentieth Century.* Berkeley: University of California Press, 1996.

Keywords: current, community, economics, megacities, postmodernism, public policy, social ecology, transportation, urban planning

Between 1970 and 1990, the population of Los Angeles County changed from 70 percent Anglo to 60 percent non-Anglo. This is just one example of the many dramatic changes that Los Angeles has witnessed in the past thirty years and which spurred the urban restructuring that is the focus of this collection. Different aspects of Los Angeles as a "post-Fordist/postmodern" metropolis are explored by means of theoretical analyses, case studies, and policy-oriented critiques. The various issues addressed include architecture, political history, transportation policy, art and the regional economy, nature, economic growth via high-technology industrial development, racial inequality, and homelessness. Some common threads that run through the fourteen articles include a debate over whether the Los Angeles pattern of growth is an exception or an exemplary illustration of late twentieth-century urbanization. As well, all of the chapters take on a geographic or spatial focus. They are concerned with policy issues and politics in hopes that more progressive forms of urban and regional planning, architecture, urban design, community development, and environmental regulation can be achieved.

427. Seamon, David. *A Geography of the Lifeworld.* New York: St. Martin's Press, 1979.

Keywords: social fabric, built environment, experience of place

"This book is an exercise in looking and seeing. It hopes to help the reader become more sensitive to his or her experiences with places and environments. Stopping to talk on the way to the corner store with a neighbor repairing his pavement, feeling sad that a local bakery has closed, adjusting to the fact that the street on which one lives has just been made one-way, getting lost in a new place, driving long into the night in order to reach home and sleep in one's own bed—situations like these are the groundstones of this book. I ask if such experiences point to wider patterns of meaning in regard to people's relationship with place and environment. Do such experiences, for example, say something about feeling responsible and caring for a place? About the essential nature of spatial behavior? About the relationship between community and place? About improving places so that they might become more livable environments, both humanly and ecologically?" This is an interesting and provocative account of the meaning of place—from a phenomenological perspective.

428. Seamon, David, and Robert Mugerauer, eds. *Dwelling, Place and Environment: Towards a Phenomenology of Person and World*. Dordrecht, Holland: Martinus Nijhoff Publishers, 1985.

Keywords: social fabric, built environment, experience of place, health

The central theme of this work is to apply the insights of phenomenology in exploring the rupture that modernity has created between ourselves and the earth as well as in our human being, a rupture that seems to stem from the very technological mastery that has allowed for human domination of the earth. The essays in this volume initiate a new approach to a consideration of this nexus between "domination and homelessness" via a conception of "dwelling" (as opposed to the mere technological construction of houses and institutions), "place" (as opposed to a homogenous and mathematized space), and "environment" (as opposed to planetary raw material). The editors frame their task as "a questioning of who we are and what we truly want and need. We must ask what human dwelling on earth is and how it is possible to have a home."

The authors in this book include three architects and an urban designer, four geographers, three philosophers, and two psychologists. Music, physics, and the phenomenology of religion are each represented by one contributor. This is a noteworthy effort and a must for anyone interested in Heideggerian and phenomenological influences in theorizing about cities.

429. Selye, Hans, ed. *Selye's Guide to Stress Research*. Vol. 2. New York: Scientific and Academic Editions, 1983.

Keywords: support, stress, health, psychological health

Selye's Guide to Stress Research, Volume 1, provided an analysis of the causes and consequences of stress, as well as methods for the reduction of stress. The second volume of *Selye's Guide to Stress Research* contains several articles that emphasize the theoretical aspects of stress and its many applications. It presents analyses of many psychosomatic implications of stress, including a discussion of hypertension, which is so intimately connected with stress; a summing up of the status of research on stress, especially as a factor in cardiovascular disease; a description of physiological instrumental stress tests; the relation of the stress response and adaptive behavior; a discussion of environmental agents as the triggering factor for all biologic responses; job stress in police officers; an attempt to sort out the confusion of terminology when anxiety is compared with stress; the implications of stress in management; a study of social adaptation in which responses to stress are examined; an examination of the psychological factors involved in coronary heart disease; stress due to weather and climate; and an investigation of the cause-and-effect relationship between the instructor in the college classroom and the health of the student. As is apparent, many of these topics have implications for an understanding of factors that affect the health of urban dwellers.

430. Sennett, Richard. *The Uses of Disorder: Personal Identity and City Life*. New York: Alfred A. Knopf, 1970.

Keywords: social fabric, community, sociology, urban design

Sennett suggests that "the freedom to accept and live in disorder represents the goal which this contemporary generation has aimed for, vaguely and inchoately, in its search for community." This, Sennett feels, can only come about in the context of cities that are designed purposely for maximum diversity which can thus "provide men with the experience of breaking from self-slavery to freedom as adults." This is a persistently thought-provoking work that provides rich linkages between theory and the practice of urban design.

431. Sennett, Richard. *The Conscience of the Eye: The Design and Social Life of Cities.* New York: Norton, 1990.

Keywords: philosophy of the urban environment, sociology

Sennett's interesting theory is that the problems of the city arise because of our separation of inner (subjective) experience and outer (physical) life. The ancient Greeks integrated their inner and outer lives and lived in vibrant cities, but Christianity brought about separation. The separation is maintained by our fear of exposing our private selves, hence preventing an integration of the private with the public. Meaningful interaction with others in public places is seldom possible.

The coming of Protestantism introduced the design of neutral spaces. Sennett notes that this reflects the fear of pleasure. As he puts it, "the designers of parking lots, malls, and public plazas seem to be endowed with a positive genius for sterility."

The author then discusses how people through the ages have dealt with questions such as "How to encompass diversity in unity? How to make the social differences contained in crowds cohere in designs that aim at . . . wholeness between people and nature? What invention could bind strangers together? What could make social diversity as abundant and instructive as was natural diversity?"

432. Shabecoff, Philip. *A New Name for Peace: International Environmentalism, Sustainable Development, and Democracy.* Hanover, N.H.: University Press of New England, 1996.

Keywords: biosphere, developing countries, ecology, economics, environmental pollution, public policy, sustainability

The title refers to a peace achieved through sustainable development and genuine concern for the Earth and all of its inhabitants. Recognizing the deeply significant relationship between the environment and economics, Shabecoff begins the book by summarizing the threats facing this peace as well as proposals for dealing with these threats. However, the principal focus of the book is the gap between rhetoric and action in the quest for a sustainable future. In this inquiry, the influence of governments, institutions, science, values, and everyday acts are explored. Obstacles and bottlenecks to sustainability are pointed out. Shabecoff states that while the obstacles are not insurmountable, he cannot be optimistic about the future. He uses his decades of journalistic experience to eloquently analyze the Rio Earth Summit and its relative ineffectiveness. The focus is not specifically urban, but the proposals and critiques of sustainable development efforts are relevant to the study of sustainable cities.

433. Shashua-Bar, L., and M. E. Hoffman. *Vegetation as a Climactic Component in the Design of an Urban Street. Energy and Building* 31, 3 (April 2000): 221-36.

Keywords: energy, urban metabolism

The cooling effect of small urban, green, wooded sites of various geometric configurations in summer is the object of this study. The authors perform a statistical analysis of 714 experimental observations from eleven wooded sites in Tel Aviv. The results demonstrate that the wooded sites had a noticeable cooling effect not only on structures within their immediate vicinity but also on buildings as far as 100 meters away. The empirical findings of this study permit development of tools for incorporating the climactic effects of green areas into urban design. Some policy measures are indicated for alleviating the "heat-island" effect in the urban environment.

434. Sheets, Virgil L., and Chris D. Manzer. "Affect, Cognition, and Urban Vegetation: Some Effects of Adding Trees Along City Streets." *Environment and Behavior* 23, 3 (1991): 285-304.

Keywords: green space, quality of life, experience of place

"Two studies explored cognitive and affective reactions to vegetation in urban settings. In Study 1, subjects viewed a line drawing of an urban street with or without the presence of vegetation (trees and shrubs). The addition of vegetation affected subjects' cognitions about the quality of life in the area as well as about the land-use of the area. Subjects also reported higher levels of positive effects when they viewed a tree-lined city street.

"In Study 2, subjects viewed slides taken before or after vegetation was added along a thoroughfare in a suburb of a large metropolitan area. Again vegetation affected perceptions of the quality of life in the area, the local land-use, and self-reported emotional responses to the setting. The results suggest that the impacts of vegetation are largely affective, but cognitions, particularly about the quality of life in an area, are also influenced by its presence. This pattern of results did not enable us to ascertain the evolutionary or cultural origins of people's responses."

435. Short, John R. *The Humane City: Cities as if People Mattered.* New York: Basil Blackwell, 1989.

Keywords: support, community, democracy, work

In part 1, entitled "Cities as if People Don't Matter," John Short outlines the current dehumanizing state of affairs in cities. He argues that this exists due to the power given to architects, planners, and administrators, instead of citizens. Part 2, "Ideas for Cities as if People Matter," suggests how greater political control of cities can be gained by the people who live in them. This principle of grassroots democracy is then applied to the workplace. Strategies for greater employee satisfaction and participation are presented as well.

436. Short, John R. *The Urban Order: An Introduction to Cities, Culture, and Power.* Cambridge, Mass.: Blackwell Publishers, 1996.

Keywords: current, case studies, economics, housing, urban ecology, urban sociology

The central issues of contemporary urbanism and city life are presented in three sections: the city and economy, the city and society, and the production of the city. The first section of the textbook explores the relationship between cities and the economy over time, over space, and in the context of internationalization. The political economy of cities is presented through a case study of Sydney, Australia. In order to consider the city as a social arena, the author analyzes the housing market, spatial differentiation based on class, ethnicity, gender and sexual identity, the household, and politics. Detailed case studies of residential mobility in Bristol, race and ethnicity in Syracuse, and writings on gender, space, and power are also included. The third and final section delves into urban metabolism and examines the flow of capital through a city, the production and reproduction of social and political power, and production and consumption. Case studies focus on Syracuse, Barcelona, and the South-East Metropolitan region of England.

437. Shoup, Donald C. "An Opportunity to Reduce Minimum Parking Requirements." *Journal of the American Planning Association* 61, 1 (Winter 1995): 14-28.

Keywords: automobiles, public policy, transportation

"To reduce traffic congestion and air pollution, California has recently enacted legislation requiring employers who subsidize employee parking to offer employees the option to take the cash value of the parking subsidy, in lieu of the parking itself. The legislation also requires cities to reduce the parking requirements for developments that implement a parking cash-out program. This study estimates how the option to cash out employer-paid parking will reduce commuter parking demand, and recommends a corresponding reduction in minimum parking requirements. To deal with spillover parking problems that may occur if cities reduce parking requirements, the article concludes with a proposal to create 'Parking Benefit Districts' where the revenues from market-priced curb parking are dedicated to paying for neighborhood public services. At market parking prices, curb parking revenue could easily exceed the current residential property tax revenue in neighborhoods subject to spillover parking." (From the author's abstract)

438. Shumsky, Neil Larry, ed. *Urbanization and the Growth of Cities.* Vol. 1. The American Cities Series. New York: Garland Publishing, 1996.

Keywords: current, built environment, economics, suburbs, United States

The American Cities Series, of which this work is a part, contains over 200 articles by many experts in the field. This series organizes and brings together articles from journals of all types, thus alleviating the problem of locating such varied literature.

The main focus throughout is on cities, their growth, politics, economy, and urban life. In this first volume, urbanization and many of its attendant processes are analyzed. Examined are such topics as the relationship between urbanization and the westward movement in North America; boosterism and urban rivalry; company towns; and a look at suburbs and their place in American urban culture since the middle of the nineteenth century.

Although this particular volume is historical in nature, some sections are very useful, such as the one on suburbs, which gives examples of projects that have made some improvements in the past and others that have not with regards to working towards making suburbs more sustainable.

439. Shumsky, Neil Larry, ed. *The Physical City: Public Space and the Infrastructure.* Vol. 2. The American Cities Series. New York: Garland Publishing, 1996.

Keywords: current, case studies, community, transportation, urban planning, water, United States

This second volume in the American Cities series examines the physical development of cities and their infrastructure. Issues discussed are city planning and its origins in the Rural Cemetery Movement, the City Beautiful movement, the role of business in advocating more rational and efficient urban places, essential aspects of the urban infrastructure, and the provision of basic services necessary for urban survival: water, sewer, and transportation systems. This book is an invaluable contribution to the history of American cities—their planning, sewage disposal, and engineering.

440. Shumsky, Neil Larry, ed. *Politics and Government.* Vol. 3. The American Cities Series. New York: Garland Publishing, 1996.

Keywords: current, case studies, democracy, public policy, United States

This third volume in the American Cities series examines politics and government. The articles deal with the following issues: how rapid urbanization in the early nineteenth century produced a chain reaction, creating first the need for new political institutions, then the rise of machine politics; reform movements that designed, advocated, and implemented new institutional structures such as the commission and city manager forms of government; the nature of intergovernmental relations at the end of the twentieth century; and the connections between the governments of cities and the governments of the regions surrounding them.

441. Shumsky, Neil Larry, ed. *The Economy.* Vol. 4. The American Cities Series. New York: Garland Publishing, 1996.

Keywords: current, case studies, economics, social ecology, work, United States

This fourth volume in the American Cities series examines the economy itself in greater detail and its development since the early ninetenth century. Three basic sectors of the economy are dealt with: trade and commerce, manufacturing and industrialization, and finance. Other issues addressed are merchants and shopping malls, flour milling and scientific management, and the Chicago Board of Trade, among others.

442. Shumsky, Neil Larry, ed. *The Working Class and its Culture.* Vol. 5. The American Cities Series. New York: Garland Publishing, 1996.

Keywords: support, case studies, economics, work, United States

The fifth volume examines the changing nature of work in American cities during the past two centuries. Specific issues discussed are: the development of the industrial and post-industrial economies; the inseparability of economic and cultural change; the differences in experience between black and white Americans, men and women, and native and foreign-born Americans; the relationship among these different groups and the kinds of actions they have taken to achieve their goals: political protests, boycotts, strikes, etc.

443. Shumsky, Neil Larry, ed. *Transportation and Communication*. Vol. 6. New York: Garland Publishing, 1996.

Keywords: transportation, telecommunications, policy, United States

This sixth volume in the American Cities series examines the relationship between technology and urban life. This is looked at in terms of development in communication and transportation that played a crucial role in the growth of cities and the nature of urban life, along with newspapers, telephones, and telecommunications, and the significance of this changing technology.

444. Shumsky, Neil Larry, ed. *Social Structure and Social Mobility*. Vol. 7. The American Cities Series. New York: Garland Publishing, 1996.

Keywords: social fabric, United States

This volume examines social class structure and social mobility. Questions addressed in the papers include: What has been the class structure of American cities during the past two centuries? How much mobility has been possible? For whom has it been possible? What has been the relationship between social and geographic mobility? How have all kinds of Americans tried to improve their social status?

445. Silverstone, Roger, ed. *Visions of Suburbia*. London: Routledge, 1997.

Keywords: social fabric, built environment, consumerism, suburbs

Cities draw many people into their midst, but they have also become a place to leave. For those who feel that the city is too much to bear, or too expensive, suburbia has become the answer. This search for the perfect marriage of nature and culture, the balanced life, and the best of all worlds is nothing new, and in fact has quite a long history. This book is about suburbia, its emergent architectural space, material environment, set of values, and way of life. Through a range of contributors, suburbia is addressed from the point of view of its production "of what," consumption "of what," and representation "of what." It is the perspective of consumerism taken by this book that makes it so important for sustainable cities, seen especially well in chapter 5: "Tupperware: suburbia, sociality, and mass consumption," and chapter 3, "A stake in the country: women's experiences of suburban development." The first two chapters look at suburbs in the past, while chapter 4 covers the suburban weekend as a vanishing dream. In chapter 6, the perils of democracy in Westchester County, New York, are explored as a deep suburban irony, and in chapter 7, the sexualization of suburbia is presented as a diffusion of knowledge in the postmodern public sphere. Suburban domesticity in postwar America is studied in chapter 8. Versions of suburbia in British popular culture are discussed in chapter 9 and suburban sensibility in British rock and pop in chapter 10. The last chapter unfolds by asking the question: Is suburbia "the worst of all possible worlds?"

446. Simmel, Georg. "The Metropolis and Mental Life." In *The Sociology of Georg Simmel*, ed. Kurt H. Wolf, pp. 409-24. New York: Free Press, 1957.

Keywords: classic, alienation, psychological health, sociology, technology

Simmel, in this classic essay, was one of the first to note that aversion or apathy and the selfish calculation of cost were both behaviors that were generated out of the exigencies of urban living. The crowded and ever-changing bustle of the urban environment was at the root of people withdrawing into themselves and developing the capacity to ignore most of what occurred around them. Without this withdrawal, Simmel suggested, people would become insane. The reduction of human motives to cost was also generated by the metropolis. Emotional strain and impersonality led people to engage in exchanges where questions such as "How much is this going to cost me?" or "Will I get something out of this?" predominated.

447. Simonds, John Ormsbee. *Garden Cities 21: Creating a Livable Urban Environment.* Toronto: McGraw-Hill, 1994.

Keywords: social fabric, community, land use, neighborhood, transportation, green space

A Garden City consists of a central intensified node surrounded by satellite communities called "new towns." The Garden City is located within a strict boundary and is abundant in greenery and wildlife, usually in a farm or forest setting. This urban model was first proposed by Sir Ebenezer Howard in the late nineteenth century. Now, Simonds presents "practical and proven" ideas on how to transform cities into Garden Cities through incorporating nature into homes by the use of houseplants, clustered homes, traffic-free neighborhoods, free-form (instead of grid block) communities, and many other interesting ideas and sketches.

448. Smith, Christopher J. *Public Problems: The Management of Urban Distress.* New York: Guilford Press, 1988.

Keywords: epidemiology, health, psychological health, sociology

This volume introduces an innovative approach to analyzing the problems currently afflicting the modern city. It provides epidemiological, geographical, and social policy approaches to selected social problems and shows how these approaches can be widely applied to the entire range of social problems. The author adopts an interdisciplinary perspective that considers the historical, political, economic, and environmental factors that influence the etiology of these problems. Three representative public problems are focused on: substance abuse, delinquency, and mental illness.

449. Smith, Michael Peter. *The City and Social Theory*. Oxford: Basil Blackwell, 1980.

Keywords: current, philosophy of the urban environment, urban sociology

"A basic theme of this book is that we often mistakenly label as 'urban problems' what are in fact a variety of society-wide ills produced by economic and social inequality. To a considerable extent, the erroneous designation of society-wide defects as urban problems stems from the ideas of the social theorists treated in this book.

"The book analyzes the diagnostic and prescriptive writings of five major theorists of urban culture and personality—Louis Wirth, Sigmund Freud, George Simmel, Theodore Roszak, and Richard Sennett. Each presents a model of basic human needs and examines the ways in which these needs are either frustrated or fulfilled by urban civilization. Each offers, finally, a plan for overcoming those conditions deemed harmful to human well-being. The theorists were chosen, in part, because they depict the modern city as a repressive social institution.

"In Wirth's view, for example, the dense and heterogeneous city creates conditions that weaken our capacity to act rationally, to determine consensual values, and to make those values the basis of planned moral and political order. In contrast, Sennett contends that density and heterogeneity are no longer hallmarks of urban life—that cities have become too orderly and that the attempt to impose harmony is bound to stifle the diversity, conflict, and disorder that people need in order to grow. The three remaining theorists also view urban life as repressive. Freud considers sexuality and aggressiveness, Simmel affection and creativity, and Roszak communal solidarity and transcendent vision as the faculties suppressed by urban civilization.

"The five theorists were also chosen because each offers a set of measures for overcoming urban alienation. Each presents a different answer to the question: 'What can be done to render the urban environment nonalienating?' In my view, this is an important and intriguing question. Yet it is also, in part, misleading, because it focuses our attention upon 'the city' as the cause of a host of social ills that can more properly by attributed to changing patterns of capitalist economic development since the Industrial Revolution." (From the author's Introduction)

450. Sorkin, Michael, ed. *Variations on a Theme Park: The New American City and the End of Public Space*. 1st ed. New York: HarperCollins, 1992.

Keywords: urban planning

The book provides an amusing examination of modern urbanism as a "non-place urban realm," and demonstrates how city planning has largely ceased its historic role as the integrator of communities in favor of managing selective development and enforcing distinction. This is an excellent critique of contemporary urbanism and city planning in North America.

451. Southworth, Michael, and Eran Ben-Joseph. *Streets and the Shaping of Towns and Cities*. Toronto: McGraw-Hill, 1997.

Keywords: neighborhood, pedestrians, public space, public policy, streets, traffic, urban planning

Although they may seem rather insignificant, street standards play a powerful role in shaping the environments we live in. A small change in pavement width, for example, can have important consequences for energy consumption, length of trips, comfort, sociability, and construction and maintenance costs. The book first studies the evolution of street standards and the role of streets in residential areas in England and the United States throughout the past 200 years. For each era, the driving forces of change, conceptual framework, design prototypes, policies, construction techniques, and design criteria are analyzed. By taking this chronological approach, the reader can appreciate the enormous impact of the automobile and the institutionalization of street standards. Chapter 5, "Streets for Living: Rethinking Neighborhood Streets," compares different street patterns and discusses issues such as neotraditional street design, shared streets, safety, cul-de-sacs, and pedestrianism. Chapter 6, "Tomorrow's Streets: Toward New Neighborhood Street Standards," makes a plea for reevaluating standards, keeping in mind that streets are not only carriers of traffic but also play an important role in neighborhood socialization and creating a sense of community.

452. Spann, Edward K. *Designing Modern America: The Regional Planning Association of America and its Members*. Columbus: Ohio State University Press, 1996.

Keywords: architecture, environmental planning, land use, urban planning

The Regional Planning Association of America (RPAA) was an influential group of thinkers on urban planning, regionalism, and environmentalism in the 1920s and 1930s. Indeed, it consisted of leading thinkers on everything related to a rapidly modernizing America, from architecture and housing, to the physical, cultural and social environment, to technology. They shared the ambition to design a radically improved America. This book studies their lives and contributions. Emphasis is given to the four men who were the "vital center" of the RPAA, namely Charles Harris Whitaker, Clarence Stein, Benton MacKaye, and Lewis Mumford. Other members who played major roles at some point are also featured. The history of the RPAA presented here is only of scholarly interest.

453. Stackhouse, John, John Barber, Rod Mickleburgh, and Paul Knox. "Global Cities Series." *The Globe and Mail*, (Toronto) June 1, 3, 4, 5, 6, 7, 1996, section A.

Keywords: case studies, developing countries, housing, population, poverty

The foci of this series of articles, published to coincide with the United Nations' Conference on Human Settlements (Habitat 2), are the challenges facing cities today. The series struggles with solutions to challenges such as overcrowding and unsanitary living conditions by inquiring into what living in each city is all about. In-depth analyses of New York City; Chongqing, China; Sao Paulo, Brazil; Bombay, India; London; Santos, Brazil; and Singapore help to give readers a feel for each city as well as the problems they are facing. Related articles such as "World's Poor Flock to Cities," "Urban Growth a Crisis, UN Says," and "Lessons for the Future" are also included.

454. Stavins, Robert N. *Policy Instruments for Climate Change: How Can National Governments Address a Global Problem?* University of Chicago Legal Forum, 1996.

Keywords: greenhouse effect, policy

In light of the "tremendous uncertainty [that] characterizes both the future damage of greenhouse warming and the costs of avoiding or adapting to such warming," this report discusses what interim measures we should be taking in our public institutions to "get the ball rolling." The report evaluates barriers to future action and examines the potential contribution of domestic and international policy instruments. This would be a useful resource for those whose work involves policy development to mitigate the impacts of climate change.

455. Stavins, Robert N., and Bradley W. Whitehead. *The Next Generation of Market-Based Environmental Policies.*, New York: Environmental Reform, The Next Generation Project, 1996. E-96-02.

Keywords: economics, policy

This report begins with the recognition that there is increased interest in market-based mechanisms to promote better environmental behavior and that these mechanisms have also, in some cases, failed to produce the expected results. The report includes a theoretical introduction to market-based mechanisms and a review of implemented market-based tools and assesses why their use has failed to produce the expected results. It makes recommendations for a new direction for efforts to develop useful market-based mechanisms. An excellent resource.

456. Stein, Richard G. *Architecture and Energy*. Garden City, N.Y.: Anchor Press, 1977.

Keywords: transformation, architecture, energy, energy efficiency

The author begins by stating, "When we speak of an energy crisis, we must also speak of an architectural crisis. The two are interwoven." The first chapter outlines the extent of these crises and considers energy consumption during the construction, use, and dismantling stages of a building. In chapter 2 (A History of Comfort with Low Technology), the author stresses that a large part of American energy use in and for buildings is unnecessary and unproductive. Chapter 3 (The Changing Form of Building) outlines the history of U.S. energy use in buildings. The following chapters explain and criticize the standard building practices in an easy to understand manner: chapter 4 (The Tall Building); chapter 5 (The Materials of Building); chapter 6 (The Systems within Buildings); chapter 7 (Lights and Lighting); chapter 8 (Piped and Ducted Systems); chapter 11 (Solar Heating Versus Electric Heating); and chapter 12 (Principles of Energy-Saving Architecture). The book also stresses the urgent need for changes and describes how these improvements can be achieved.

457. Stoker, Gerry, and Stephen Young. *Cities in the 1990s: Local Choice for a Balanced Strategy*, ed. John Benington and Mike Geddes. Harlow, Essex: Longman Group UK Ltd., 1993.

Keywords: case studies, urban planning

Chapter 5 (the chapter most relevant to healthy cities) "reviews the experience of the last two decades and argues that area or decentralisation initiatives should continue to play a part in the approach of city policy-makers in the 1990s. . . . It concludes that area or decentralisation approaches tend to attract unreasonably high expectations but if they are seen as one part of a wider strategy they can make a valuable contribution. The scope and limitations of that contribution are then discussed in the third section of the chapter by reference to the most comprehensive decentralisation initiatives attempted so far—the radical experiment launched by the London Borough of Tower Hamlets in 1982."

458. Stokols, Daniel, ed. *Perspectives on Environment and Behavior.* New York: Plenum Press, 1977.

Keywords: social fabric, architecture, community, crowding, emotional needs, environmental planning, noise—psychosocial effects

"Learning theorists and engineering psychologists have conducted extensive research on the reinforcement properties and behavioral constraints of the physical environment, while clinical and social psychologists have studied the impact of the social environment on behavior. To what extent then, do the newly emerging domains of ecological and environmental psychology differ from the more traditional areas of psychological research?"

This book explores this question, and is one of the classic texts in the field of environment-behavior studies. See especially sections 3 and 4. Section 3 reviews research in the area of environmental psychology, which combines the perspective of ecological psychology with a greater emphasis on personal as well as social mediators of environment-behavior transactions. Theoretical and empirical developments in research on such topics as human crowding, response to noise, environmental cognition, and environmental simulation and assessment are discussed. Section 4 examines applications of behavioral research to the fields of architecture and community planning, with particular emphasis on the concept of behavior-environment congruence as a basis for environmental design.

459. Strasser, Susan. *Satisfaction Guaranteed: The Making of the American Mass Market.* New York: Pantheon Books, 1989.

Keywords: consumerism, economics

This book describes the historical processes that have created the material world that we live in. Our culture is flooded with product images and the feelings derived from products and the symbols attached to them. Advertisements manipulate people and, since Vance Packard's "The Hidden Persuaders," Americans have become even more comfortable with the situation. Since people show demand with dollars, the demands of the poor are unseen. However, the fundamental concepts of the present system face increasing challenges. Industrial catastrophes are numerous and bring into question underlying production decisions.

460. Stren, Richard E., and Rodney R. White, eds. *African Cities in Crisis.* Boulder: Westview Press, 1989.

Keywords: developing countries, poverty, urban design, urban ecology, urban planning

Many African countries are experiencing severe problems with inappropriate urban management in the face of massive growth. Unplanned shanty towns and deterioration of health facilities and public transport, as well as rising unemployment, are the result. Based on fieldwork done by African researchers and funded by the International Development Research Center, this book assesses the problem of managing rapid urban growth by analyzing seven case studies in representative African countries, from which general conclusions are drawn. Nigeria, the Ivory Coast, Kinshasa, Dakar, Tanzania, Greater Khartoum, and Nairobi are studied.

The articles outline the reasons for the failure of various policies to alleviate the situation. In general, it is suggested that the failure of tactics such as subsidizing the urban food supply, administrative decentralization, and the generation of community self-help groups have not succeeded because of weak institutional structures incapable of implementing the initiatives. The situation is further aggravated by the financial inability of local and regional governments to provide critical services and the lack of skilled personnel to deliver these services, even when funds are made available. The crumbling urban infrastructure combines with rapid population growth and already high levels of poverty to raise the situation to crisis proportions. This book is invaluable in the identification of the critical areas that need to be addressed in African urban development.

461. Stren, Richard, Rodney White, and Joseph Whitney, ed. *Sustainable Cities Urbanization and the Environment in International Perspective.* Boulder: Westview Press, 1992.

Keywords: case studies, developing countries, energy, food, greenhouse effect, green cities, health, housing, sustainability, transportation, waste, water

"The objective of the authors is to explore the various dimensions of sustainable development as they relate to human settlements and to indicate how urban sustainable development can be attained through a re-structuring of international, national, regional, and local economic and social systems. Without these structural changes, all of the attempts to realize the objectives of the Brundtland Report through 'green' cities, recycling resources, greater efficiency of energy and materials use, and so on will be nullified.

"The papers in this volume address two major questions. What is the relationship between cities and the natural environment in both the developed and the developing world? How can cities play a more constructive role in responding to the major environmental issue—that of 'sustainability'—faced by our planet today? The first is an empirical question, while the second is a policy question. An important aim of this volume is to bring empirical analysis into the service of public policy.

"The structure of this volume responds to two major concerns. First, in presenting 'state of the art' papers on most of the major regions of the less developed and more developed world, we wish to show that northern and southern regions can be related. Thus, each of the three sections presents both northern and southern regions, related by a single introduction written by one of the three editors. A common format is used in all papers. The major elements of this format include an introductory argument dealing with the relationship between sustainable development and human settlements in the region, an outline of demographic and urban geographical features of the region, scenarios of possible 'global warming,' an analysis of what we call 'pressure points' (such as urban food supply, waste disposal, transport, health, water, energy use, and shelter), a discussion of the political economy of urban environmental policy, and a conclusion which suggests 'future prospects and policy proposals.'" (From the editor's Introduction)

This collection includes case studies material relating to projects in several countries, including Canada.

462. Stren, Richard, ed. *Urban Research in the Developing World, Vols. 1-4.* Toronto: University of Toronto Press, 1994.

Keywords: developing countries, public policy

This series, supported by the Ford Foundation, seeks to address the question of the role of research in urban development. The series is the result of a large international project begun in 1991, involving fifty countries. The common introductory chapter in all four volumes discusses the four major findings of the research regarding the level of scientific production in urban research, verifying "disciplinary clusters" in different regions, the dispersion of research activity, and new research modalities such as NGOs. In addition, Richard Stren attempts to answer the question, "Does urban research benefit development?"

Volume 1 presents the findings of the first phase of this project in South and Southeast Asia and China. Volume 2 deals with Northern, Eastern, and Southern Africa and the Francophone and Anglophone countries of West Africa. Volume 3 focuses on Latin American findings. In each of these three volumes, the significance and structure of urban research is determined. The work that has been taking place since the 1960s is studied, as well as future research needs.

Volume 4, entitled "Perspectives on the City," contains ten articles that aim to integrate the findings of the project into conclusions. The first three articles are concerned with historical and institutional urban questions. Local institutions, law and development, and governance are their themes. Chapter 4 deals with the issue of governance and its value as an interface between government and civil society. Some factors such as urbanization and the economy, globalization and world cities, and the environment seem to affect cities systematically, regardless of their history or institutional set-up. These factors are the subjects of chapters 5, 6, and 7. The subsequent chapter on gender and urbanization looks at considerable research to determine if gender and urban development issues have been incorporated into the mainstream research on cities. A chapter on children in Latin American cities and on useful research methods conclude this volume.

463. Szelenyi, Ivan. *Cities in Recession: Critical Responses to the Urban Policies of the New Right.* London: Sage Publications, 1984.

Keywords: housing, public policy, urban sociology

The group of papers that make up this book were presented at a conference on August 20, 1982. They were all written from a left-liberal perspective, and are critical responses to the urban policies of the New Right. The book begins in part 1 by looking at why the policies of the New Right are unlikely to work. In part 2 a critical analysis is given of different aspects of neo-conservative urban policies, and the contradictions and failure of the policies of the New Right are detailed with attention to: housing, local government financing, public transportation, and "reindustrialization." Part 3 reports on the success/failure of the left-wing local governments in different national settings, including

France, Italy, Great Britain, and South Wales. The final section contains a paper on the kind of urban sociology one will need when neo-conservatism begins to decline, and a new, third paradigm is outlined for urban sociology.

464. Tabibzadeh, I., A. Rossi-Espagnet, and R. Maxwell. *Spotlight on the Cities: Improving Urban Health in Developing Countries*. Geneva: World Health Organization, 1989.

Keywords: support, developing countries, health, health care

The aim of this text is to outline the scale, nature, and urgency of urban poverty and to point out the importance of including the urban poor in health care planning. It is a message to ministries of health, city hospitals, health departments, the medical profession, and political leaders. A key characteristic of successful action to improve urban health as reflected by actual local experience is community involvement. A rapidly growing number of people are living in cities, especially in developing countries. To improve the health of people receiving poor, if any, health services, strong action and political commitment are needed. The health system must be directed to the needs of poor people. An appropriate general strategy for the health care problem is suggested and involves the following:
-simple preventive actions with proven results
-intersectoral action rather than concentration on medical care services alone
-involving people in their health care and accounting for their priorities
-not ignoring the widespread problem of poverty and ill health by settling for small experimental action
-working towards a national pattern of health care.

465. Talbot, Janet Frey, and Rachel Kaplan. "Needs and Fears: The Response to Trees and Nature in the Inner City." *Journal of Arboriculture* 10, 8 (August 1984): 222-28.

Keywords: emotional needs, green space

"Interviews were conducted with 97 Detroit residents living in primarily Black low- and moderate-income areas, in order to assess the preferences of inner city residents for different types of natural areas. The participants rated 26 photographs for preference, and also answered questions about the particular elements that made certain outdoor areas especially liked or disliked, and about the importance they placed on their own opportunities to enjoy the natural environment. The results indicated that well-maintained areas incorporating built features were preferred over more untouched and densely wooded areas, which were often associated with fears of physical danger. The participants' responses also indicated that these residents placed a very high value on their opportunities to enjoy the outdoors. Few differences in preferences or in value perceptions were found when stratifying the sample according to demographic characteristics. The results emphasize the importance of appropriate management of urban forestry resources, and suggest that outdoor spaces should be planned for ease of visibility as well as for pleasing arrangements of natural features." (Authors' Abstract)

466. Talbot, Janet Frey, and Rachel Kaplan. "The Benefits of Nearby Nature for Elderly

Apartment Residents." *International Journal of Aging and Human Development* 33, 2 (1991): 119-30.

Keywords: emotional needs, green space

"Few studies have examined the potential value of nearby nature for elderly adults. In the current study, elderly residents of two apartment complexes were interviewed about the availability of and the importance of different nearby natural settings. They were also asked how involved they were with various 'nature compensations'—indoor activities, such as growing houseplants or watching nature programs on television, which might substitute for more strenuous outdoor activities. The results indicate that elderly adults consider access to nature near their homes to be very important. Nature compensations were frequently pursued but did not affect satisfactions. Satisfaction levels were significantly higher among residents whose apartments overlooked natural settings, and among those who lived closer to certain kinds of outdoor settings." (Authors' abstract)

467. Tarr, Joel A. *The Search for the Ultimate Sink*. Akron: University of Akron Press, 1996.

Keywords: input, public policy, suburbs, transportation, waste

This book explores the technical solutions to waste disposal, and the policy issues involved in the trade-offs among public health, environmental quality, and the difficulties and costs of pollution control. This discussion is held in the context of ongoing changes in civic and professional values. The "City to Suburb" chapter provides a useful background for those unfamiliar with the role transportation technology has played in shaping the form of cities.

468. Teaford, Jon C. *The Twentieth-Century American City*. 2nd ed. The American Moment. Baltimore: Johns Hopkins University Press, 1993.

Keywords: social fabric, suburbs, urban planning, United States

Jon Teaford traces the perception of urban problems and the search for solutions from the turn of the century through the present, and examines the ways in which obstinate urban realities have stymied social planning. This is the second edition of *The Twentieth-Century American City,* and it brings the story of urban America up to date through the early 1990s, with an analysis of recent attempts to revive aging central cities and a look at a new form of development known as "technoburbs" or "edge cities."

469. Technical Workgroup on Traffic Calming and Vehicle Emission Reduction. *Evaluating the Role of the Automobile: A Municipal Strategy*. Toronto: Healthy City Office, 1991.

Keywords: automobiles, environmental pollution, quality of life, sustainability, traffic, transportation, Canada

The Technical Workgroup on Traffic Calming and Vehicle Emission Reduction was established in Toronto in February 1989. The members of the workgroup were representatives from municipal government, environmental groups, ratepayers, and businesses.

Their purpose was to assist Toronto's City Council in developing strategies to achieve a more livable city via a reduction of traffic volume and vehicle emissions. The workgroup proposed seventy-four recommendations to reduce the social, health, and environmental impacts of automobiles in Toronto, thus achieving its purpose.

These recommendations are rooted in the principles of sustainability, coordination and integration at the community and government level, quality of life, social equity, and community involvement. Using these principles, 3 goals were set for the city of Toronto: (1) to reduce automobile carbon dioxide emissions, (2) to reduce automobile carbon monoxide, nitrogen oxide, and hydrocarbon emissions, and (3) to reduce the volume of traffic and its impact on the quality of life. From these goals, broad strategies were set including the enhancement of public transit, promoting bicycle use and walking, expanding the rapid transit system, changing land use, and public education to reduce car use. The seventy-four specific recommendations were then derived from these broad strategies. Although the statistics presented in this report are sometimes inaccurate, the recommendations made are innovative as well as feasible.

470. Tempest, W., ed. *The Noise Handbook*. London: Academic Press, 1985.

Keywords: transformation, efficiency, health, home environment, noise—physiological effects, noise—psychosocial effects, transportation

"*The Noise Handbook* aims to give a current picture of the effects of noise upon man, the incidence of noise in various environments and situations and the protection afforded by the law and by what is technically feasible in the way of noise control. The book should be of value to audiologists, architects, town planners, public health and factory inspectors, industrial hygiene staff, environmentalists, sociologists, psychologists, and engineers." (From the editor's introduction) Topics include: noise measurement, health, hearing, communication, efficiency, and annoyance. Noise in industry, transportation, and the home is considered as well.

471. The Metropolitan Planning Department. *Towards a Livable Metropolis: A Discussion Paper in the Metropolitan Plan Review Series*. The Metropolitan Planning Department, 1991. Metropolitan Plan Review Report No. 13. Toronto: Queen's Printer, 1991.

Keywords: support, public policy, sustainability, urban planning, Canada

"The purpose of this report is to provide a framework for the new Metropolitan Official Plan that reflects the values and aspirations of the citizens of Metropolitan Toronto for a livable metropolis . . . this report offers an alternative approach to managing growth and the use of public resources. As a discussion paper, it also presents ideas, suggestions and proposals concerning innovative ways of dealing with the issues currently confronting communities. The report also emphasizes what is needed to achieve a healthy environment, a component of livability that has been under great strain."

472. Thomas, June Manning. *Redevelopment and Race: Planning a Finer City in Postwar Detroit*. Baltimore: Johns Hopkins University Press, 1997.

Keywords: support, case studies, neighborhood, poverty, urban planning

Why there are still so many problems in cities when we have such a large number of urban planners trying to find solutions? This book takes a close look at this question and gives reasons for the slow progress and numerous failures, such as a lack of implementation tools and administrative structures, the frustration of fighting the market, weak and ineffective policies, and the conflicting efforts of other parties. Two themes addressed in the book are the stunting of redevelopment through "weak and local policy tools and structures," and the negative effect that racial justice had on redevelopment and conversely, how race relations were in turn negatively affected by redevelopment. Part 1, "The Optimistic Years," addresses the roots of postwar development in the first chapter, and postwar planning in the second. Part 2, "Renewal and Loss," looks at various issues such as the problem of slums and how to eliminate them as well as the problems associated with them; racial flight and an experiment to try to maintain neighborhoods; and revisioning urban renewal. Part 3, entitled "Progress Amidst Decline," examines the origins of Detroit's civil disturbances and why they could not be prevented, the Detroit mayor Coleman Young and his part in redevelopment, planning a better city, and racial disunity. A conclusion, on "Moving Toward a Finer City" closes this book. Despite the Detroit focus of this book, there are good lessons offered for other cities.

473. Tjallingii, Sybrand P. *Ecopolis: Strategies for Ecologically Sound Urban Development*. London: Backhuys Publishers, 1995.

Keywords: input, output, environmental overload, pollution

This book examines the input and output flows that preserve the city system and the resultant number of environmental problems that occur. It is centered around three themes: the responsible city, the living city, and the participating city. In the responsible city model, the flow of water, energy, waste, and traffic are all considered as chain models where things flow into and out of the city. In the living city model, the author investigates how spatial demands can be connected to plans and ecological potential. In the participating city model, guidelines for self-organization and involvement of environmental issues for all parties in the process of urban development are considered. Good case studies are included.

474. Todd, Nancy Jack, and John Todd. *From Eco-Cities to Living Machines: Principles of Ecological Design*. 2nd ed. Berkeley, Calif.: North Atlantic Books, 1993.

Keywords: ecology, energy, green cities, urban design, water

This book presents the ecologically based working designs and prototypes of the authors, who have become well known for their leadership in the restoration of polluted water, the bioremediation of wild aquatic environments, food production, and urban design. Here, the authors further develop the idea of Eco-cities—designs for integrating agriculture and pure flowing water in green urban settings based on the principles of biodiversity. As well, examples of Living Machines, a family of technologies for purifying wastewater without chemicals, are presented in case studies. The book encompasses site-specific technological interventions and systems-wide ecological thinking. It is a revised edition of *Bioshelter, Ocean Arks, City Farming* (1984).

The authors present an interesting look at what is possible with the use of living machines. Although the tone is somewhat preachy, the book nevertheless succeeds in showing how radically cities could be transformed if ecological principles are applied in planning and design.

475. Tolley, Rodney, ed. *The Greening of Urban Transport: Planning for Walking and Cycling in Western Cities.* London: Belhaven Press, 1990.

Keywords: pedestrians, sustainability, traffic, transportation

Urban traffic threatens both the social and environmental sustainability of urban life. Never before has there been such a great need to provide car-free transportation such as cycling and walking. After the environmental protests of March 1990, Britain is following in the footsteps of European countries such as Germany, which are the innovators of non-polluting forms of transportation. Other countries, such as the United States, suffer increasing car dependence and are far from attempting European innovative practices. This work is a collection of essays whose combined purpose is to bring together accumulated knowledge which would otherwise be inaccessible, to introduce planning for "green modes" of transportation, to analyze the strategy of planning principles, and to examine their application in a variety of locations. The book is divided into four sections: principles, strategy, practice, and a summary.

The first section on principles (chapters 1-7) focuses on methods of traffic calming via traffic and transport planning in addition to urban planning that will enhance facility accessibility. Emphasis is placed on revealing the ignorance of modern statistical methods used to assess the danger of traffic.

The section on strategy (chapters 8-12) examines green policy and the obstacles to be expected in a German context. Success in Holland is used as an example for Western cities. The design for walking networks within the city are discussed along with the lack of these in the United States. The planned integration of walking and public transport is also emphasized.

The section on practice examines the experiences of different cities and countries in their attempt to encourage "green modes" of transportation. The Delft bicycle network is discussed along with the failure to increase bicycle use in the United Kingdom. The encouragement of cycling in the Netherlands is examined, as is the innovative approach of creating "bicycle-friendly towns" in Germany. The "Safe Routes to School" Project in Odense and its relevance for Western cities is also described.

The final section provides conclusions and proposes policy directions.

Although this is a collection of essays by different authors, all pieces of work are intimately linked to one another. They are placed so that they follow a specific train of thought, each continuing where the other left off. Furthermore, they all strongly support the primary themes presented by the whole.

476. Tolley, Rodney, and Brian Turton. *Transport Systems, Policy and Planning: A Geographical Approach.* Harlow, England: Longman Scientific and Planning, 1995.

Keywords: sustainability, transportation

This book contains a review of the spatial aspects of transport systems around the world, with an in-depth analysis of transport problems in both urban and rural areas. It has been prepared to meet the needs of second- and third-year courses concerned with transport geography and was given to many students for feedback. An overview of principal aspects of transport systems in a geographical context and an outline of recent infrastructure, policy, and planning developments is provided. There is also an evaluation of major social, environmental, and policy issues generated by modern transport systems. The book is divided into the following four parts, each considering an aspect of transport geography:

1) basic geography examining spatial structures focussing on contributions to industry, agriculture, and urban development

2) specific national and international transport systems drawn from studies of western industrialized nations

3) specific examples drawn from developing and developed countries as well as former planned economies to contrast difficulties of transport systems in urban and rural areas.

4) significant contemporary transport issues like the environmental and social impacts of rising personal mobility.

The authors state that since the book is structured sequentially, it must be read the same way. Other key topics include transportation planning, environmental and social issues, as well as transport policy and sustainability.

477. Tomalty, Ray, Robert B. Gibson, Donald H. M. Alexander, and John Fisher. *Ecosystem Planning for Canadian Urban Regions*. Winnipeg: ICURR publications, 1994.

Keywords: case studies, ecology, green cities, Canada

This survey and analysis presented by the ICURR (Intergovernmental Committee on Urban and Regional Research) on ecosystem planning contains a review of the literature and an examination of approaches toward green cities and healthy communities. Fifteen case studies and a generic five-step planning framework to implement ecosystem planning were developed. The ICURR and its sponsors, the Ministry of Municipal Affairs and the Canadian Mortgage and Housing Corporation, have identified sustainable development as a key issue.

This report demonstrates how ecosystem planning can be used to guide the management of urban growth. Existing plans and policies as well as interviews with key people were used as resources. Chapter 1 defines ecosystem planning and compares it to conventional planning. Chapter 2 reports on a survey identifying constraints and barriers to ecosystem planning. Each case study includes the plan description, comments on its strengths and weaknesses, and finishes with an outline of the main results. Chapter 3 explores other methods similar to the ecosystem approach. An outline of how ecosystem planning can be promoted in Canada is contained in chapter 4. For the proposed solutions to be implemented, either the recommended initiatives must be adapted to current institutions or the present institutions will need modification for the solutions to be implemented. The insights from other chapters are used to form a basis for implementing ecosystem planning.

478. Tomalty, Ray. *The Compact Metropolis: Growth Management and Intensification in*

Vancouver, Toronto and Montreal. Winnipeg: ICURR, 1997.

Keywords: urban planning, Canada

Advocates of compact urban form believe that by planning more compact urban and suburban regions, agricultural land can be preserved, the impact of urbanization on the environment can be reduced, more vibrant communities can be created, and the financial costs of growth can be minimized. This report investigates the positive and negative impacts resulting from attempts to promote more compact urban form and looks at the dynamics between various levels of government. Using case studies of Canada's three largest metropolitan areas, this report provides an in-depth investigation of intensification efforts. The book provides an introduction to town and country planning by examining the physical, social, legal, economic, visual, and environmental dimensions as they relate to planning. Its target audience is the beginning student from a variety of backgrounds. It incorporates a discussion of planning, urban design, urban geography, housing, surveying, and estate management. This report is an excellent reference for those who are confronting growth management issues in their work.

479. Transnet. *Energy, Transport and the Environment*. London: Calvert's Press (TU) Co-operative, 1990.

Keywords: air pollution, energy, energy efficiency, technology, transportation, Britain

The use of energy in transport has the largest impact on global emissions of CO_2. In previous decades, the depletion of nonrenewable fuel resources was the major transport concern; now transport is also associated with the adverse environmental effects of energy use. These effects include global warming, acid rain, health problems, and pollution.

Energy consumption in the transport sector is not limited to the use of fuel to propel vehicles, but also involves the energy used in vehicle production, maintenance, building the transport infrastructure, and producing fuels. It is suggested that new models are needed to assess the environmental costs of transport. The goals of this report are to investigate the energy consumption and environmental impact of the transport sector and to recommend strategies to reduce this impact and make better use of energy resources.

Part 1 outlines the transport-energy problem and provides estimates of transport's contribution to air pollution and energy use. Part 2 examines several solutions to the problems of air pollution, energy use, and transport under these headings: alternative fuels, catalyst technology, energy efficiency, encouraging intermodal shift, land use planning, and a variety of taxation and pricing policies. The focus is on air pollution from the UK transport system. The report concludes that traditional technical fixes are not sufficient to solve the transportation problem. To alleviate the environmental impact of the transportation sector, urgent implementation of broad-based strategies with a commitment from the government is essential.

480. Travis, Curtis C., and S. Crystal Cook. *Hazardous Waste Incineration and Human Health*. Boca Raton, Fla.: CRC Press, 1989.

Keywords: output, health, hazardous waste, risk assessment, toxins,

This book offers an extensive analysis of hazardous waste management. By using various risk assessment procedures, the investigators attempt to clarify the nature and magnitude of the health risk resulting from hazardous waste incineration.

Chapter 1 introduces some of the complexities involved in defining, measuring, and regulating hazardous waste. Questions addressed include: What is waste? Who generates hazardous waste? What type of hazardous waste, and how much is incinerated annually? What chemicals are most often detected in incinerated waste? Chapter 2 provides brief descriptions of the hazardous waste incineration process and the presently available incinerator types. Chapter 3 summarizes the data base from incinerator test burns conducted by or for the EPA. Chapter 4 contains a description of the four components of risk analysis and discusses the predictive methodology employed in quantitative risk assessment. Chapter 5 includes a series of sections that present risk estimates for exposures to hazardous waste incinerator emissions. Chapter 6 is a discussion of inhalation exposure to incinerator stack releases of heavy metals.

481. Turiel, Isaac. *Indoor Air Quality and Human Health.* Stanford: Stanford University Press, 1985.

Keywords: transformation, indoor pollution, energy efficiency

This volume provides general information on indoor air pollution sources and the pollutants commonly found indoors, as well as the potential health effects arising from exposure to these pollutants. Formaldehyde, other household contaminants, radon, particulates, combustion products, and second-hand smoke are investigated. The final chapters deal with energy efficient buildings, office buildings, controlling indoor air pollutants, and their legal and regulatory issues.

482. Turner, John F. C. "Uncontrolled Urban Settlement: Problems and Policies." In *The City in Newly Developing Countries: Readings on Urbanism and Urbanization*, ed. Gerald Breese, pp. 507-34. Englewood Cliffs, N. J.: Prentice-Hall, 1969.

Keywords: developing countries, poverty, support

This article was one of the first to suggest that squatter settlements ("autonomous urban settlements") are actually a normal and important part of a growing city. The conventional belief of the time, still prominent today, is that squatter settlements are a problem that must be extinguished. Turner explains the reasoning behind his argument against the conventional belief using four hypotheses:

1) "We do not consider the existence of urban settlements to be the problem, but the fact that they are uncontrolled and that their forms are so often distorted." In other words, during urbanization, the new immigrants must have *somewhere* to live; if this somewhere is in shantytowns, it is better than out on the street.

2) "Autonomous urban settlements are both the product of and the vehicle for activities which are essential in the process of modernization." These activities include giving the person a place in society, shelter, and the ability to change locations as necessary to follow jobs around. With temporary squatter settlements, this is easy. The worker could not change residences as easily with a house and mortgage, and this would limit his job opportunities.

3) "Autonomous urban settlement (in the major cities of urbanizing nations) is the product of the difference between the nature of the popular demand for dwellings and those supplied by institutionalized society." This reinforces the second hypothesis—that permanent government dwellings with significantly higher costs are undesirable for most newcomers, who have little money and must stay close to employment opportunities.

4) "The institutional control of urban settlement depends on the encouragement and support of popular initiatives through the government servicing of local resources." Governments, especially those that do not have adequate resources, can not substitute for local action by squatters, but should support it.

483. Udy, John M. *A Value Basis for Urban and Regional Planning.* Lewiston, N.Y.: Edwin Mellen Press, 1995.

Keywords: current, philosophy of the urban environment, sociology

This book seeks to fill the gap between the values expressed in the theory of planning and the practicalities of planning implementation. Values discussed in this book include: equality, health, liberty, comfort, safety, community, economic, stability, political, and the pursuit of happiness. The author believes that this discussion of values is important if we are going to plan better communities.

484. Ulrich, Roger S. "The Psychological Benefits of Plants." *Garden* (Winter 1984): 16-21.

Keywords: emotional needs, green space, psychological health

"About three quarters of the U.S. population lives in cities or urban areas. Unfortunately—despite a widely-held notion that natural scenes with trees, grass and flowers are good for people—much of our highly urbanized landscape offers very little vegetation.

"Most of the people responsible for urban development—the politicians and the planners—probably agree that plants contribute to environmental quality. Yet in the cost-benefit analyses that so often shape development decisions—where the benefits, as well as the costs, must be demonstrated and quantified—the intuitive arguments in favor of plants carry little weight. As a result, the politicians often give only lip service to plants and dismiss planting programs as unwarranted luxuries.

"The paucity of urban plantings attests to a wide gap between our needs, which cannot be expressed in numbers or dollars, and our planning processes.

"Recently, however, researchers from several disciplines have begun investigating the benefits of contact with plants. The research to date, still relatively meager but growing, has already deepened our understanding of the positive experiences plants make possible and the needs they satisfy. Such studies, giving plants a measurable value, may eventually enable urban planners to give vegetation the high priority it deserves." (From the author's Introduction)

485. United Nations Environment Programme and World Health Organization. "Air Pollution in the World's Megacities." *Environment* 36, 2 (March 1994): 4-37.

Keywords: air pollution, environmental pollution, megacities

"To assess the problems of urban air pollution in the world's largest cities, the World Health Organization and the United Nations Environment Programme (UNEP) initiated a detailed study of air quality in 20 'megacities.' The study was carried out within the framework of the WHO/UNEP urban air quality monitoring and assessment program known as GEMS/Air, which is a component of the Global Environment Monitoring System. For the purposes of this study, megacities were defined as urban agglomerations with current or projected populations of 10 million or more by the year 2000." The study presents an analysis of the sources, dispersion and impact of pollutants, air quality trends, and control strategies for air pollution. Small case studies of the following areas are included within these pages: Beijing, LA, Mexico City, India, Cairo, Sao Paulo, and Tokyo. The article contains edited excerpts from the GEMS/Air report, *Urban Air Pollution in Megacities of the World*, published on behalf of WHO and UNEP by Blackwell Publishers in 1992.

486. United Nations University and IFIAS. *Industrial Metabolism: Restructuring for Sustainable Development*. New York: United Nations University and IFIAS, 1989.

Keywords: ecology, economics, efficiency, sustainability

This report contains the various contributions of participants in the Human Dimensions of Global Change workshop entitled "Industrial Metabolism: Restructuring for Sustainable Development," organized by the United Nations University. The workshop was divided into a number of themes, each of which produced a keynote address and a number of statements. The themes include ecological restructuring of the economy; preventive environmental policy; ecological orientation of economic policy; clean technology; and sharing global environmental costs.

487. Uno, Kimio. *Environmental Options: Accounting for Sustainability*. Dordrecht: Kluwer Academic Publishers, 1995.

Keywords: energy, environmental pollution, land use, public policy, quality of life

This book is an attempt to develop a systematic statistical framework for studying the environment in relation to technology, economy, and society, for an analysis of the impact of human activities on the environment, and to operationalize the concept of sustainable growth. Energy consumption, resource use, pollution, technology, recycling, and pollution prevention are among the topics covered. Environment, technology, economy, and society are interrelated so that a statistical system encompassing all these areas is proposed. We must seek technological and lifestyle changes to make our society and environment sustainable.

Not only is a global model provided, but the proposed framework can serve as a guide for industry and various social groups and for forming environmental policy in developed and less developed countries. The Japanese experience is included in a case study, in which a general statistical framework is used to carry out a quantitative analysis of policy scenarios aimed at sustainable growth. Also included are attempts to estimate a "Given GNP," to take into account both positive and negative growth, and a cost-benefit analysis when the cost is environmental degradation. This book contains five parts: (1) Policy Issues, (2) Energy, (3) Pollution Prevention, (4) Changes in Land Use and International

Linkages to Trade in Resources, and (5) The Relationship between Quality of Life and the Environment. The final chapter examines the framework encompassing environment, economy, technology, and society is closely related to the Integrated Environmental and Economic accounting proposed by the United Nations.

488. Vale, Brenda, and Robert Vale. *Green Architecture: Design for a Sustainable Future*. London: Thames and Hudson, 1991.

Keywords: architecture, case studies, energy efficiency, green cities

Building strategies for improving energy efficiency, minimizing waste and new resources, working with climate, and respecting users and the site are presented through amply illustrated case studies. This volume recognizes the fragility of the environment and the interdependency of people on one another and the environment. The city is seen as a series of interacting systems for living, working, and playing. This book outlines how a design for a few can affect many.

According to the principles of Green Architecture, the design must satisfy the client, stay within budget, and be approved by peers, but architects must also realize the responsibility involved in designing a part of the built environment. Green architecture's attitude to materials and resources should be based on vernacular architecture, and available and compatible materials in the contexts of the structure should be used. The following six basic principles for green architecture are examined: energy conservation, working with climate, minimizing new resources, respect for users, respect for the site, and using a holistic approach.

489. Vanderburg, Willem H. *The Labyrinth of Technology*. Toronto: University of Toronto Press, 2000.

Keywords: sustainability, energy, urban metabolism, technology, sociology

A detailed diagnostic study of engineering education in particular and professional education in general along with a comparison of conventional and state-of-the-art practices for dealing with the social and environmental implications of technology reveals a professional ethos that concentrates on technological development in terms of performance ratios such as efficiency, productivity, profitability, and GDP, that masquerade as social values. Such input-output ratios provide us with no indication as to whether any improvement in performance is partly or wholly achieved at the expense of human life, society, and the biosphere. These considerations are attended to in an end-of-pipe or after-the-fact manner resulting from the intellectual division of labor and corresponding institutions that first create problems and then seek to resolve them. These problems are compounded by an economic bookkeeping that makes no distinction between gross and net wealth creation.

The above diagnosis leads to a possible prescription. Preventive approaches gather information about how technology interacts with and depends on human life, society, and the biosphere in order to adjust design and decision-making to ensure that our goals and aspirations are not compromised. After developing a conceptual framework for preventive approaches (including individual and organizational prerequisites), basic intellectual tools and values are set out. Next, three dimensions of sustainability form the basis for decision matrices to ensure that solving a problem in one area will not create others else-where. Finally, preventive approaches are developed in four areas of application: materials and production, energy, work, and cities.

490. Van der Ryn, Sim, and Peter Calthorpe. *Sustainable Communities: A New Design Synthesis for Cities, Suburbs, and Towns*. San Francisco: Sierra Club Books, 1986.

Keywords: case studies, ecology, sustainability, urban design

The first part of this book is a series of case studies of American cities including Sacramento, Philadelphia, and Sunny Vale, Colorado. The second part discusses the various contexts of sustainable design.

This book evolved out of a week-long design workshop where many of America's leading innovators in ecology and community design deliberated on what sustainability means for urban design. Some strategies for changing our cities (from being designed for consumption into sustainable habitats) are forwarded. One such strategy is to shift from a mass economy to an information economy. Other issues discussed are the notion of a post-industrial culture, the importance of cultural diversity, sustainable agricultural practice, and sustainable transportation strategies. The authors make a convincing argument for the development of more compact, mixed use, transit-oriented communities housed in energy- and materials-efficient homes that are environmentally compatible and are designed with a sensitivity to the site's uniqueness. Various other practical means to achieve sustainable communities through design are outlined as well.

491. Van der Vegt, Henri, Henk ter Heide, Sybrand Tjallingii, and Dick van Alphen, eds. *Sustainable Urban Development: Research and Experiments*. Delft: Delft University Press, 1994.

Keywords: current, case studies, energy, green cities, green space, neighborhood, public policy, sustainability, transportation, urban design, urban ecology

Case studies, especially a substantial collection of them, can be very useful in determining the necessary pre-conditions for and the results of ecological city strategies. These proceedings of the workshop "Sustainable Urban Development: Research and Experiments" put together by the Consultative Programming Committee for Spatial Research (PRO) provide such a set of case studies. In part 1, "Introduction," the workshop is outlined along with The Dordrecht Ecology Week in 1993, of which the workshop was a part. Strategies and guiding models for eco-city design are included here as well. Part 2 contains case studies of Curitiba, Oslo, Sheffield, Dordrecht, Örebro (Sweden), and Breda (Netherlands) which outline existing urban sustainability projects. The importance of thinking of the city as an ecosystem is emphasized throughout. Part 3 reports on detailed strategies and models for energy emissions, neighborhoods, flow management, traffic reduction, and other aspects of sustainability through case studies of Nottingham, the state of Brandenburg and other areas of Germany, Dordrecht, and the area between Nijmegen and Arnheim in the Netherlands. Directions for future research and cooperation agreements conclude the book.

492. Van Vliet, David R. *Sustainable Subdivision Planning and Design: Analysis, Lit-*

erature Review and Annotated Bibliography. Winnipeg: Institute of Urban Studies, 1994.

Keywords: sustainability, urban design, urban planning

This is a brief report on current research and practice concerned with sustainable sub-division planning and design. The study is focused on Canada, but examples from the United States, Australia, and Europe are included. A list of projects—built, in progress, and proposed—is included along with an annotated bibliography for further reference. An attempt is made to document efforts and research in the emerging field of sustainable subdivision planning and design, with which to build new projects and evaluate existing ones. Present planning approaches are criticized and alternatives are proposed based on the principle of sustainability. For the implementation of improved plans and policies, the need for a broad ecosystem approach is emphasized.

It is also noted that site planning and subdivision design require a wide range of expertise, and the shortcomings of "single expert" approaches by urban planners, engineers, landscape architects, and environmental scientists are pointed out. It is emphasized that achieving sustainability requires each professional to broaden their scope of expertise and to involve other professionals. Although local urban communities in Canada have begun to demonstrate their concerns about reducing the environmental impacts of their actions, the Canadian delivery system for sustainable planning and design is slow. Three obstacles are noted: (1) the lack of a precedent of a fully sustainable community, (2) inflexible municipal procedures, codes, and engineering standards that do not allow innovations, and (3) established consumer demand. These issues must be addressed on both a local and government level if sustainability is to be achieved.

493. Vig, Norman J., and Michael E. Kraft, ed. *Environmental Policy in the 1990s: Reform or Reaction?* 3rd ed. Washington, D.C.: CQ Press, 1997.

Keywords: biosphere, environmental pollution, public policy, sustainability

In the 1960s, at the beginning of the environmental movement, urban environmental protection didn't seem so difficult; it was postulated that tough laws would force polluters and exploiters to clean up or get out of business. In reality, however, this was not the case. This book comments upon American environmental policy developments and politics since the 1960s by studying underlying trends and institutional shortcomings. Part 1, "Environmental Policy and Politics in Transition," provides a framework for analyzing policy changes in the United States. The role of federal institutions in environmental policy-making is examined in part 2, which contains chapters reporting on the impact of Reagan and Clinton, the EPA, and the role of the courts. Part 3, "Public Policy Dilemmas," considers economics, incentives, risk-based decision-making, environmental justice, and the "greening" of industry. The fourth part, unlike the rest of the book which has an American focus, looks at environmental policies in the European Union, the Southern countries, and general global trends. Global environmental diplomacy and the effects of trade are also addressed.

494. Vitullo-Martin, Julia, ed. *Breaking Away: The Future of Cities—Essays in Memory of Robert F. Wagner, Jr.* New York: Twentieth Century Fund Press, 1995.

Keywords: support, economics, health care, housing, neighborhood, poverty, transportation

At the outset, this work, written by Julia Vitullo-Martin and "beloved" New York politician and public figure Bob Wagner, was going to be a book about innovative approaches to dealing with urban problems. After Bob Wagner's sudden death during field research for the book, the format of the book was changed. It now consists of a prologue on Wagner's life and sixteen chapters by Julia Vitullo-Martin and other contributors who worked and were friends with Bob Wagner. These chapters are divided into three perspectives, representing three dimensions of Bob Wagner's life: the scholarly perspective, the new policy perspective, and the field perspective.

The Scholarly Perspective Section deals with fiscal, economic, and racial problems in American cities. More specifically, political scientist Phil Thompson looks at theories about the causes and the effects of urban poverty, especially the consequences for African-Americans. Economist Dick Netzer shows that there has been an increase in economic activity and services available in cities. Ester Fuchs, on the other hand, believes that cities are now in "permanent fiscal crisis."

In the New Policy Perspectives section, Diane Ravitch suggests ways of providing equality of opportunity and quality of instruction in New York City's schools. Christopher Stone discusses the merits of community policing, community prosecution, community courts, and neighborhood defenders. Julia Vitullo-Martin examines the successes and failures of the public housing program in Chicago. Ways to reinvigorate the social welfare system are explored in Ellen Chesler's chapter. She advocates the model of social settlement houses of the progressive era as a solution. Finally, the chapter by Paul Goldberger explores what attracts people to cities.

The Perspectives from the Field section contains papers on hands-on lessons from the field regarding various urban problems. For example, Donna E. Shalala argues for the importance of public health education and disease prevention. The former chairman of New York's Metropolitan Transportation Authority, Robert R. Kiley, explains the problems he faced and the solutions he implemented during his tenure. Similarly, Joseph Fernandez discusses his experience as chancellor of the New York City Board of Education. Public investment in the arts promotes economic development, as well as spiritual well-being, argues Nathan Leventhal in his contribution. Finally, Stanley Brezenoff and Roger Cohen present a eulogy of the Wagner family.

495. Vogel, Ronald K, ed. *Handbook of Research on Urban Politics and Policy in the United States*. Westport, Conn.: Greenwood Press, 1997.

Keywords: community, housing, poverty, public policy, suburbs, transportation

There is a constant host of problems requiring solutions facing all those with a stake in the urban system. Through a varied series of works by experts from many areas, this text attempts to provide an abundant source of information for urban policy-makers in order to help them deal with the problems at hand. Each chapter follows a general pattern consisting of an overview of the field and how it has evolved; then the major methodological issues and/or theoretical issues of concern to researchers are considered; and lastly, the current state of the field and directions for future research are discussed. In part 1, "Theories, Methods and Concepts," the issues discussed are theoretical models in urban politics, research methods in urban politics and policy, urbanization, community, power in urban America, race and ethnicity in the city, class and inequality in the city, and gender in the city. Part 2 focuses on "Governance and Politics," with chapters on urban government, participation in local politics, neighborhoods, central cities and suburbs, metropolitan government, urban service delivery, urban management, and budgeting in the city. Urban economy, urban planning and development, and economic development are dealt with in Part 3, "Development." In part 4, entitled "Problems and Policy," the following topics are addressed: policy process; housing; urban poverty, public policy, and the underclass; urban education, politics, and policy; police, crime, and crime prevention; urban health, politics, and policy; equal opportunity in the city; urban transportation; cities and the environment; and national urban policy. This is an invaluable resource on the workings of American cities.

496. Wagner, Fritz W., Timothy E. Joder, and Anthony J. Mumphrey Jr., eds. *Managing Capital Resources for Central City Revitalization.* New York: Garland Publishing, 2000.

Keywords: inner cities, transformation, economics

This is an examination of the various ways in which central cities in the United States attempt to stimulate economic growth and development. A number of different strategies are examined for their effectiveness on the vitality of the city as a whole as well as the targeted neighborhood and its adjacent areas.

The core of the book is a detailed analysis of three development strategies: reusing temporarily obsolete, abandoned, and derelict structures (TOADS); establishing business improvement districts; and siting sports stadia. The conclusion is that there are five factors that make for successful central city revitalization: "developing public-private partnerships; making a commitment to physical revitalization to improve the quality of life for central city residents; taking a holistic view of the benefits to the entire region; involving all actors in the planning process; and crafting strategies to take advantage of the unique strengths of each central city."

497. Wallis, Brian, ed. *If You Lived Here: The City in Art, Theory, and Social Activism.* Seattle: Bay Press, 1991.

Keywords: broader sociological issues

This volume documents the present crisis in American urban housing policies and portrays how artists, within the context of neighborhood organizations, have fought against government neglect, shortsighted housing policies, and unfettered real estate speculation. Through essays, photographs, symposiums, architectural plans, and the reproduction of works from the series of exhibitions, the book serves a number of functions. It is a practical manual for community organizing, a history of housing and homelessness in New York City and around the United States, and an outline of what a humane housing policy might encompass for the American city.

498. Walmsley, D. J. *Urban Living: The Individual in the City.* New York: Longman Scientific and Technical, 1988.

Keywords: emotional needs, experience of place

The emphasis here is on how individuals cope with urban living. Four main issues are addressed here: how individuals come to know the city in which they live; how they feel about the urban environment; the extent of their travel patterns within the city; and the influence of place on behavior. In seeking to explore these issues the book asks a number of important questions: How well do people know the urban environment? How do they find their way around? What makes a city memorable? How do people feel about the city in which they live? Are there basic human needs that city living is expected to fulfill? Why do city dwellers develop a sense of emotional attachment to particular places? What makes certain urban landscapes appealing? How extensive are people's travel patterns within the city? To what extent are urban dwellers territorial animals? What effect does the character of the local neighborhood have on its inhabitants? Does high-density living create stress and social problems? Do certain sorts of urban environment foster crime, delinquency, and vandalism?

This book does not push one particular theoretical orientation. Rather, it covers both research in "mainstream" social science and newer initiatives that are commonly described as "humanistic."

499. Walter, Bob, Lois Arkin, and Richard Crenshaw, eds. *Sustainable Cities: Concepts and Strategies for Eco-City Development.* Los Angeles: Eco-Home Media, 1992.

Keywords: current, architecture, case studies, community, ecology, green cities, neighborhood, pedestrians, quality of life, sustainability, transportation, urban ecology

This useful book evolved out of the First Los Angeles Ecological Cities Conference in 1991. The 350 pages are filled with ideas on what Los Angeles could and should be and how to achieve this vision of an eco-city. It includes bustling, tree-lined, pedestrian-oriented urban centers, economic vitality, social cohesion, and a healthier environment. The foundation for achieving the transformation to an eco-city was laid down in the conference; the book adds to this by providing more details regarding the principles, structure, infrastructure, planning, politics, and economics of eco-cities.

Following the introductory section is a section entitled "Overall Design Parameters—A Foundation to Build On" in which the principles of eco-city development are considered. Calthorpe's pedestrian pockets, Kaplan's retrofitting, healthy building design, and high-density mixed use land development are just a few of the approaches presented here. The next section, "Sustainability," contains various approaches to sustainable urban development, and contains an article by Sim van der Ryn. The section "Ecological Design Components" provides a wealth of practical information on solar design, water management, urban landscaping (including farming), waste management, transportation, and sustainable technology. Economic strategies such as neighborhood co-ops and others are the subject of the subsequent section. Next, the citizen-planner interface and proposed policy changes are presented. The section "Work in Progress" contains five proposals for eco-community projects. In the final section, a future scenario of Los Angeles is presented by Sim Van der Ryn, and the question, "Where do we go from here?" is asked.

500. Watson, Ann Y., et al. *Air Pollution, The Automobile and Public Health.* Washington, D.C.: National Academy Press, 1988.

Keywords: air pollution, automobiles, disease, health, transportation

This volume was sponsored by the Health Effects Institute (HEI), Cambridge, Massachusetts. HEI is an independent nonprofit corporation structured to define, select, support, and review research that is aimed at investigating the possible health effects of motor vehicle emissions. More specifically, effects of automobile emissions on pulmonary emphysema, respiratory infections, and behavior are studied.

501. Wayson, Roger L., ed. *Transportation Planning and Air Quality: Proceedings of the National Conference.* New York: American Society of Civil Engineers, 1992.

Keywords: air pollution, technology, transportation

This book consists of papers presented at the national conference sponsored by the Urban Transportation Division of the American Society of Civil Engineers. These papers are concerned with the improvement of air quality by controlling mobile sources of pollution. With current statistics showing that most carbon monoxide and about half of the nitrogen oxides and hydrocarbons come from mobile sources, new laws, regulations, and procedures have been implemented to address these concerns. Key issues addressed are: the Federal Clean Air Act and transportation planning, the effectiveness of transportation strategies, emissions modeling, trends in mobile source emissions modeling, air quality at intersections, and innovative approaches to transportation and emission.

502. Weinstein, Carl Simon, and Thomas G. David, eds. *Spaces for Children: The Built Environment and Child Development.* New York: Plenum Press, 1987.

Keywords: support, growing up, built environment, children, home environment

There has been a neglect of physical variables in mainstream child development research that reveals a tacit view of the physical setting as an unimportant backdrop. This volume challenges that view. The authors believe that the developmental process can be influenced by the physical setting. This is particularly true for very young children, who have limited control over their surroundings and who spend much of their time engaged in interaction with the physical, rather than the social environment. The authors also believe that systematic knowledge about children and their interaction with the built environment can be used to improve the design of children's settings. They focus on two questions: first, what do we know about the nature of children's interactions with the built environment; and second, how can we apply our knowledge of children and the developmental process to the design of spaces for children? The chapters deal with issues such as development of place identity, the physical environment and cognitive development in child-care centers, the environment as organizer of intent in child-care settings, institutions, designing settings for infants, the developmental implications of home environments, designing preschool classrooms to support development, designing playgrounds for able and disabled children, children's participation in planning and design, and imaging and creating alternative environments with children.

503. Weinstein, Malcolm S. *Health in the City: Environmental and Behavioral Influences.* New York: Pergamon Press, 1980.

Keywords: health, psychological health, urban planning

"The modern city developed out of man's need to cope with his physical environment. Many of today's urban health problems arose during the period of accelerated urbanization brought about by the industrial revolution in the nineteenth century. . . . City governments were forced to react to health concerns. . . . Physical problems were given a great deal of early attention while the needs of social and health problems resulting from overcrowding and poor housing were ignored. Today's health in the city reflects this early priority of physical over social needs. This book argues that health and city planning today must correct this imbalance if we wish to improve the level of health in the city tomorrow." (From the author's Introduction)

504. Welch, Bruce L., and Annemarie S. Welch, eds. *Physiological Effects of Noise*. New York: Plenum Press, 1970.

Keywords: transformation, noise—physiological effects, psychological health

This volume is based upon papers that were presented at an international symposium on the physiological effects of audible sound. It brings together the major elements of existing information on the effects of audible sound upon cardiovascular, reproductive, endocrine, and neurological functions. Reports on the studies that have thus far been conducted on the effects of sonic booms are also included.

505. Wells, Donald T. *Environmental Policy: A Global Perspective for the Twenty-First Century*. Upper Saddle River, N. J.: Prentice-Hall, 1996.

Keywords: biosphere, air pollution, energy, environmental pollution, sustainability, waste, water pollution

Environmental protection is not a choice; it is a necessity. Our actions have consequences that are far-reaching in both time and space. These are the two themes that guide this discussion of the ecological basis of life in relation to environmental policy around the world. After providing an overview of the environment as a public policy issue, the relevant institutions, actors, and strategies involved are described. The following seven chapters describe and analyze policies regarding air pollution, water pollution, chemical dependency and environmental degradation, nuclear waste, solid waste, energy, and land. The final chapter reiterates the need for viewing the environment as a unitary global system and for cross-national policies.

506. White, Rodney, and Ian Burton, eds. *Approaches to the Study of the Environmental Implications of Contemporary Urbanization*. Man and the Biosphere (MAB), a UNESCO Programme. Paris, France: UNESCO, 1983.

Keywords: built environment, developing countries, sustainability

This volume represents part of an attempt to develop a new intellectual and practical approach to the rapidly escalating problems of the larger cities in developing countries. The main theoretical planks of this approach are the adoption of an ecological viewpoint and an evolutionary perspective. Fundamental research questions addressed include "Are very large cities sustainable in the long run?" "Can the massive scale of urbanization, now underway in many developing countries, be guided so that cities achieve a viable relationship with their natural environment and become resilient assets to their own nations and the international community?" and "To what extent are cities—particularly the expanding cities of the third world—in danger of becoming permanent drains on national and international economies, destroying the productivity of their hinterlands?"

507. White, Rodney R. *Urban Environmental Management: Environmental Change and Urban Design*. Chichester, West Sussex: John Wiley & Sons, 1994.

Keywords: environmental pollution, urban ecology, urban metabolism, urban planning, classic

"The aim of this book is to examine the problems of urban planning and management from an environmental perspective. The city is analyzed as part of the cycle of organisms, elements and nutrients that make up the natural environment. Thus we can identify the metabolism of our cities—the ways in which they ingest, process, and extrude elements of these natural cycles. The general conclusion is that we need to manage our cities more 'intelligently,' meaning that the city lives symbiotically within the environment, rather than at its expense." This is perhaps an excellent even paradigmatic work on the topic of urban metabolism or urban ecology.

508. Whitehand, J. W. R. *The Making of the Urban Landscape*. Cambridge, Mass.: Blackwell Publishers, 1992.

Keywords: urban design, urban planning

A sequel to *The Changing Face of Cities* (1987), this volume considers those responsible for making the urban landscape. A range of issues concerning the makers and making of urban forms are brought together. A weakness of this approach is that some areas, such as industrial landscapes and housing, receive little attention. Information from previously published papers by the same author, as well as unpublished theses and dissertations that the author supervised, were all sources of information. Building and planning applications, correspondence, and many meetings with public and institutional bodies were also examined. A study of the English cities of Northampton, Watford, and London is included. The physical form of urban areas, referred to as urban morphology, shapes the ways in which people and society interact and evolve, and a lot of money is expended on it, not always to our benefit.

This study focuses attention on people and organizations responsible for urban development. A detailed analysis of selected parts of urban areas is included, the findings of which have general significance.

509. Whitelegg, John. *Inequalities in Health Care*. Nottingham: Straw Barnes, 1982.

Keywords: support, health, health care, social ecology

Despite the economic and social "development" made in industrial societies, there exists social dysfunction, inequality and poverty in the decade of the '80s comparable only to that of the Great Depression. In this book, it is argued that inequalities in health care are a good indicator of social dysfunction and are intimately linked to inequalities in recreation, mobility, employment and housing. Understanding these connections can only be arrived at by examining its wider social and economic contexts. This book establishes a wide frame of reference within which to examine inequalities in health care by looking at common features of all inequalities. Chapter 1 establishes the framework that links inequalities in health, education, housing, employment, and income. Chapter 2 focuses on health care, on its use as an indicator of social dysfunction, and on the possibilities for major improvements. Chapter 3 examines the issue of health care accessibility, while chapter 4 is concerned with a study linking accessibility problems to inequality in the UK. Chapter 5 critiques existing health care delivery and suggests ameliorative measures arising from a clear understanding of accessibility problems. Chapter 6 concludes with a review of policy issues related to achieving an equitable society.

510. Whitelegg, John. *Transport for a Sustainable Future: The Case for Europe.* London: Belhaven Press, 1993.

Keywords: air pollution, greenhouse effect, transportation

"This book makes a clear break with previous transport texts and sets the policy debate within the widest possible framework of economic, social and environmental arguments in Europe. . . . This well reasoned and ultimately damning assessment of the current shortcomings of European transport policy, is grounded in substantial arguments about the philosophy of transport while presenting important viable alternatives." It is a comprehensive study of the effects of transportation including not only global warming, air pollution and noise, but also time pollution and other concerns.

511. Whyte, William H. *City: Rediscovering the Center.* New York: Doubleday, 1988.

Keywords: social fabric, community, experience of place, land use, public space, urban design

William Whyte focuses on the design and management of urban spaces with the end goal being the creation of a better living environment. Topics include: the social life of the street, street people, the design of spaces, the role of the natural environment, carrying capacity, the decline of downtowns, and an analysis of various planning policies. His approach is easy to follow and well regarded in planning circles.

512. Williams, Colin C., and Graham Haughton, eds. *Perspectives Towards Sustainable Environmental Development.* Aldershot, England: Avebury, 1994.

Keywords: current, ecology, environmental planning, green cities, sustainability, urban design, urban planning

This book provides a discussion, from four different perspectives, on how the concept of sustainable development can become reality: economic, business, planning, and political perspectives. Three of the chapters in the planning section deal with healthy cities.

Cities' contributions to global sustainability and recommended changes in urban management are discussed in chapter 8 by Graham Haughton and Colin Hunter. They present a summary of the guiding ecological principles for sustainable development which are elaborated upon in their book *Sustainable Cities* (also in the bibliography). Chapter 9 advocates a local "corporate" approach to sustainable development. The response of the British planning system to the concept of sustainable development is the subject of chapter 10. Specifically, the experience of Yorkshire is described and recommended. Suggested amendments to the planning system are put forth. These three chapters all point to the fact that a political will must be present for sustainable planning practices to be realized.

513. Williams, John S., et al. *Environmental Pollution and Mental Health*. Washington, D.C.: Information Resources Press, 1973.

Keywords: quality of life, environmental pollution, housing, noise—psychosocial effects, psychological health

While acknowledging the fact that "no experimental model of conventional epidemiological analysis can encompass the full complexity of the environmental impact on mental health," the authors attempt to summarize what is known about the subject. The focus is on the effects of the degradation of the physical environment, and sociocultural aspects of the environment are purposely omitted.

The book is the product of a large literature search. Part 1 ("Research Trends and Needs") provides a very brief survey of findings of the effects on mental health of pollutants, noise, housing, and recreation.

Part 2 ("Abstracts") contains 110 abstracts from journal articles that deal with "at least one stimulus or agent rising from man-made degradation of the physical environment, a consequent influence on man, and a measurement of this influence on man's mental health." These are categorized into the headings of general, pollutants (subdivided into lead and other pollutants), noise, housing, and recreation. A list of bibliographies on the topic of environment and mental health follows.

514. Willson, Richard W. "Suburban Parking Requirements: A Tacit Policy for Automobile Use and Sprawl." *Journal of the American Planning Association* 61, 1 (Winter 1995): 29-42.

Keywords: automobiles, suburbs, transportation

"Suburban parking requirements have largely unrecognized effects on travel behavior, development density, development cost, and urban design. Case studies of suburban Southern California office buildings reveal that zoning codes cause parking to be oversupplied, and that automobile commuters are shielded from the economic cost of parking. These circumstances increase automobile commuting, lower building density and land value, and create automobile-oriented urban design. Taken together, such site effects contribute to the automobile-oriented, low density character of suburban areas. Suburban parking requirements thus work at cross-purposes with efforts to reduce traffic congestion and air pollution." (Author's abstract)

515. Wilson, Richard W., et al. *Health Effects of Fossil Fuel Burning: Assessment and Mitigation.* Cambridge, Mass.: Ballinger Publishing, 1980.

Keywords: air pollution, fossil fuels

This volume analyses strategies for controlling air pollution. Technical control options, operational controls, and siting methods are discussed. The authors consider the importance of generic solutions to reduce all pollutants since we cannot be sure which have the most serious effects on human health. Not surprisingly, the choice of control strategy is often made on political grounds, rather than technical, economic, or humanitarian grounds.

In the introduction, the authors discuss the history and scope of the problem. Chapters 2 to 4 deal with specific pollutants such as particulate matter, certain gases and organic matter, and the pollutants of coal combustion. In chapter 5, human health effects are explored. The topic of chapter 6 is the difficult issue of health effects at low exposures. Chapters 7 to 10 deal with pollution reduction, regulations, pollution pricing, and the legal problems of pollution control.

516. Wintle, Michael, ed. *Rhetoric and Reality in Environmental Policy: The Case of the Netherlands in Comparison With Britain.* Aldershot: Avebury, 1994.

Keywords: biosphere, case studies, energy, environmental pollution, public policy, sustainability, transportation, waste

The Dutch are renowned for their progressive environmental policies. Britain is considered "the dirty man of Europe." But what lies behind this rhetoric of reputation? The tension between these public images and reality is what this book explores. It contains three articles by established experts on Dutch environmental politics and policy. In contrast to their broad analytic approach, the other four pieces focus on specific policy areas, namely transport, energy, household waste recycling, and nitrates. They provide detailed studies on Dutch policy, how it came about, what it is achieving, and how it compares to British policy.

517. Wohlwill, J.F., ed. and Willem van Vliet, co-oeditor. *Habitats for Children: The Impacts of Density.* 1st ed. Child Psychology Series. Hillsdale, N.J.: Lawrence Erlbaum Associates, 1985.

Keywords: children, crowding, housing, psychological health

The main theme of this work is well summarized in the author's own words: "Much has been written from the diverse perspectives of the economist, the sociologist, the designer and planner, and others about the pros and cons of different patterns of housing and settlement for our population. Yet rarely have the implications and consequences of these different residential contexts for the behavior, development, and well-being of the children living in them been systematically considered." The effects of residential density, crowding, and noise on perceptual-cognitive development, play, family interaction, peer interaction, and social adjustment are also discussed at some length.

518. Wojtowicz, Robert. *Lewis Mumford and American Modernism: Eutopian Theories for Architecture.* New York: Cambridge University Press, 1996.

Keywords: current, architecture, modernism, utopia

Mumford believed in the betterment of society through sound design in architecture, the practice of housing reforms, comprehensive planning at the regional level, and social reform. As a idealistic modernist he wrote substantially on architecture and urbanism. This book presents his views on utopia including: living within our means, connecting with nature, avoiding a blind faith in technology, and working together for the greater good of our communities and the betterment of life.

519. World Environment and Resources Council. *The Environment of Human Settlements.* Brussels: Pergamon Press, 1976.

Keywords: current, built environment, case studies, democracy, technology, urban design, urban planning

The conference proceedings are outlined in five sections. Section 1 is entitled "Modern Technology for Cities of Today" and explores Ontario's Resource Recovery Programme, accessibility, and interstate highway interchange communities as sites of future settlements. Section 2 deals with the political, legal, and economic considerations when designing for human well-being. Specific issues considered here include: noise control, minimizing pollution, and case studies of policies for clean urban environments. The optimization of urban density, the provision of low-cost housing, citizen participation, and others are the topics addressed in section 3 ("Urban and Land Use Planning"). Section 4 inquires into urban design that aids in solving urban problems. Finally, the future of well-being in cities is discussed in section 5.

520. World Health Organization. *Health Hazards of the Human Environment.* Geneva: World Health Organization, 1972.

Keywords: air pollution, food, health, home environment, noise—health effects, psychological health, toxins, water pollution, work environment

"This publication is addressed primarily to health authorities called upon to deal with environmental problems, although much of it will be of interest to others concerned with deterioration of the environment. The human environment is considered here as comprising those external physical, chemical, biological, and social influences that have a significant and detectable effect on the health and well-being of the individual or of communities of people."

This is an overview of the relationship between health and air, water, food, soil, land, insects, rodents, the home environment, the work environment, climate, altitude, transport hazards, pollutants, mutagens, carcinogens, ionizing radiation, non-ionizing radiation, and noise.

521. World Health Organization. *Urbanization and its Implications for Child Health: Potential for Action.* Geneva: World Health Organization, 1988.

Keywords: support, growing up, air pollution, children, health, housing, poverty, water pollution

"This book explores present trends in urbanization, the effect of these trends on the physical and social environment, and the impact of this environment on child health. It aims to increase awareness of the severe and pervasive impact on health of the deteriorating environmental conditions produced by too rapid urbanization, and to promote widespread consideration of policies and actions that could improve the situation." The importance of healthy housing, neighborhood organizations, and the local government is emphasized.

522. World Health Organization. *Environmental Health: Guidelines for Healthy Housing.* Vol. 31. Copenhagen: World Health Organization, 1988.

Keywords: housing, indoor pollution

"The purpose of these guidelines is to remind Member States, Ministries of Health and Architecture, policy-makers, environmental health officers, sanitarians, planners, architects and others concerned about housing hygiene in relation to 'traditional' and 'new' slum housing. The guidelines are aimed at encouraging administrations to formulate a sound housing policy that helps to solve basic health-related housing problems and to meet WHO's objective of healthful housing for all by the year 2000. The guidelines are aimed particularly at developing middle-income countries in Europe. However, the principles of healthy housing have universal applicability as most countries of the developed world have areas of slum or otherwise insanitary housing."

These guidelines focus mainly on requirements in the home and the micro-residential environment rather than the wider macro-environment despite the obvious interrelationship between them. Other WHO publications cover the broader environmental health aspects of human settlements. Similarly, the lack of detailed epidemiological information related to conditions in developing countries and the wide disparities in geography, culture, social habits, and political priorities mean that these guidelines are inevitably very generalized.

523. World Health Organization. *A Guide to Assessing Healthy Cities.* Vol. 3. WHO Healthy Cities Papers. Copenhagen: FADL, 1988.

Keywords: health, public policy

This project may be thought of as seeking answers to the following three questions: What is a healthy city? How do we get one? How well are we doing? The manual is intended to be useful to community members, Healthy Cities Project staff, politicians, journalists, researchers, and others interested in the healthy city. It does not provide a complete blueprint for community evaluation and should not be viewed as such. Instead, it should be used as one important tool in defining what a healthy city is, initiating a healthy city project and evaluating its progress, complemented by other tools such as indicators that are yet to be developed.

524. World Health Organization. *Spotlight on Cities: Improving Urban Health in Developing Countries*. Geneva: World Health Organization, 1989.

Keywords: community, developing countries, health, health care
Until recently, the plight of the urban poor has largely been ignored by health planners and decision-makers. This volume draws attention to the scale, nature, and urgency of the situation in many cities and advocates a fundamental shift in health care priorities towards the widespread application of primary health care. Community involvement, health-related development, and the struggle for universal coverage are discussed.

525. World Health Organization. *The New Public Health in an Urban Context: Paradoxes and Solutions*. Vol. 4. WHO Healthy Cities Papers. Copenhagen: FADL, 1989.

Keywords: health, health care, public policy, quality of life

This booklet evaluates the work of municipal health departments and public health policy, reviews the history of urban health, compares the healthy cities movement with epidemiology, and suggests strategies to better achieve health for all.

526. World Health Organization. *Healthy Cities Project: A Project Becomes a Movement*. Copenhagen: FADL Publishers, 1990.

Keywords: health, sustainability

The WHO Healthy Cities project was initiated in 1985 with the objectives of making health a priority for decision-makers in the cities of Europe and encouraging public health at the local level. These objectives grew out of the general goal of improving the physical, mental, environmental and social well-being of the citizens of European cities. The project has now grown to a movement that includes thirty project cities in Europe, seventeen national networks, and the involvement of over 400 cities in Europe, Australia, and North America. This report is an account of the development of the project. It includes a description of various initiatives for health already in effect in the thirty project cities that encourage equity and sustainability. An account is given of the many achievements of the project and of the challenges that lie ahead.

527. Xu, S. "Urban Ecosystems: A Holistic Approach to Urban Analysis." *Environment and Planning B: Planning and Design* 16 (1989): 187-200.

Keywords: urban ecology, urban planning

Urban and regional planning are increasingly concerned with the concept of integrated analysis. This paper presents the benefits of integrated analysis when based on a holistic view of an urban system and suggests that adopting a holistic view is a prerequisite to the integrated analysis of a city. The holistic concept is explained using the principles of ecology in the context of the urban ecosystem. This is followed by a presentation of the "urban behavior matrix," a framework that may be used for holistic urban analysis and which contains both spatial and behavioral information. The application of this urban behavior matrix to an urban ecosystem is discussed. The interactions between urban areas

are investigated in terms of three types of urban behavior: the environmental, the resource, and the socioeconomic. The importance of pursuing integrated analysis as a solution to problems associated with each type of behavior is stressed.

528. Yiftachel, O. "Towards a New Typology of Urban Planning Theories." *Environment
and Planning B: Planning and Design* 16, 1 (Jan. 1989): 23-39.

Keywords: urban planning

In this review paper, the author attempts to solve the problem of a confusing and im-
practical urban planning theory. He proposes a new typology of urban planning theory
that he hopes will act as a useful guide for planners. He formulates a specific (rather than
general) theory of the evolution, tasks and properties of urban land use. The new typology sees urban land use planning as composed of three debates: the "analytical" debate
(over the sociopolitical role of land use planning), the "urban form" debate (regarding
land use solutions to urban problems), and the "procedural" debate (over decision-making
procedures). The author establishes the need for a new approach in urban planning theory, reviews previous clarification attempts and presents his new typology. The history of
the three debates is discussed, followed by the possible future development of urban
planning theory.

529. Zeisel, John. *Sociology and Architectural Design*. 2nd ed. New York: Russell Sage
Foundation, 1975.

Keywords: architecture, sociology, urban design, urban planning

"Sociologists have long shown interest in the way the physical environment relates to
people. Nevertheless, sociology of the built environment has not, until recently, developed into a distinct field of study. When social scientists applied social research to decision-making about the physical environment they often overlooked architectural problems, working instead at a larger scale on planning problems. The trends are now
changing.
"A group of social scientists is working to establish a new specialty of environmental
sociology; some of these people focus their attention on applying social research to architectural design.
"This book outlines roots of this development in sociological theory and research and
then analyzes more recent work to show how one gap has been bridged between social
research and architectural design." This volume represents a very brief, concise summary
of early developments in the application of social science research to architecture and to
urban planning and design.

530. Zuckermann, Wolfgang. *End of the Road: The World Car Crisis and How We Can
Solve It*. Post Mills, Vt.: Chelsea Green Publishing, 1991.

Keywords: automobiles, pedestrians, public policy, traffic, transportation

The first section of this excellent book describes the seriousness of the car crisis. The
second section provides a good overview of strategies that can help to develop more sus-

tainable transportation patterns. Many practicable policies are suggested, drawing on the experience of case studies. The chapter on the car in the city is heavily influenced by *The Death and Life of Great American Cities* and is therefore not very original.

AUTHOR INDEX

Note: This index is to annotation numbers.

KEYWORD INDEX

Note: This index is to annotation numbers.

ABOUT THE AUTHORS

Willem H. Vanderburg is the founding director of the Centre for Technology and Social Development in the faculty of applied science and engineering at the University of Toronto and holds cross-appointments in the Institute for Environmental Studies and the department of sociology. He is the editor-in-chief of the *Bulletin of Science, Technology & Society,* and the author of *Perspectives on Our Age: Jacques Ellul Speaks of His Life and Work* (House of Anansi Press, 1997), *The Growth of Minds and Cultures* (University of Toronto Press, 1985), and *The Labyrinth of Technology* (University of Toronto Press, 2000).

Namir Khan is a lecturer at the Centre for Technology and Social Development in the faculty of applied science and engineering at the University of Toronto. He is the managing editor of the *Bulletin of Science, Technology & Society*.